FRENCH HAND SEWING FOR INFANTS

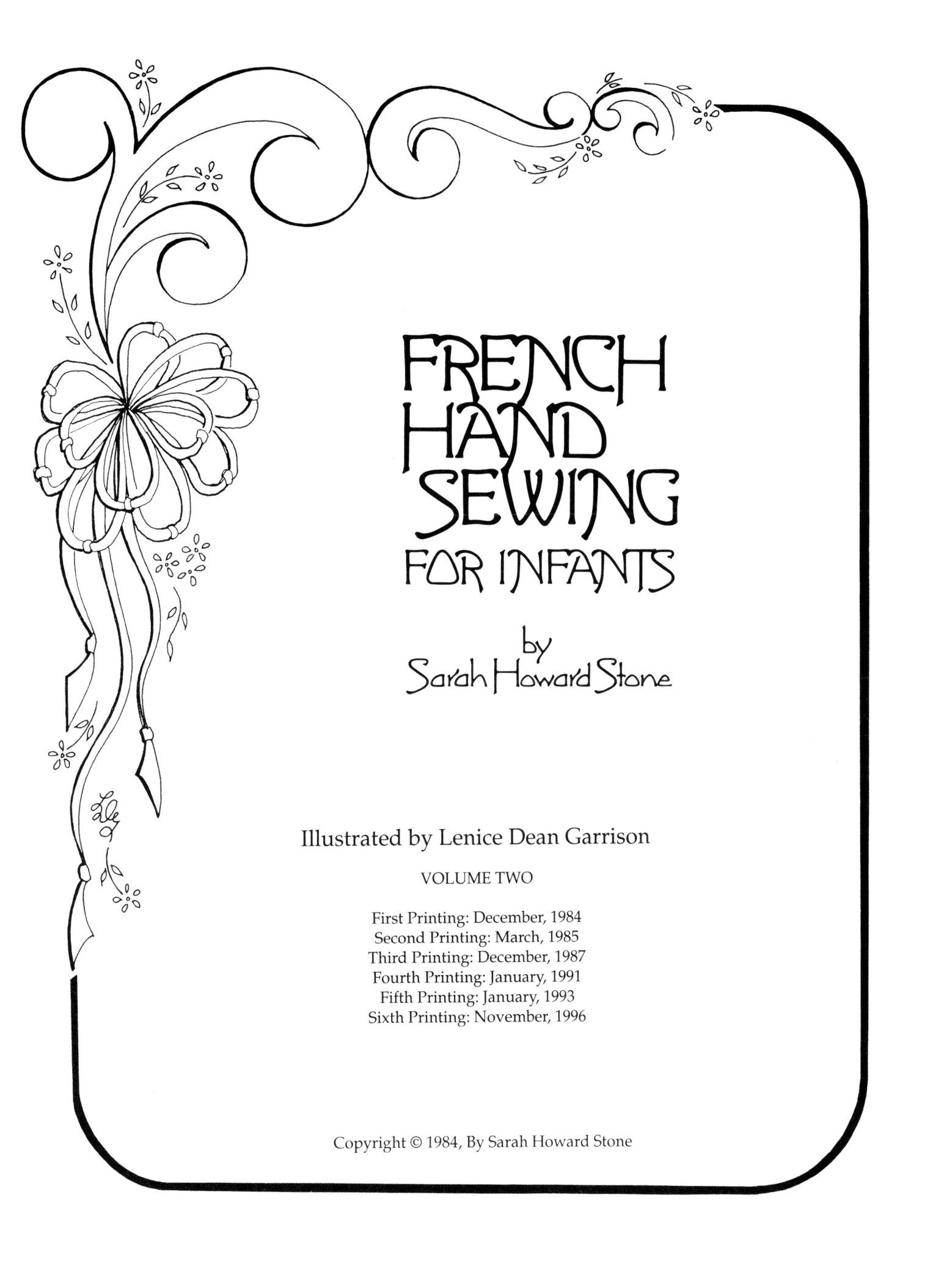

by
Sarah Howard Stone

Illustrated by Lenice Dean Garrison

VOLUME TWO

First Printing: December, 1984
Second Printing: March, 1985
Third Printing: December, 1987
Fourth Printing: January, 1991
Fifth Printing: January, 1993
Sixth Printing: November, 1996

Copyright © 1984, By Sarah Howard Stone

*This book is dedicated to Oliver,
my first and only love.*

LCCN-82-110193
ISBN 0-937773-02-6 (vol. 2)
ISBN 0-937773-00-X (total volume series)

CONTENTS

Christening Gowns 6
Caps and Bonnets 70
Daygowns 90
Trousseau Treasures 110
Babette and Baby Dresses 140
Boy Dresses 156

INTRODUCTION

The lovely handsewn clothing for infants shown in this book has its beginnings in the Victorian era. This was a time in which tiny babes wore long, generously-skirted dresses until their first toddling steps dictated shortened styles. Even then, boys as well as girls were dressed in beautifully hand-embellished dresses through the earliest years of childhood.

The materials used, like this list of suggested fabrics for a little girl's dress from a turn-of-the-century **Delineator,** roll off the tongue like bits of verse: "India linon, French gingham, dimity, and chambray . . . French lawn, fine batiste, or organdy." And the tiny garments were replete with tucks, laces, embroidery, and other fancy work. (Another early journal, **American Motherhood,** suggests with a charming blend of sentiment and practicality that baby clothes be embellished with "handwork, and the odds and ends of lace insertion that you have left from the making of your trousseau.") As the period photographs scattered through this book so touchingly suggest, our grandmothers' handsewing captured the special grace of childhood in clothes that were airy, comfortable, and yet very beautiful.

And thanks to the revival of interest in the fine art of handsewing, mothers and their children are once again enjoying the treasures of a handsewn layette — and garments that are not just **as** beautiful as the fine antiques, but actually lovelier. Handsewers today still rely on time-honored stitches and techniques. But unlike the turn-of-the-century sewer, who often had only the eyelets and simple laces she herself could make, modern needleworkers have access to a wide range of fine imported fabrics and trims. And while Victorian styles could sometimes be heavy, filled with detail, and elaborate to the point of gaudiness, present-day garments are better-designed and balanced, lighter and more appealing to the eye. Handsewers today are free to preserve the best of the heritage, choose among the styles and techniques of many periods, and express them, with contemporary flair, in the wonderful materials now available.

Some may wonder if handsewing, with its seemingly endless stitches, has a real place in today's busy home. Just as comfortable a place, we reply, as the rocking chair in the nursery. In the same way that the gentle motion of the rocker soothes both infant and mother, the repetitive stitches of handsewing offer a calming and pleasant occupation for the busy modern mother, while providing her the opportunity to make unique and treasured clothing for a special child.

You need not be an accomplished seamstress or have strong machine sewing skills to succeed at French handsewing. The basic stitches are few in number and soon mastered, and may then be combined in projects as simple or elaborate as you please. Some of my best students have had almost no sewing experience prior to enrolling in handsewing classes.

And handsewn clothing for infants, for all its delicate beauty, offers durability and old-fashioned practicality because of the fine materials used. Cotton garments can be bleached and refreshed for a brand-new look, even after much wear. And the extra care that natural fabrics require will be repaid with years — possibly generations — of beautiful service. Without doubt, the increasing interest in fine handsewn clothing is part of a widespread desire for a return to quality and durability in the clothing and other things that touch our lives.

After all, every new mother wants the most wonderful things possible for her child. As **The Ladies' Home Journal** for October, 1904, puts it, "The outfit for her baby is a work into which each mother puts her whole heart." Of course, ideas about the composition of the ideal layette vary considerably from time to time. One modest turn-of-the-century list of necessities for the newborn calls for "four pinning blankets, three nightdresses, cambric waists, three shirts, three pairs of stockings, and two flannel skirts." Another, more elaborate layette is found in **The Ladies' Home Journal** for November, 1905. In addition to a flannel nightgown, kimono, sacques, dimity dress, little shirts, pretty bibs, petticoats, and cashmere cloak, this ready-for-anything listing calls for "a flannel bath-apron with a large pocket into which the baby is placed, to protect him from draughts while being bathed . . . a drooling bib made of heavy linen or of Canton flannel; a rubber diaper for outdoor wear; a cover for the hot-water bag, made of flannel or outing-flannel; a flannel bag for the nursing-bottle; a bootee made of heavy woolen material; and a cap for the baby with protruding ears."

For the modern baby's ideal layette, we suggest a christening gown, slip, and cap; two pretty dresses, one fairly elaborate and one less elaborate; six permanent-press daygowns; six more elaborate batiste daygowns; six pairs of booties or little socks; three or four short sacques (made of challis for the winter baby and silk for the summer); three or four kimonos; six drawstring gowns; three little caps; six diaper shirts; six very pretty top sheets; one fancy pillow; one less elaborate pillow; fourteen plisse and flannel receiving blankets; and two challis squares with wide lace ruffles.

In the following chapters, you will find ideas for making and embellishing almost every type of clothing or layette accessory needed for babies to age eighteen months or for the treasured doll. The basic stitches and techniques of handsewing required for making these items, unless included here, can be found in **French Handsewing, Volume 1.** (Look there, for example, for more information on tucks, puffing, lace work, and embroidery.) Here we give general instructions for different types of clothing, and specific instructions for those features which give each design its unique character. These sketches will provide a treasure trove of inspiration for anyone who wishes to combine the rich heritage of handsewing with her own creativity in making memorable infant's clothing.

THE BABY

Where did you come from, baby dear?
Out of the everywhere into the here.

Where did you get your eyes so blue?
Out of the sky as I came through.

What makes your cheek like a warm white rose?
Something better than anyone knows.

Whence that three-cornered smile of bliss!
Three angels gave me at once a kiss.

Where did you get that pearly ear?
God spoke, and it came out to hear.

Where did you get those arms and hands?
Love made itself into hooks and bands.

Feet, whence did you come, you darling things?
From the same box as the cherubs' wings.

How did they all just come to be you?
God thought about me, and so I grew.

But how did you come to us, you dear?
God thought of you, and so I am here.

George MacDonald

CHRISTENING GOWNS

Round Yoke Dresses

Puffing and Embroidered Panels 9

Spoked Yoke with Teardrops Encircling Skirt 15

Pin Stitch 15

Round Yoke and Panel with Lace Medallions 19

Lace Medallions 20

Eyelet, Lace, and Tucks 25

Basic Construction of Round Yoke Dress
 in Twelve Steps 26

Square Yoke and Shaped Square Yoke Dresses

All Lace with Pointed Collar 29

Pointed Yoke and Panels 31

Tucked Yoke and Bands 37

Puffing Yoke and Panel 39

Tatted Butterfly Panel 43

Basic Construction of Square Yoke Dress
 in Nine Steps 48

Empire Dresses

Lace and Eyelet Yoke and Panel 49

Lace Yoke and Skirt Ovals 57

Basic Construction of Empire Dress in Ten Steps .. 59

A Special Gift 61

Slips in Varied Styles 63

Right: Benton Douglass Stone
Son of Mr. & Mrs. William Oliver Stone

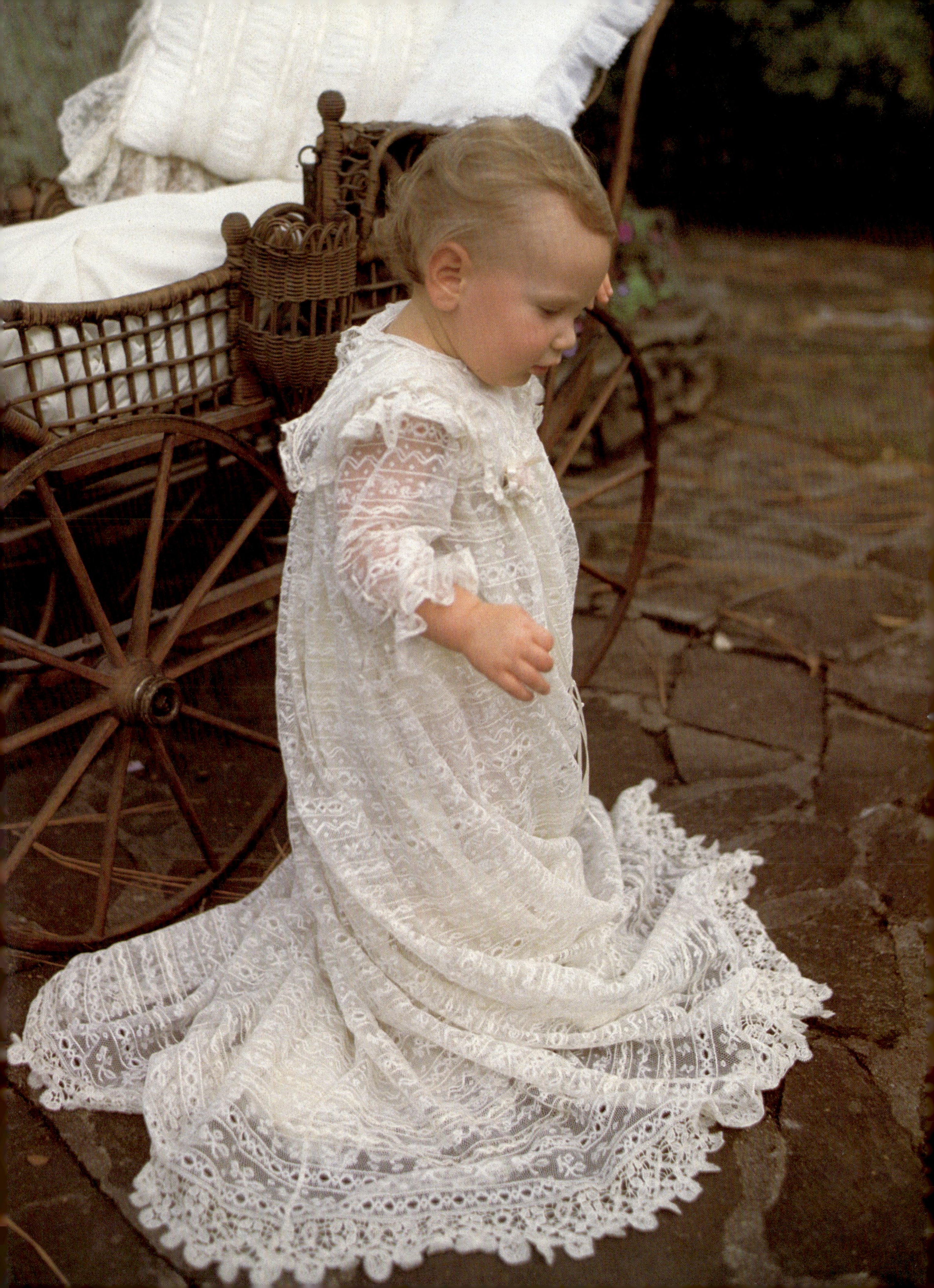

INTRODUCTION

The time of christening is a special, shining moment in a childhood, bringing infant, family, and friends together in a ceremony of joy. Special and shining, too, is the christening dress. It is likely to be the most elaborate garment in a child's wardrobe, the one upon which most care is lavished, and the one most likely to be saved and shared with succeeding generations.

The christening dress may be as simple or as elaborate as you wish. Use your own creativity to fashion a unique and personal garment. Do take care, however, not to try for a particularly "feminine" or "masculine" look. You are creating an heirloom piece. Chances are that grandchildren and great-grandchildren — girls **and** boys — will share in this lovely legacy. The christening ensemble can be completed with a girl's bonnet or a boy's cap. Make one of each to be put away and kept with the dress.

Designs for the christening dresses we show begin with a variety of yoke styles. The yokes may be embellished with tucks, puffing, lace work, embroidery, or any combination of techniques you choose. (These yokes will serve as the starting point, too, for the baby dresses and Babettes sketched in another chapter.) The suggestions which follow will get you started.

Puffed sleeves can be used for girl's dresses, but I prefer to use long sleeves. Baby's long sleeves can be finished with a ruffle or with beading, with ribbon ties to adjust the wrist opening. A 6-inch beading should be sufficient for a newborn to a one-year-old size.

The length of the christening dress should be 27, 36, or 42 inches, measured from the top of the neck band to the finished hem. The dress may be longer, if desired, but no shorter. The skirt width should be 66 to 72 inches, proportionate to its length. Ruffles at the hem should be 3 to 5 inches deep. As a general rule, the length of ruffle fabric should be 1½ times the measurement around the bottom edge of the dress; but the deeper the ruffle, the fuller it should be.

Strive for balance in the skirt design, with pleasing proportions of fancy work and plain areas. As a general rule, if the skirt is an elaborate one, with a great deal of lace, puffing, or tucks, at least one-third of the skirt, at the top, should be plain. If, on the other hand, embellishment is reserved for a band at the hem, that embellished area should make up at least one-third of the total skirt.

The slip may be either A-lined or yoked. On a yoked slip, the neck should be trimmed out 1/2 inch, the top of the shoulder 1/4 inch. The bottom edge of the slip should be finished with lace or a ruffle comparable to that of the dress. The slip skirt should finish one inch shorter than the dress. As an alternative to a slip, you may wish to make a skirt liner, attached to the gathers inside the dress.

Fasten the christening dress with gold beauty pins, which can be purchased at your jeweler's. The slip can be fastened with tiny pearl buttons.

ROUND YOKE DRESSES

Puffing and Embroidered Panels

The yoke on this dress has three rows of lace insertion (one at neck edge, one at bottom edge, and one equally spaced between the top and bottom). The seam allowance should be trimmed from the neck and bottom edges of the yoke pattern before making the paper guide. (Fig. 1)

The skirt is made up of six puffing and lace panels and six embroidered panels. The panels are tapered at the top of the skirt to fit the yoke, and the top of the sleeve is gathered to fit between the notches. (Fig. 2) In order to make the back panels slightly longer than the front, the top row of puffing on these will be longer. The rest of the

BACK YOKE
INVISIBLE PLACKET

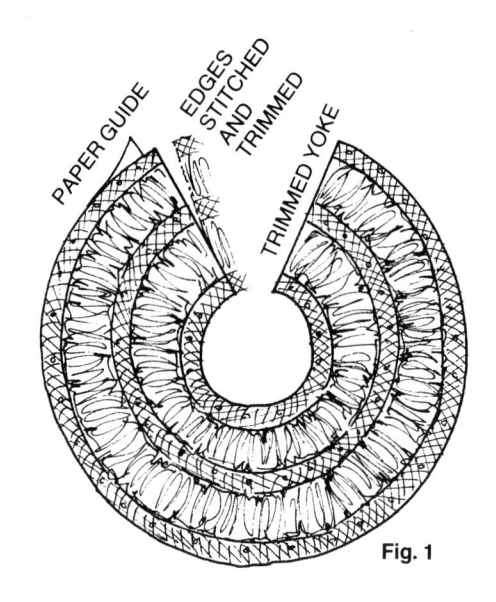

lace has been attached to panel. Trim to stitching line. (Fig. 5)

Draw the embroidery panels on pieces of fabric. (Do not cut panels out.) Hand baste on the pencilled outline. Transfer the embroidery design to the panel with a No. 2 lead pencil. Embroider. Wash and iron panels before cutting them out. (Fig. 6)

Lay the lace insertion on the embroidered panels in the same manner as on the puffing panels. Finish in the same way.

Whip the panels together, forming the skirt.

Whip the entredeux to the bottom lace scallops. (Fig. 7A) Puff a strip of fabric to the entredeux on the bottom edge. (7B) NOTE: The puffing is two times the bottom edge, and each section should be puffed on a paper guide. Attach entredeux to the bottom of the puffing. (7C) Attach lace insertion to the entredeux and entredeux to the bottom of the insertion, (7D-E) still using the paper guide.

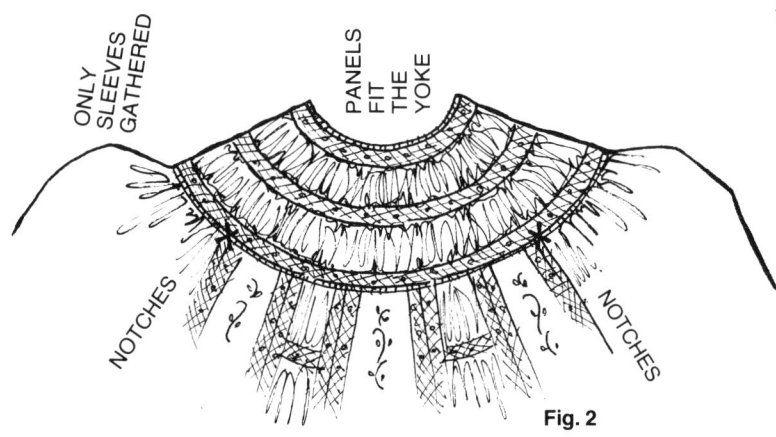

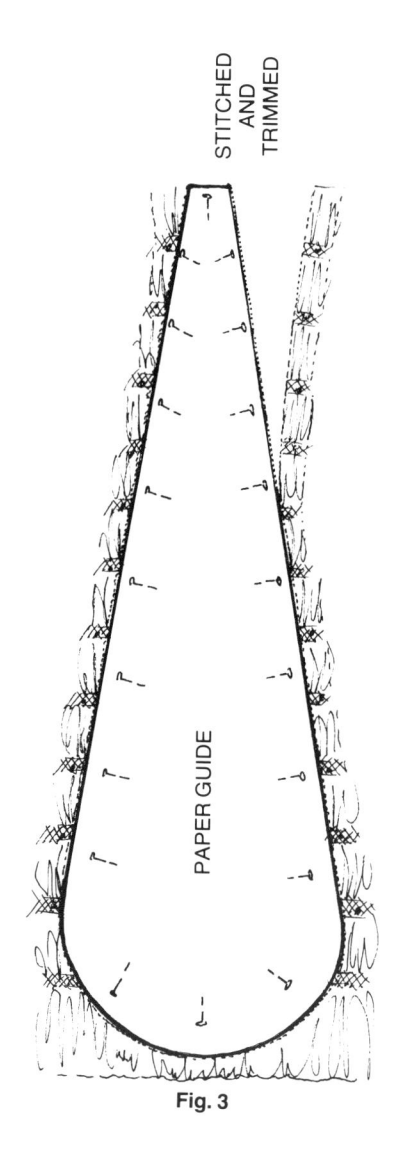

puffing and lace should be the same, front and back, all the way down.

The bottom puffing strips on the panels should be made to extend beyond the bottom edge of the pattern. Machine stitch with a tiny zigzag or a very short straight stitch just at the edge of the paper guide. NOTE: When using a straight machine stitch, stitch three times — one stitching on top of the other. Trim the excess fabric and lace as close to the stitching line as possible. (Fig. 3)

Lay lace insertion around the puffing panel with the outer edge of the lace even with the edge of the panel. Pull a thread in the heavy line of the lace to gather and ease lace around the bottom curve. Tiny baste the inside of the lace insertion (in the heavy line) (A) and zigzag or buttonhole the lace to the panel. (B) (Fig. 4)

Lay insertion back on panel. Machine stitch with a straight stitch or zigzag 1/8 inch from where

Fig. 4

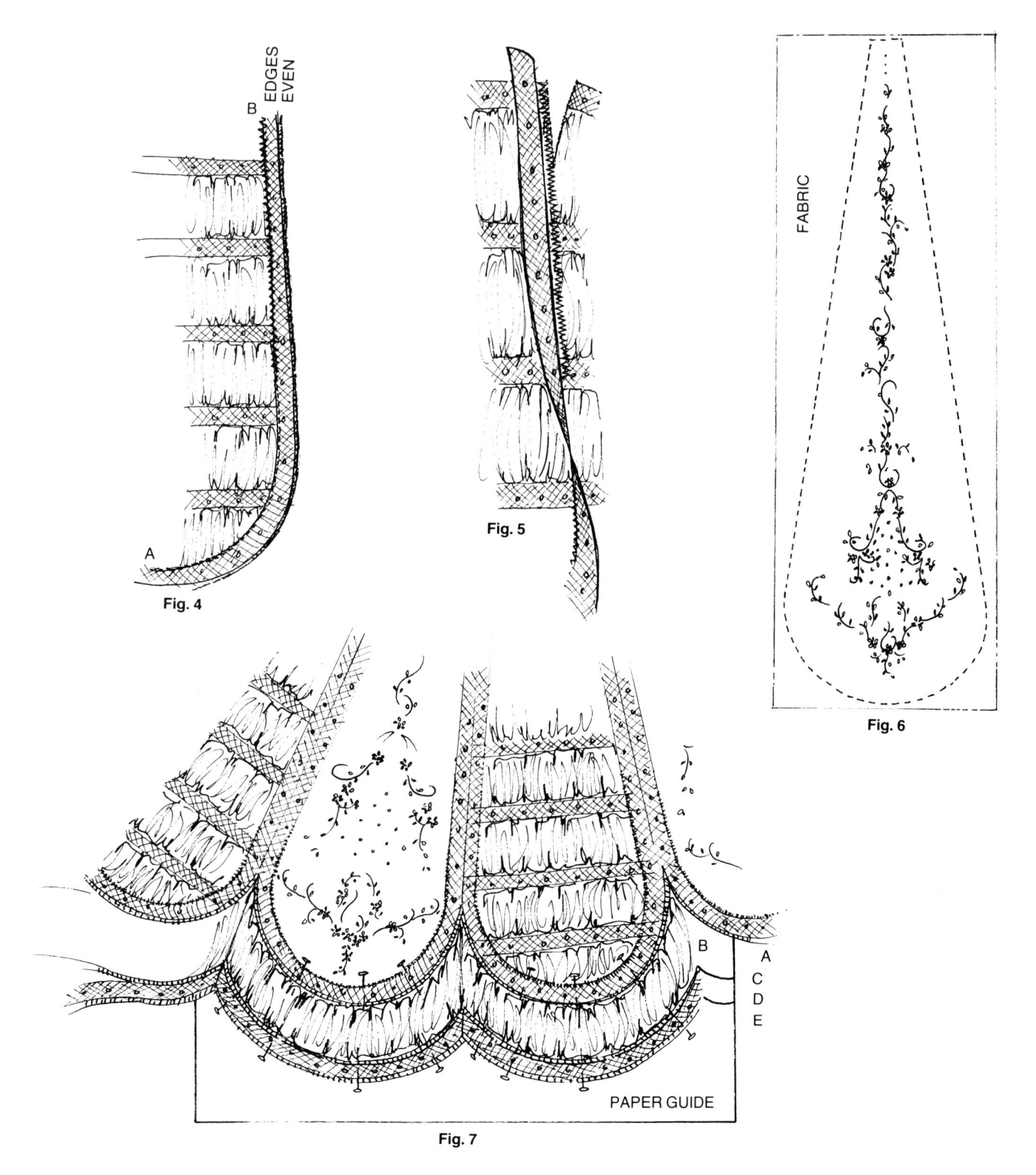

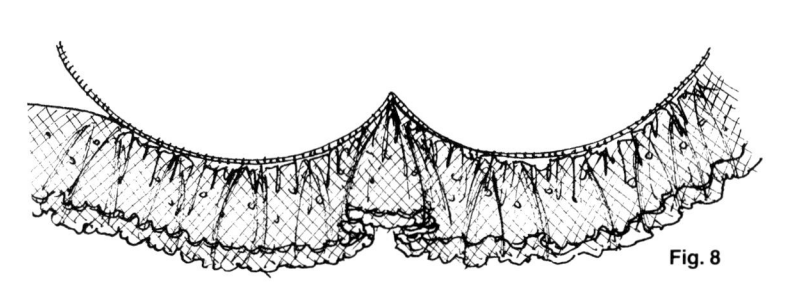

Fig. 5

Fig. 6

Fig. 7

Fig. 8

Whip wide gathered lace edging to the bottom of the entredeux. Measure around the skirt at the bottom of the scallops and allow 1¾ times that length of lace for fullness. NOTE: You need more than 1½ times the length to gather and add fullness at the points. If you are using wide lace or a fabric ruffle, you might gather 2 times for fullness. (Fig. 8)

The sleeves and yoke are enhanced with a lace ruffle.

LAY THIS DAISY ON TOP OF THE DAISY AT THE BOTTOM OF SECTION 1.

SECTION 1 DESIGN FOR PUFFING AND EMBROIDERED PANELS CHRISTENING GOWN.

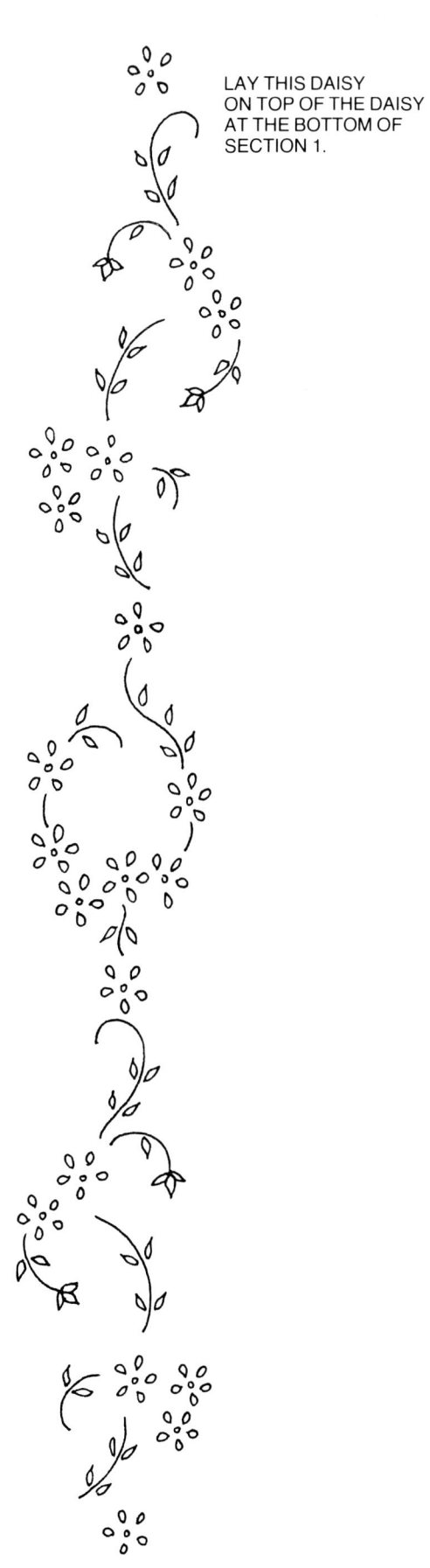

SECTION 2 DESIGN FOR PUFFING AND EMBROIDERED PANELS CHRISTENING GOWN

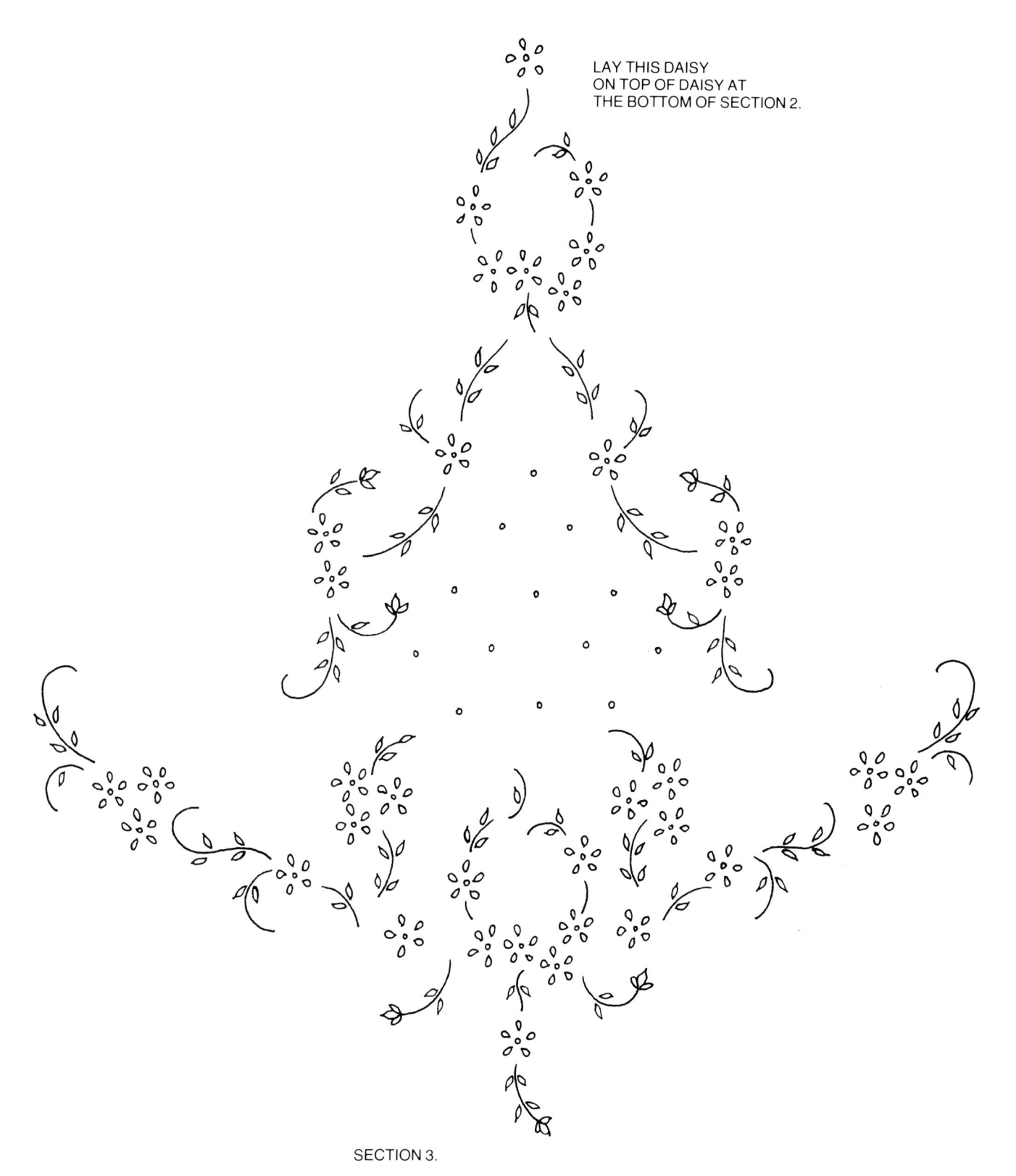

LAY THIS DAISY
ON TOP OF DAISY AT
THE BOTTOM OF SECTION 2.

SECTION 3.

DESIGN FOR PUFFING AND EMBROIDERED PANELS
CHRISTENING GOWN.

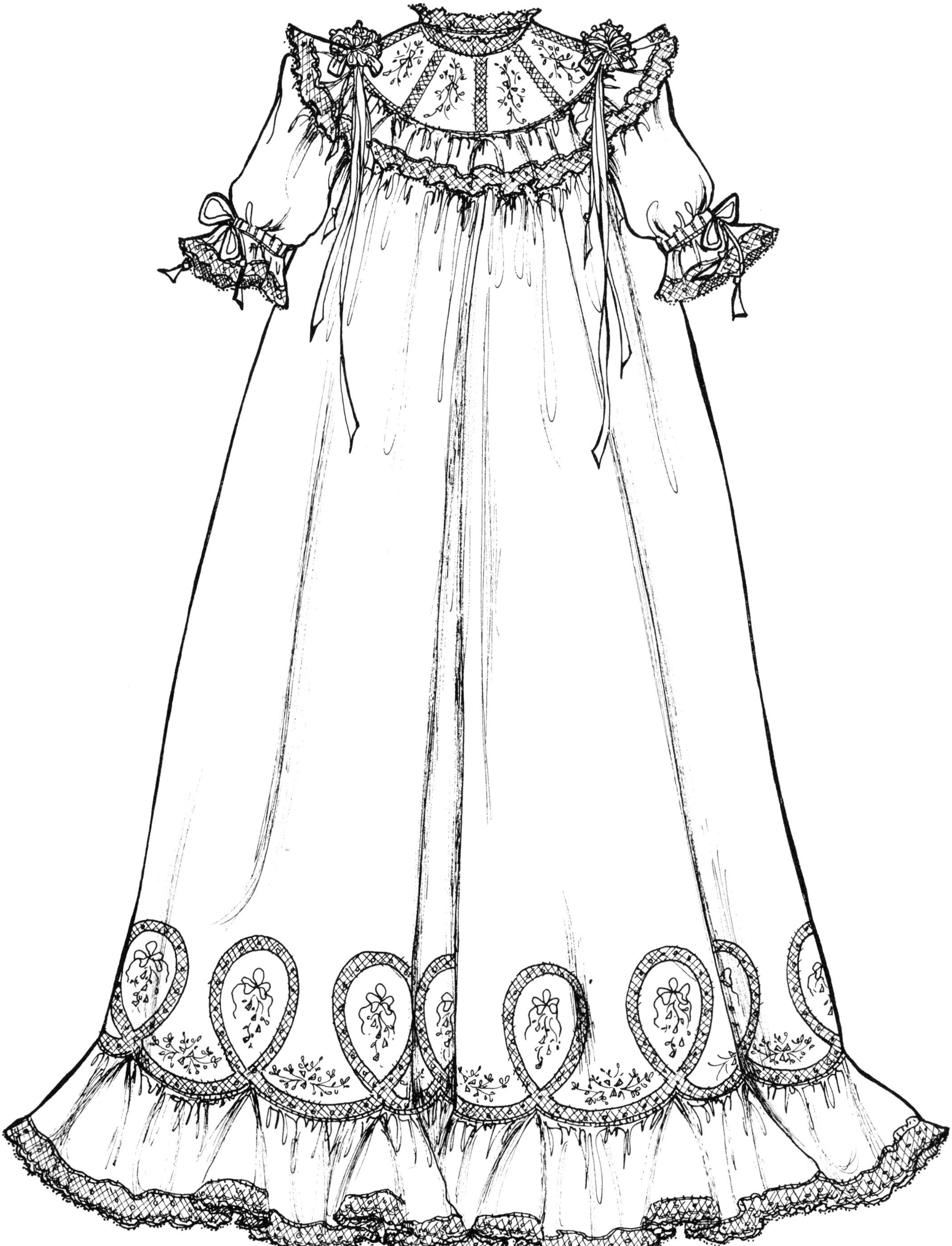

Spoked Yoke with Teardrops Encircling Skirt

The yoke of this dress (one front and two backs) should be drawn on a strip of fabric. Lines should be drawn where the lace will be placed vertically. One strip of lace will be in center front, one will cover each shoulder seam, one equally spaced between each of the above; and the placket will be double lace insertion (one piece of lace sewn on top of the other).

Hand baste the outline of the yoke and transfer the embroidery design onto the fabric with a No. 2 lead pencil. (Fig. 9) Embroider design; wash and iron the fabric strip. Sew the lace insertion onto the yoke, excluding the strips at the shoulder and at the placket edge. Tiny baste the lace to the fabric in the heavy lines. Zigzag, buttonhole, or pin stitch the lace to the fabric. (Fig. 10)

Pin Stitch

Tiny baste the lace to the fabric. (11A) Machine stitch the fabric (with an unthreaded needle) as close to the lace as possible. (11B) NOTE: This step will help you keep your stitches even until you master this technique.

Bring the needle and thread up through the end of the lace (Fig. 11C) before taking the first stitch. Proceed with stitches as shown in Fig. 12, 13 & 14.

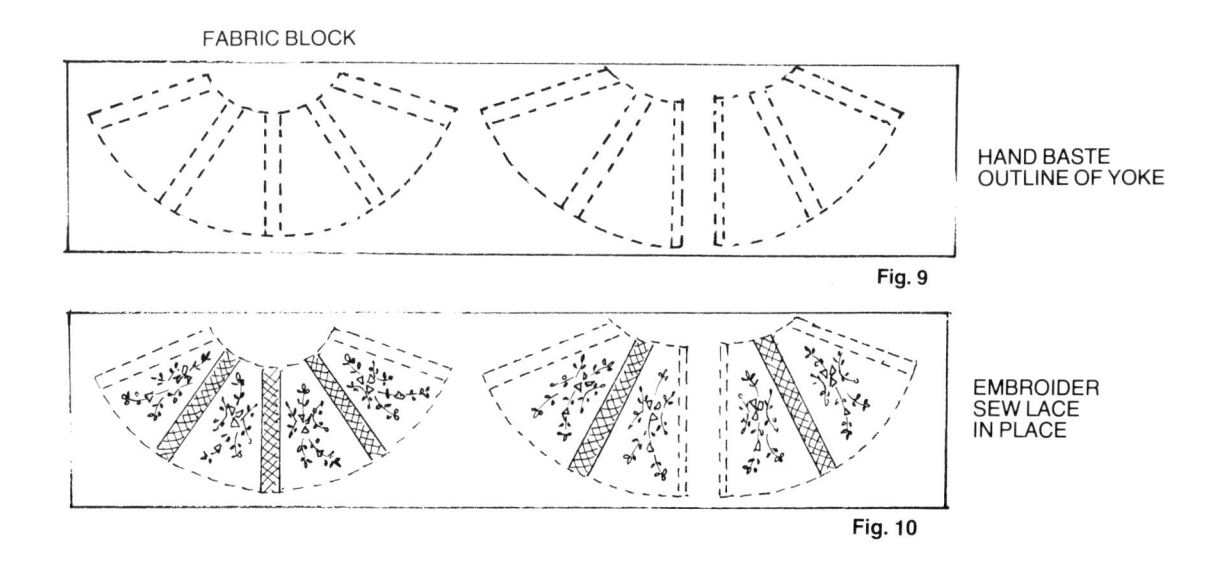

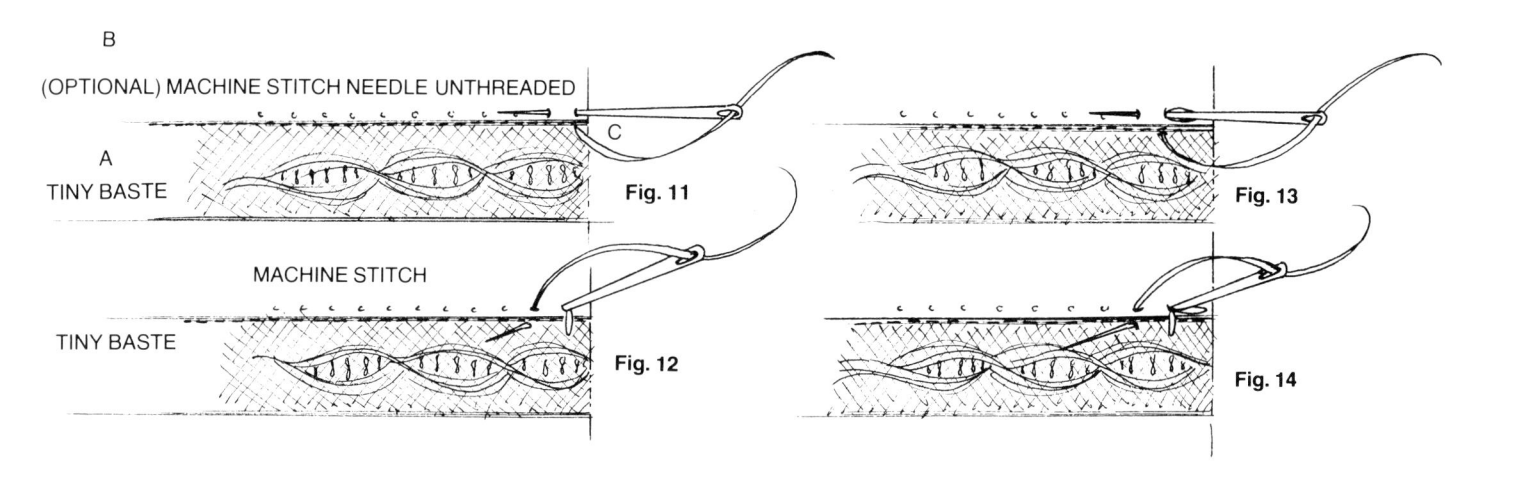

15

Cut the yoke pieces out, leaving 1/8 inch beyond center back on back yoke pieces. Trim the fabric away from behind lace. Cut each back yoke 1/8 inch beyond center back. Sew the shoulder seams. Center the lace insertion on top of the shoulder seams and apply in the same way you applied the other lace strips. (Fig. 15)

Roll and whip the 1/8 inch fabric extending beyond center back. Whip the double lace insertion to the rolled edge, or leave the 1/8 inch fabric unrolled and lay the double lace 1/8 inch upon

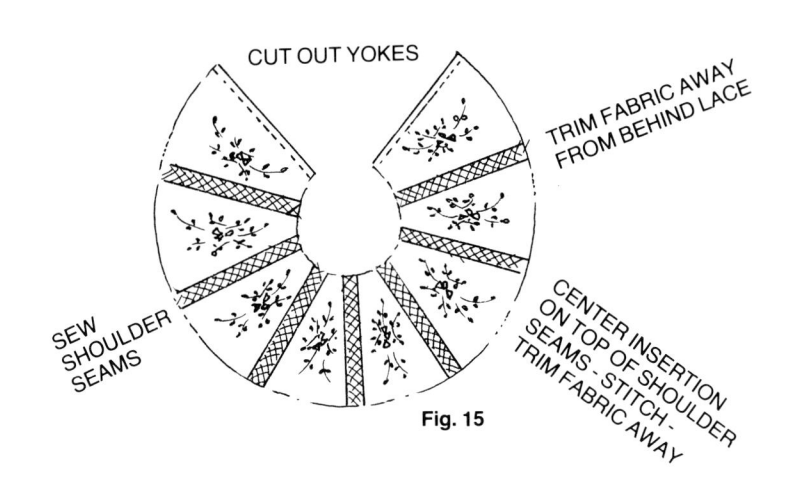

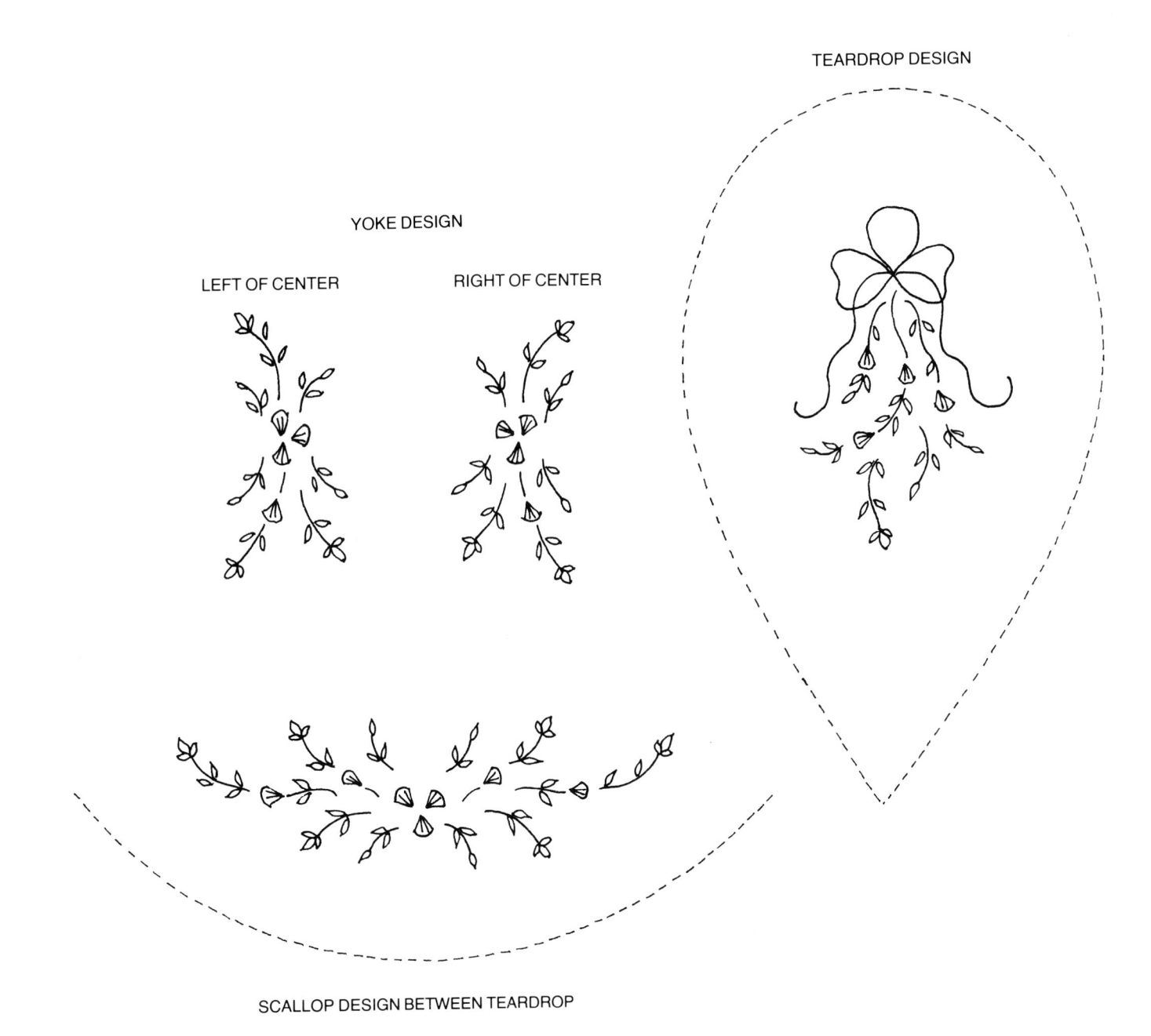

Fig. 15

TEARDROP DESIGN

YOKE DESIGN

LEFT OF CENTER

RIGHT OF CENTER

SCALLOP DESIGN BETWEEN TEARDROP

fabric. Tiny baste the inside line and finish with zigzag, buttonhole, or pin stitch. (Fig. 16)

Roll and whip neck and bottom edge of yoke. NOTE: To keep neck and bottom edge from stretching, roll and whip and gather, then release gathers.

Cut two lengths of fabric for skirt. Divide skirt into equal sections. Draw teardrops on the skirt. Draw scallops to join the teardrops. Hand baste the outline of the teardrop and scalloped edge. Transfer the design to the skirt. Embroider. Wash and iron fabric and then apply lace.

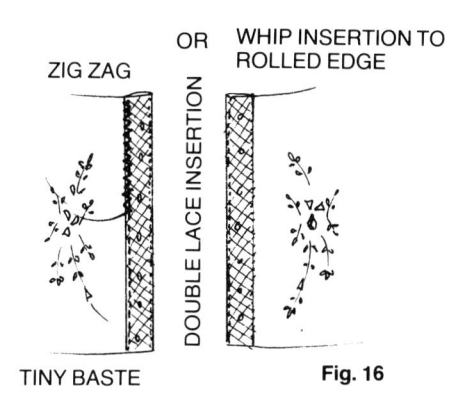

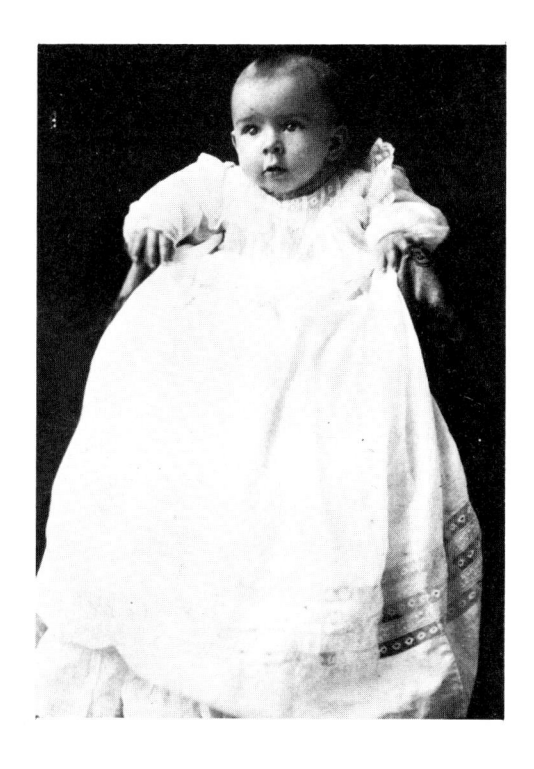

Fig. 16

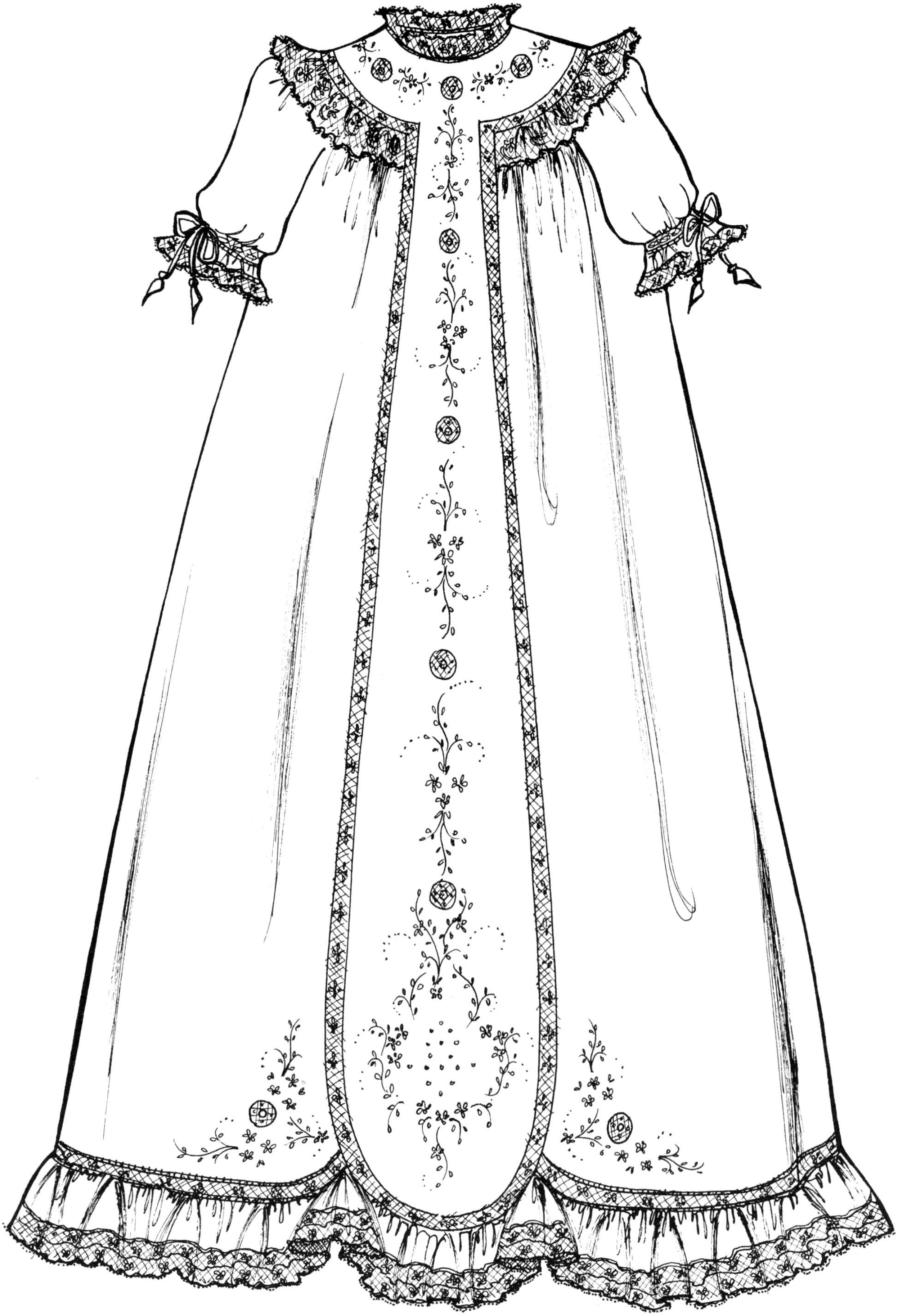

Round Yoke and Panel with Lace Medallions

This gown is embellished with lace medallions and embroidery. The front yoke and panel are one piece. The back yokes are cut on the straight of the fabric and are french seamed to the front yoke at the shoulders. (Fig. 17)

Lace insertion is applied to the entire outer edge of the yoke and panel.

The bottom of the skirt is scalloped at the points where the skirt meets the panel. (Fig. 18) Where the scallops of the skirt meet the panel, the lace is joined with a buttonhole stitch.

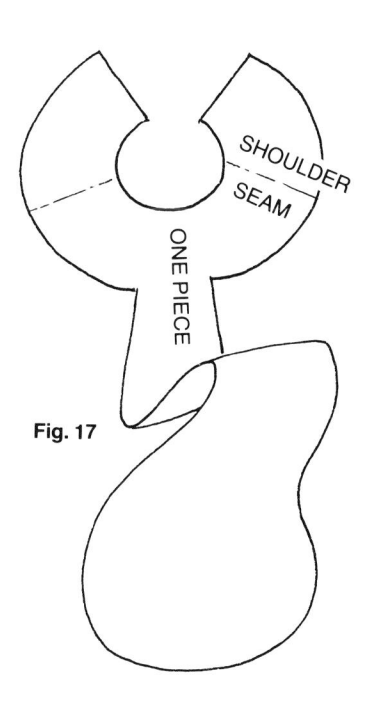

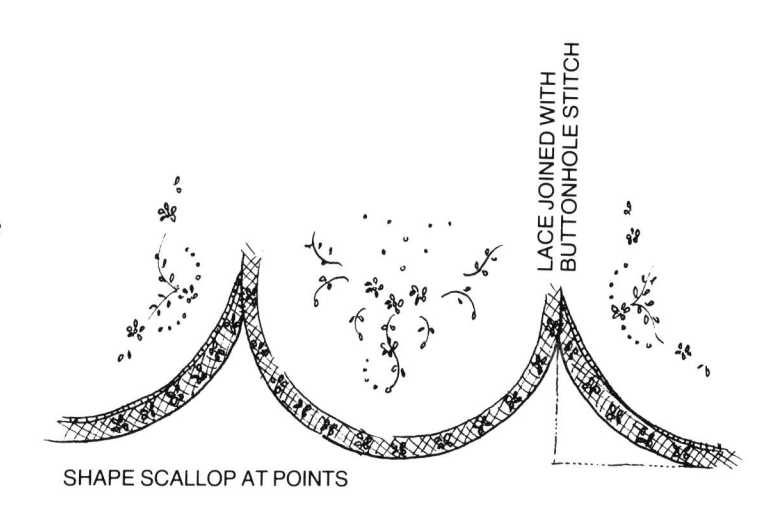

SHAPE SCALLOP AT POINTS

Fig. 18

Fig. 17

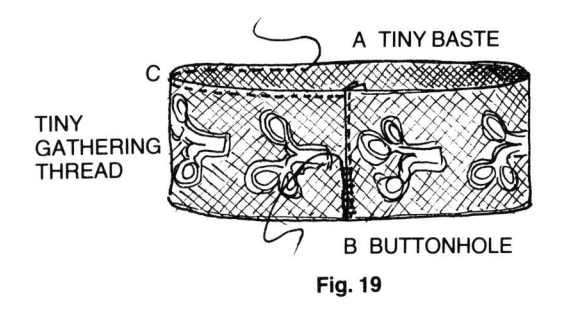

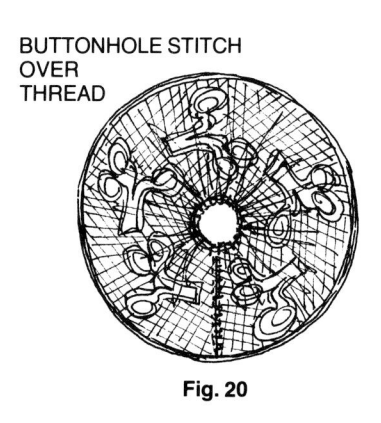

Lace Medallions

Cut a strip of insertion long enough to gather and make a circle the size you want plus 1/2 inch.

Fold one end under 1/4 inch and lay the folded edge 1/4 inch on top of other edge. Tiny baste (A) and buttonhole to secure. (B) Using the same needle and thread, run a tiny gathering stitch inside circle. (C) Pull the gathering thread, forming a small hole in the center of the medallion. (Fig. 19) NOTE: The inside should be gathered enough so that the outside will lay flat without gathers. Buttonhole stitch over the gathering thread to secure. (Fig. 20)

Lay the medallion on the fabric. (Fig. 21) Tiny baste (A) the outer edge and finish with a buttonhole (B), pin (C), or satin stitch (D). Cut the fabric away from behind the medallion within 1/8 inch of the lace edge. (Fig. 22)

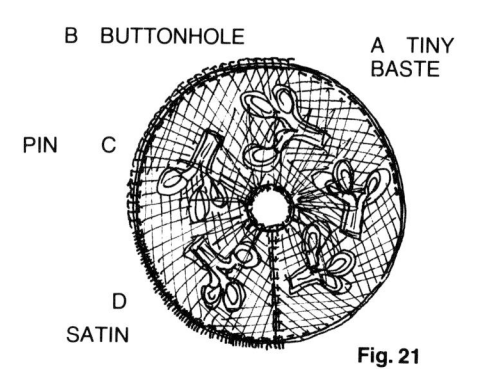

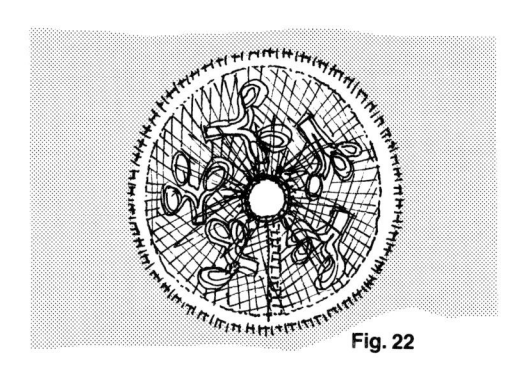

LACE
MEDALLION

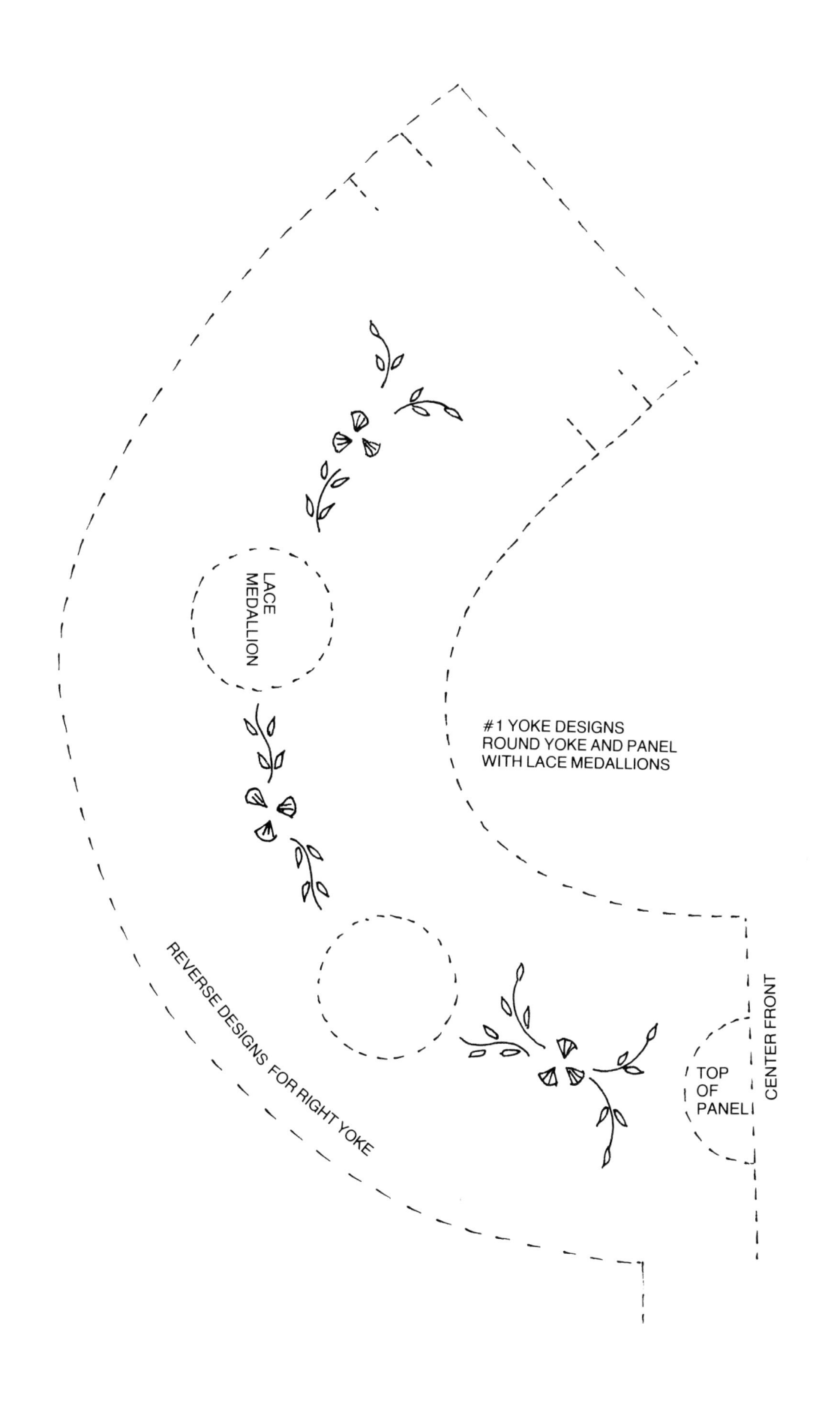

#1 YOKE DESIGNS
ROUND YOKE AND PANEL
WITH LACE MEDALLIONS

REVERSE DESIGNS FOR RIGHT YOKE

TOP
OF
PANEL

CENTER FRONT

#2
TOP OF PANEL
CENTER FRONT
YOKE

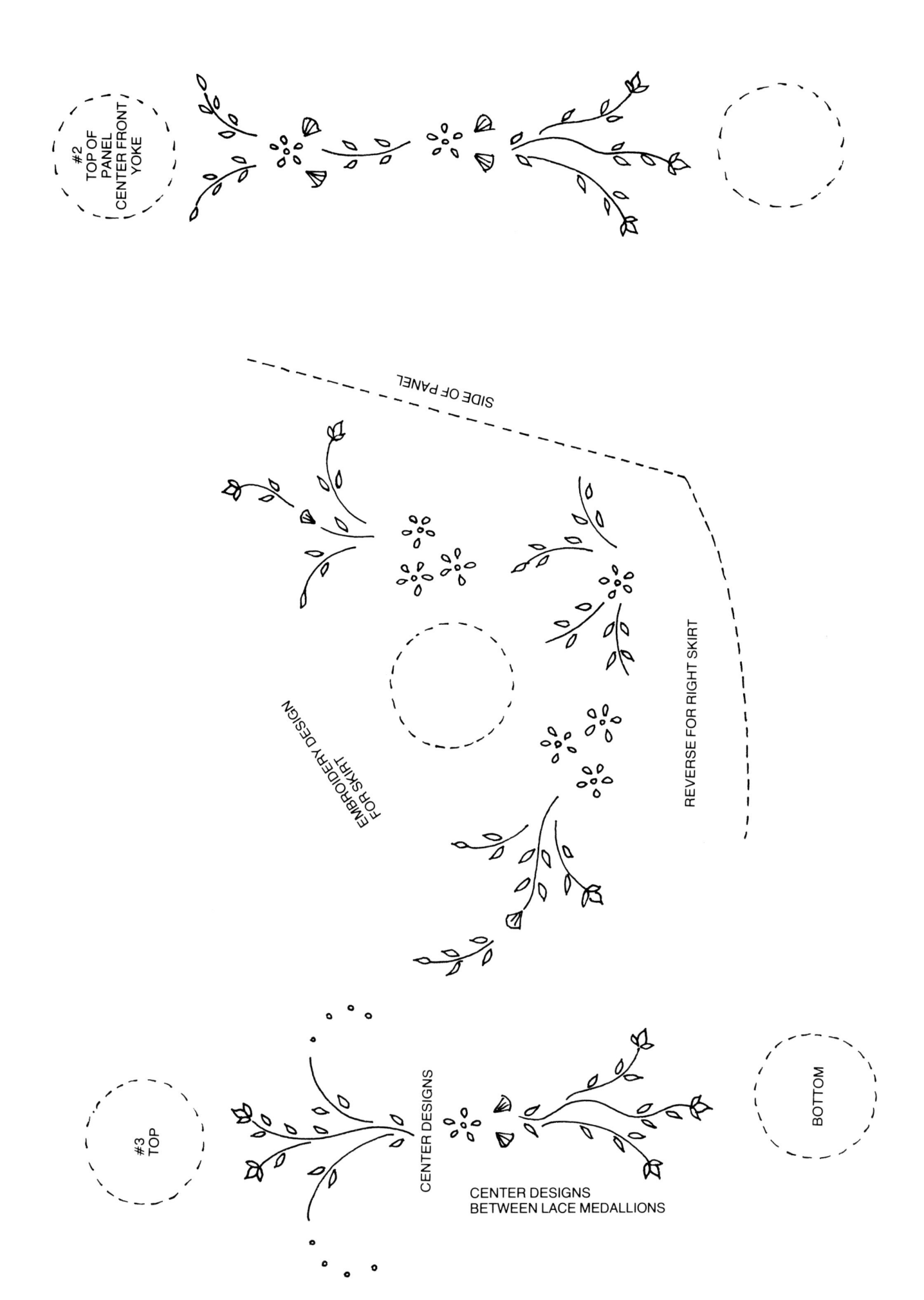

SIDE OF PANEL

EMBROIDERY DESIGN
FOR SKIRT

REVERSE FOR RIGHT SKIRT

#3
TOP

CENTER DESIGNS

CENTER DESIGNS
BETWEEN LACE MEDALLIONS

BOTTOM

PANEL DESIGN FOR
ROUND YOKE AND PANEL WITH
LACE MEDALLIONS

#4

BOTTOM OF PANEL

BACK YOKE

24

Eyelet, Lace, and Tucks

On the yokes of many antique dresses, the trim is sewn vertically in the front, but appears diagonal when viewed from the back. This effect is achieved by making a block of trim large enough that the entire yoke can be cut from it.

Begin by cutting an entire yoke pattern from brown paper (front and back put together at the shoulders). Trim the back edges 1/8 inch beyond center back. (Fig. 23) Trim the seam allowance away from the neck and the bottom edges of pattern. Lay the paper pattern on the block of trim and pin securely. (Fig. 24)

Machine stitch with a tiny zigzag or short-length straight stitch as close to the paper as possible without catching the paper in the stitching.

Take the paper guide off the block and sew once again on top of the first stitching. NOTE: This machine stitch will act as a rolled edge. Trim away excess as close to the stitching as possible. (Fig. 25)

For double lace placket on the back yoke, lay two pieces of insertion (length needed) one on top of the other and whip together on one side. Cover 1/8 inch seam allowance at center back with top piece of insertion. Tiny baste and machine stitch to secure. (Fig. 26A) Underneath, whip the bottom insertion strip 1/8 inch over to the stitching line. (B) This forms the placket.

Whip entredeux to the neck and bottom edges of the yoke using the machine stitch as a rolled edge.

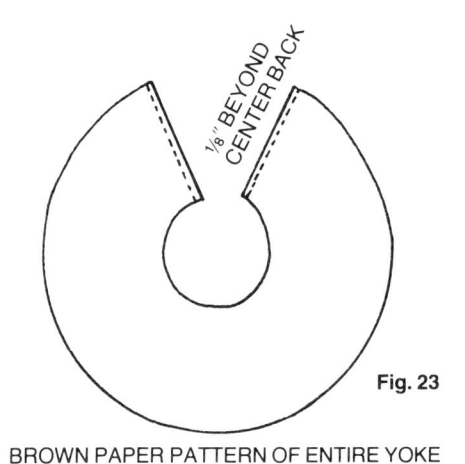

Fig. 24

MACHINE STITCH AROUND PAPER PATTERN THEN AGAIN AFTER REMOVAL OF PATTERN

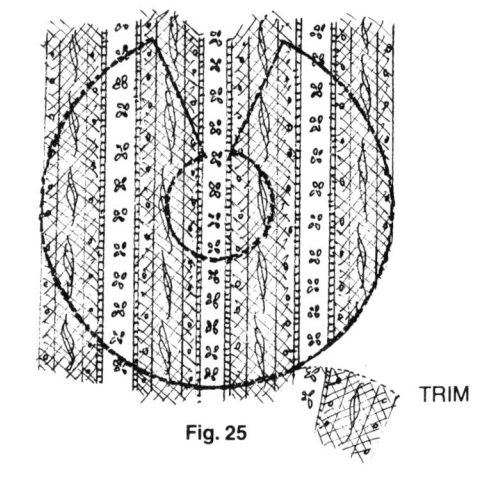

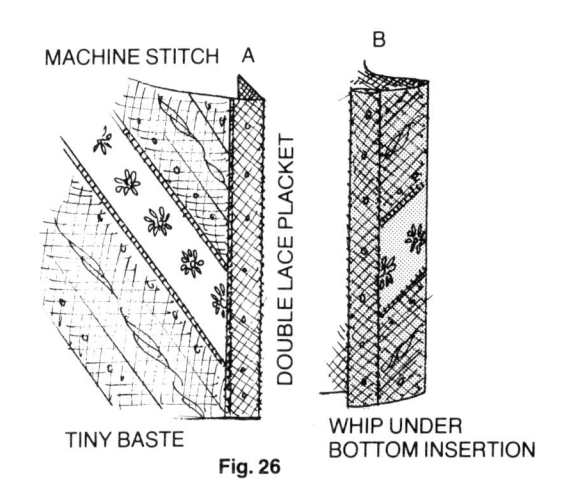

TRIM

Fig. 25

Fig. 23

BROWN PAPER PATTERN OF ENTIRE YOKE

1/8" BEYOND CENTER BACK

MACHINE STITCH A   B

DOUBLE LACE PLACKET

TINY BASTE   WHIP UNDER BOTTOM INSERTION

Fig. 26

Fig. 27

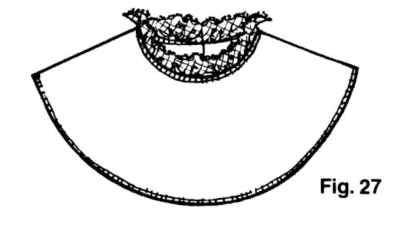

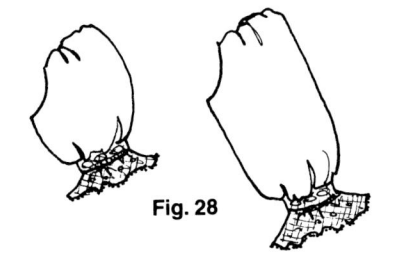

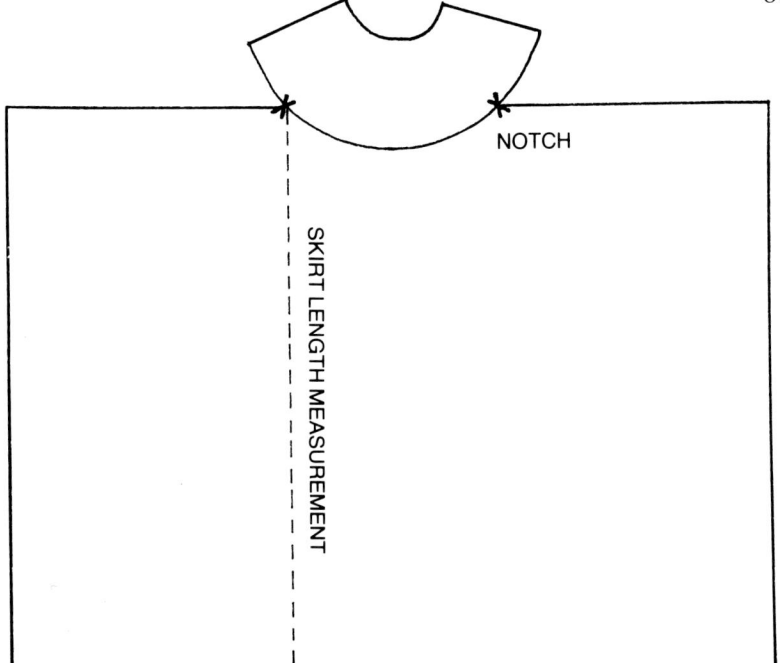

Fig. 28

Basic Construction of A Round Yoke Dress in Twelve Steps

1. Make the yoke of your choice. (Fig. 27)
2. Make the sleeve of your choice. (Fig. 28)
3. Make the skirt of your choice. NOTE: The skirt length measurement should be taken from the point where the armhole joins the yoke or at the notch or x on yoke. (Fig. 29)
4. Put the side seams together and cut to shape the top of the skirt, using the skirt guide and armhole guide for a round yoke. (Fig. 30)
5. Roll and whip the skirt part of the armhole. (Fig. 31A)
6. Whip entredeux to the rolled edge of the armhole. (Fig. 31B)

NOTCH

SKIRT LENGTH MEASUREMENT

Fig. 29

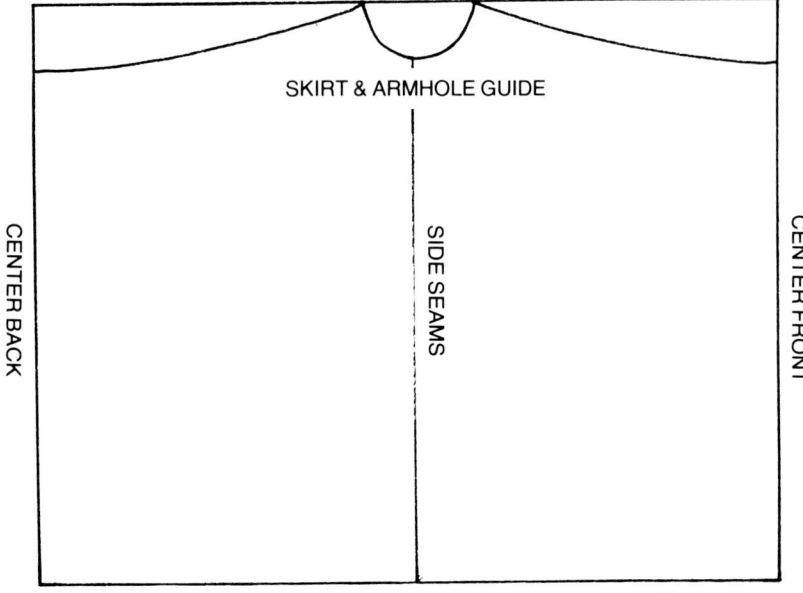

SKIRT & ARMHOLE GUIDE

CENTER BACK

SIDE SEAMS

CENTER FRONT

Fig. 30

Fig. 31

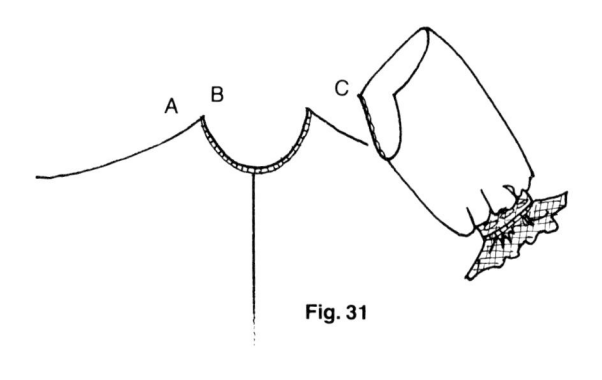

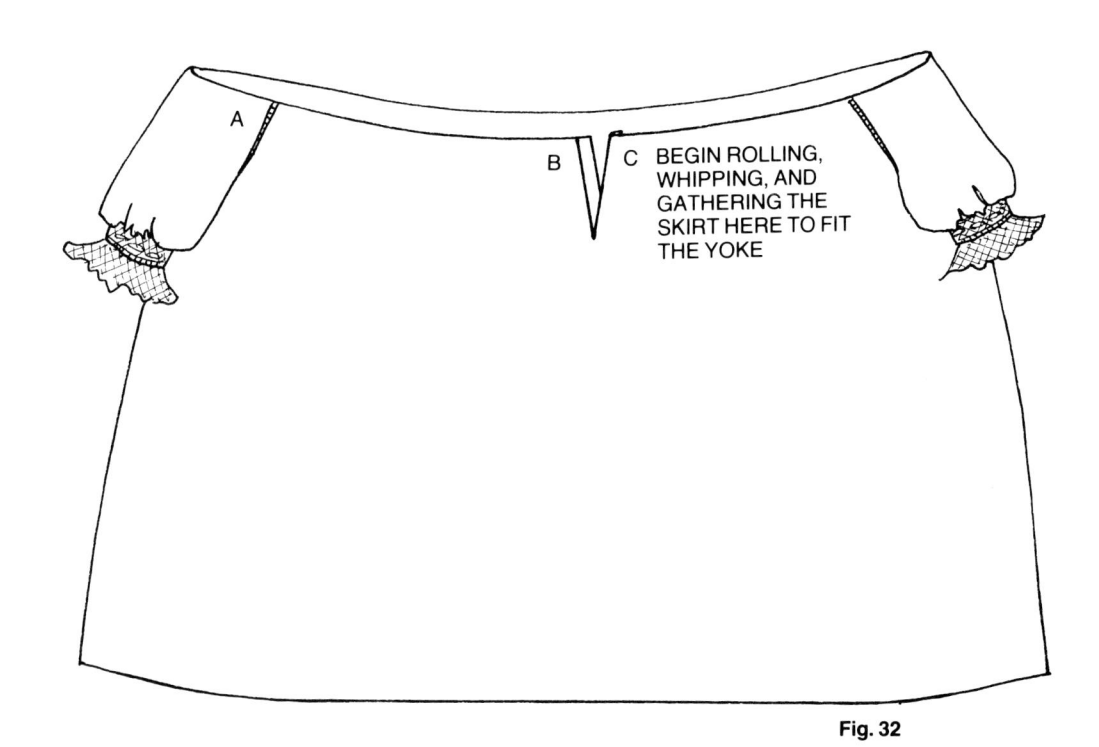

Fig. 32

7. Roll and whip the armhole part of the sleeve. (Exclude the top edge.) (Fig. 31C)
8. Whip the rolled part of the sleeve to the entredeux in the armhole. (Fig. 32A)
9. Put a continuous placket in top center back of skirt. (Fig. 32B)
10. Pin the top of the skirt to the bottom of the yoke, matching the armhole seams to the notches on the yoke pattern and center front as well as placket edges. (Fig. 33A)
11. Roll and whip and gather the top of the skirt to fit as pinned. With another needle and thread, whip the top rolled edge of skirt to the entredeux on the bottom of the yoke. (Fig. 33B)
12. Whip lace, eyelet, or fabric ruffle to the outer edge of the yoke. (Fig. 33C)

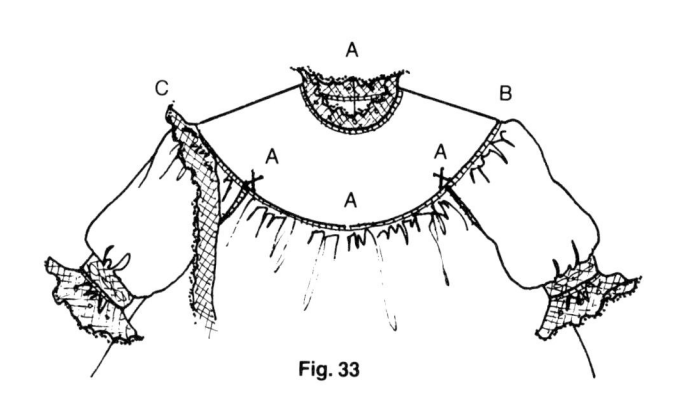

Fig. 33

28

SQUARE YOKE AND SHAPED SQUARE YOKE DRESSES

All Lace with Pointed Collar

The basic square yoke of this dress is made of ecru swiss batiste. NOTE: You would use white batiste with white lace and ecru batiste with ecru lace.

The collar is made from the yoke pattern. For front of collar, draw the front yoke pattern on a piece of brown paper and add two triangles at the bottom edge to form collar points. For back collar patterns, fold back yoke pattern at center back line. Draw two back yoke pieces (left and right) on brown paper. On each, subtract width of lace edging to be used from center back. Draw a triangle at bottom edge of each pattern to make collar points the same depth as those on the front. (Fig. 34)

Make a lace block for the front collar and two for the backs. On the front collar block, start with one vertical strip of lace at center front, and add lace strips, left and right, whipping them together as you build the block outward. Use a variety of laces for interest. Match lace patterns that will be used in skirt. On blocks for back collar pieces, start with the shoulder edge and build in, arranging laces so that they will match those of front collar. (Fig. 35)

Lay collar pattern pieces on lace blocks so that laces will match, front and back. Pin securely. Machine stitch bottom, neck, and shoulder edges. (Fig. 36)

Pin shoulder seams together. Baste, stitch, and trim seam allowances to 1/8 inch. Center a piece of lace insertion over seam and tiny baste. (Fig. 37A) Straight stitch or zigzag by machine. Remove paper pattern and zigzag again over stitching. Trim away excess lace as close as possible to the stitching line.

Whip entredeux to the entire outer edge, excluding neck edge. (37B) Whip gathered lace edging to the entredeux. (37C)

MAKE BROWN PAPER PATTERN FOR COLLAR

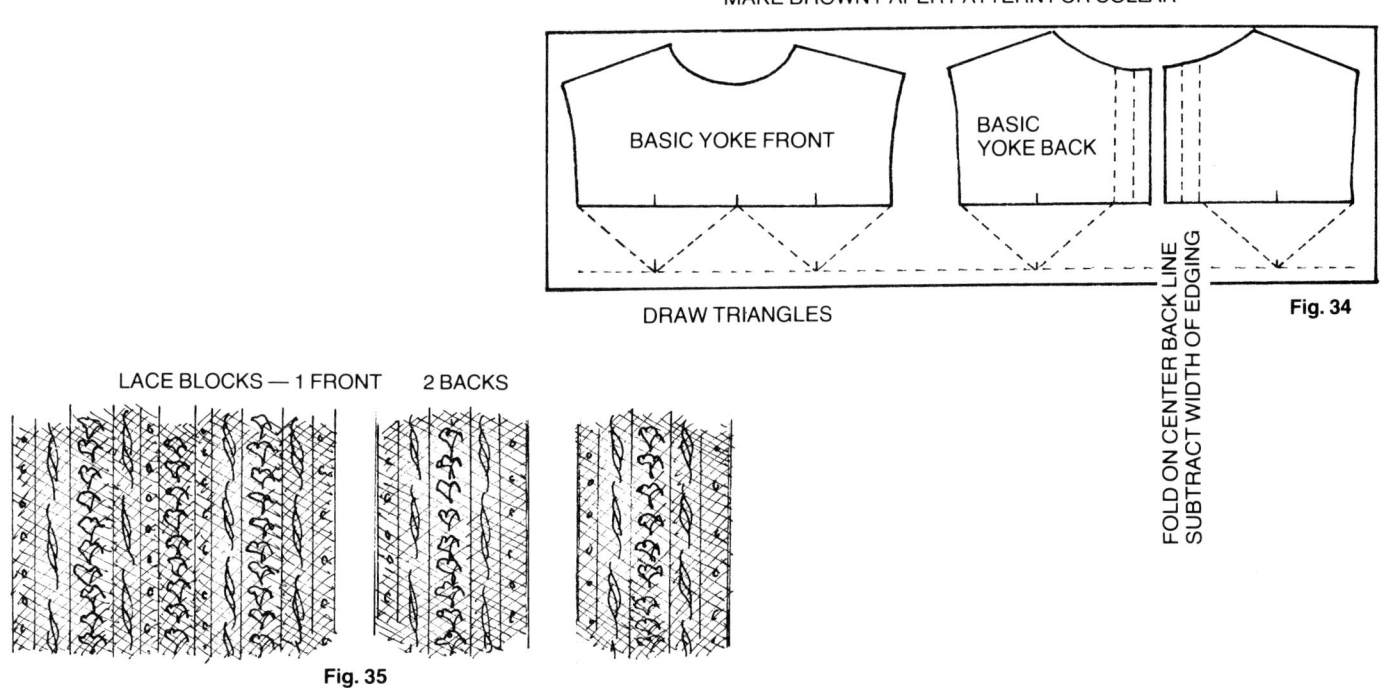

BASIC YOKE FRONT

BASIC YOKE BACK

DRAW TRIANGLES

FOLD ON CENTER BACK LINE
SUBTRACT WIDTH OF EDGING

Fig. 34

LACE BLOCKS — 1 FRONT   2 BACKS

Fig. 35

MACHINE STITCH SHOULDER, NECK, AND BOTTOM EDGES

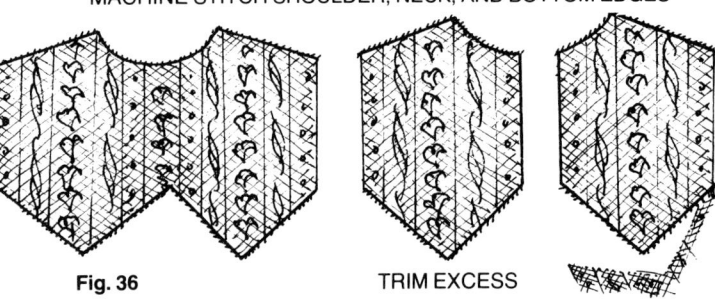

Fig. 36   TRIM EXCESS

Fig. 37
A CENTER LACE INSERTION OVER SEAM

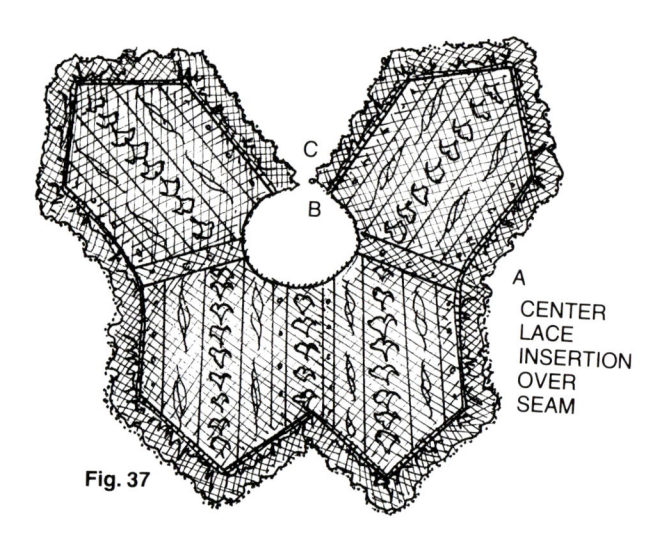

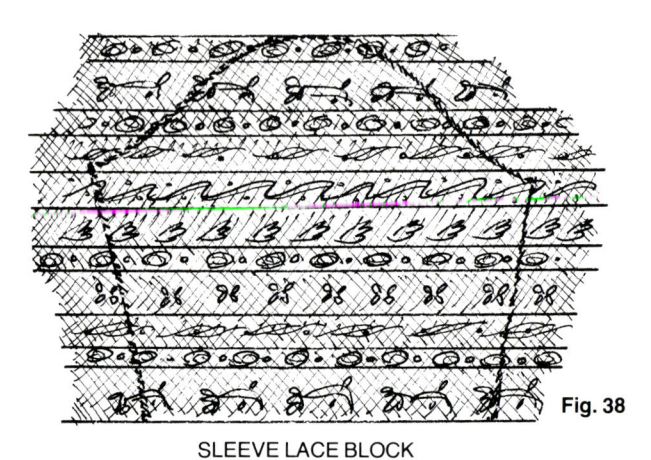

Fig. 38
SLEEVE LACE BLOCK

Fig. 39

Fig. 40

The sleeves are cut from a lace yoke block with the lace sewn horizontally. (Fig. 38)

The skirt is 60 inches at the top and 3½ yards at the bottom edge. This fullness is achieved by pressing the bottom of each row of lace after it has been sewn to the row above. The pressing stretches the lace.

I found that it was easier to work the skirt in three sections. Make a third of it and french seam it into a circle. Make the next section in like manner and join it to the first section in equal fourths. Finally, the third section is made and put on in the same manner. The continuous placket is made with cotton net.

The collar is put onto the yoke and machine stitched 1/4 inch down around the entire neck. Trim to the machine stitching and whip entredeux to the neck edge using the machine stitch as a rolled edge. Whip gathered lace edging to the entredeux.

The ruffles across the shoulder are shaped at each end (Fig. 39) and attached to the shoulder edge of the yoke. (Fig. 40)

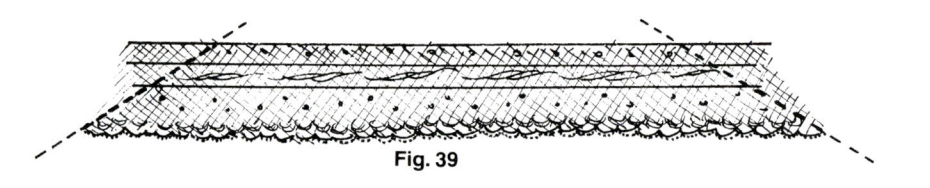

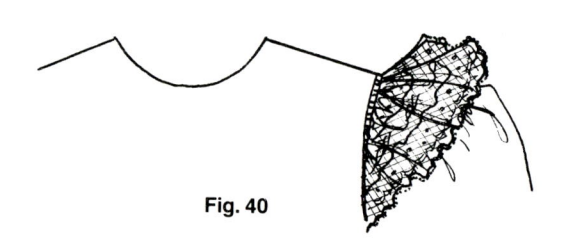

Pointed Yoke and Panels

The front and back yokes are french seamed, and the lace insertion goes from front to back across the shoulders. The front yoke is pointed and the back yoke is cut straight.

Draw front yoke and back yokes (left and

BACK YOKE

right) on a block of fabric. Do not cut out. Transfer embroidery designs and hand baste lines for lace insertion. (Fig. 41)

Embroider, wash, and iron fabric. Cut out yokes.

French seam shoulder seams.

Lay lace insertion on basted lines. Tiny baste lace to the fabric in the heavy lines. Zigzag, buttonhole, or pin stitch the lace to the fabric. Trim away fabric to stitching. Finish the bottom of the front yoke in the same way and add entredeux to the bottom of the lace. (Fig. 42) (A1-2)

Add entredeux, lace, and entredeux to the bottom edges of the back yoke. (Fig. 42B)

NOTE: Roll and whip the back yoke. Whip entredeux and lace insertion to the rolled edge before turning the placket on the fold line. Finish the placket 1/2 inch wide. Blind stitch to secure and add entredeux to the bottom lace insertion.

The skirt is made of ten panels 6½ inches wide. The lace insertion is put on each panel in the same way as for the first dress, but the bottom lace is mitered to form the points. (Fig. 43) The panels are joined by whipping the lace on the sides together. You must pin the panels to a paper guide so that they can be sewn in evenly.

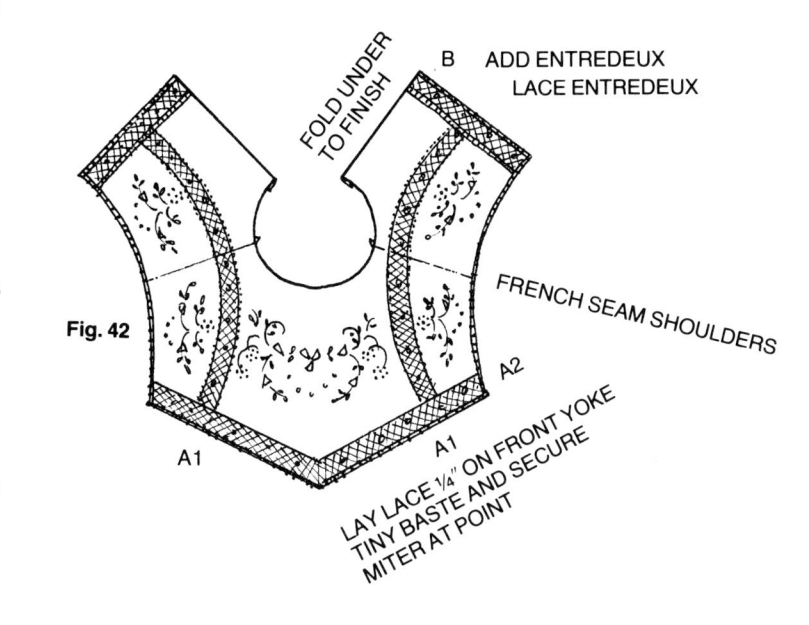

Fig. 41 — HAND BASTE LACE LINES — TRANSFER EMBROIDERY DESIGN

Fig. 42

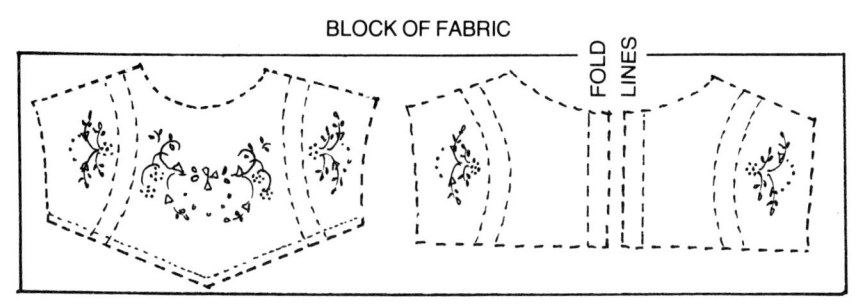

Fig. 43

As an alternate method of making the skirt, cut 2 lengths of material x 32½ inches. Pull a thread vertically every 6½ inches. Do not cut. Draw the points on the fabric with a No. 2 lead pencil. Hand baste the outline of the points with a pastel thread. Transfer the embroidery designs onto each panel. Embroider. Then wash and iron fabric. Lay insertion on each panel. Secure lace on inside line. Cut panels apart and trim fabric to 1/8 inch of lace. (Fig. 44)

Whip entredeux to the bottom edge of skirt. (Fig. 45A) Whip gathered lace edging to the entredeux. (45B)

The ruffle is attached to the slip. The lace edge on the bottom of the points should come to the top of the insertion on the ruffle.

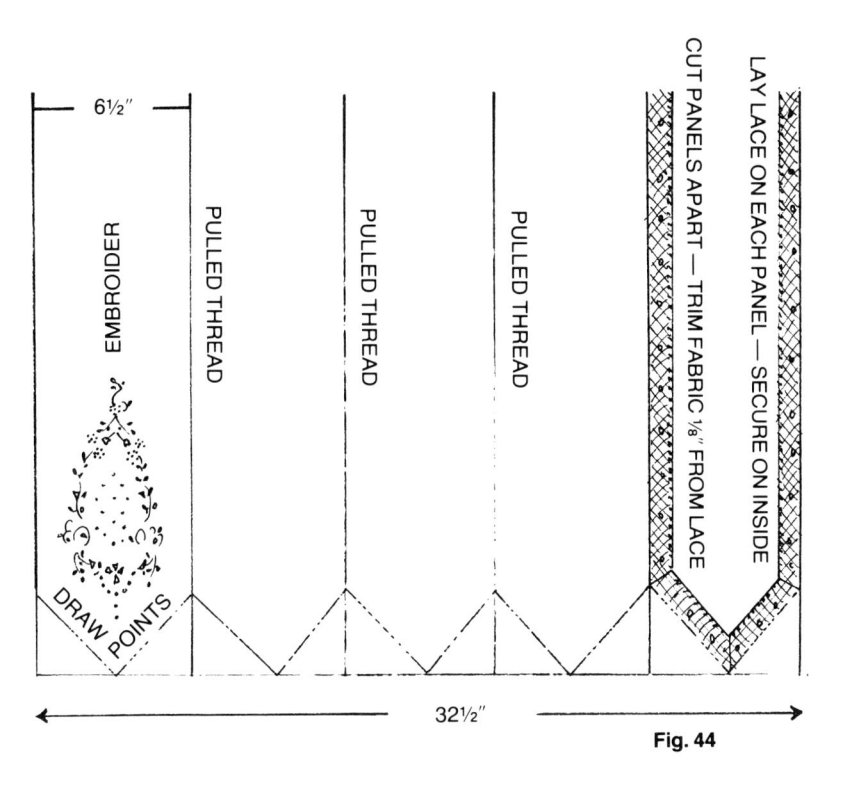

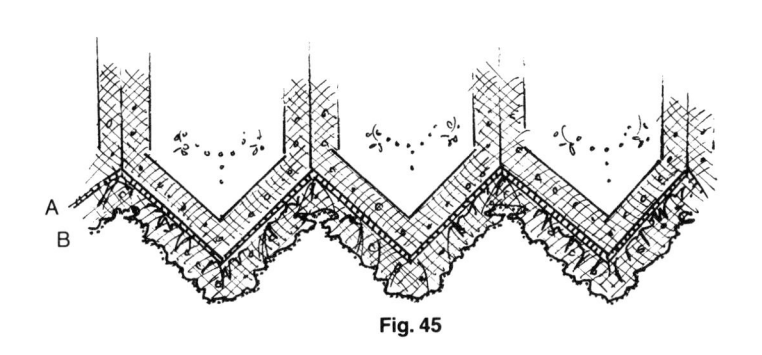

Fig. 44

Fig. 45

USE THIS DESIGN FOR BACK YOKES ALSO

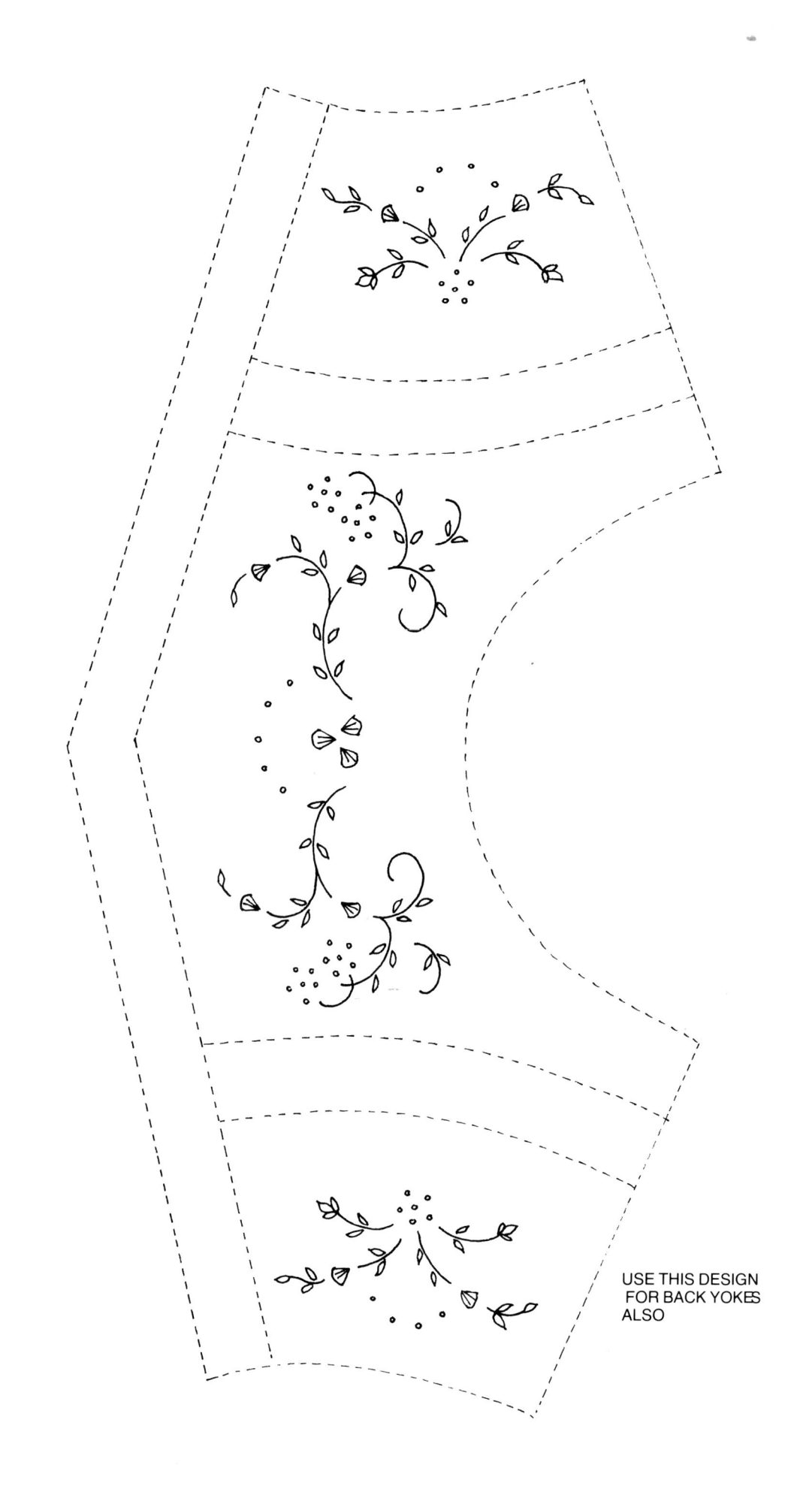

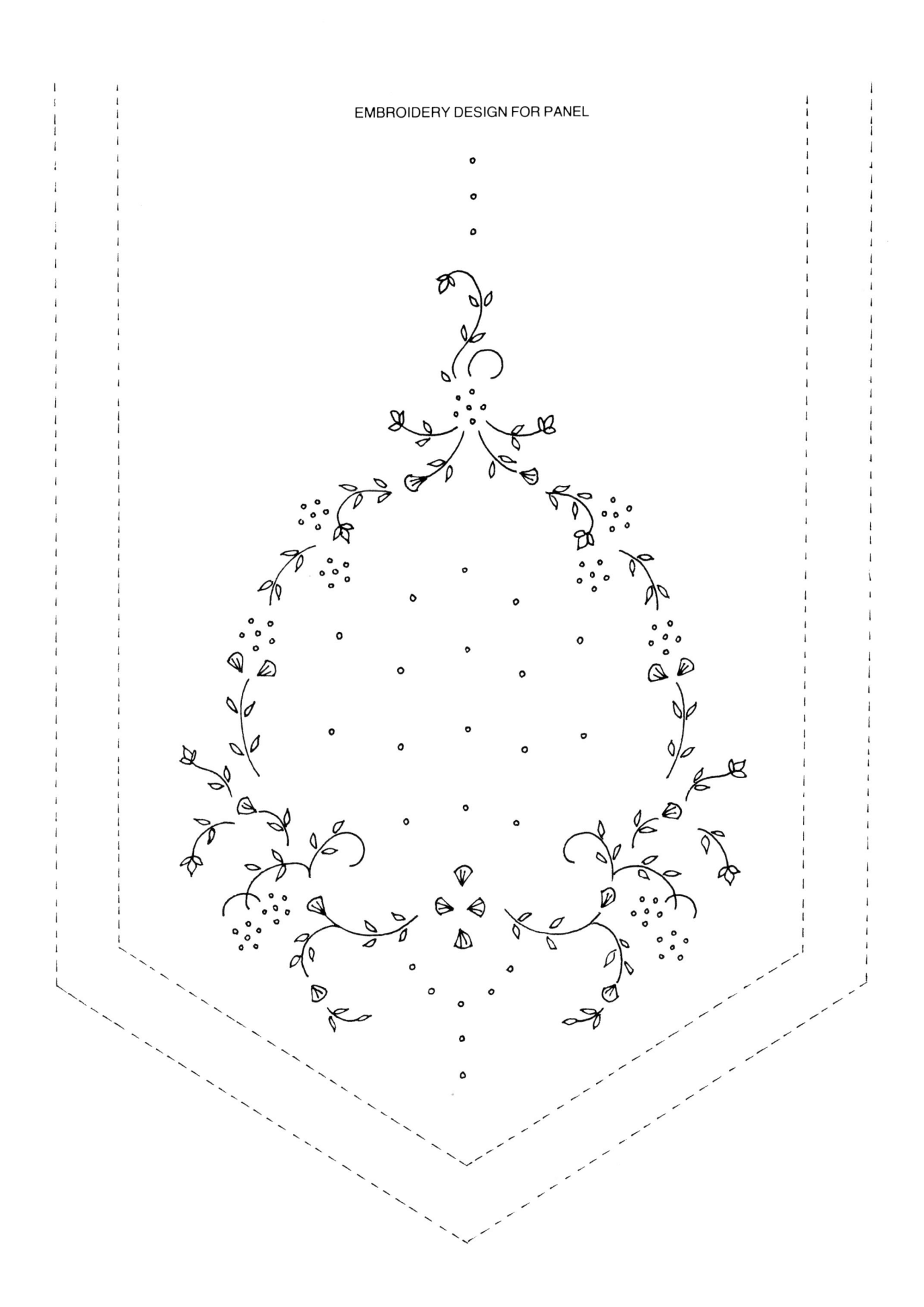

EMBROIDERY DESIGN FOR PANEL

BACK YOKE

Tucked Yoke and Bands

The front and back yokes of this dress are formed of vertical rows of lace insertion and bands of fine pin tucks, joined together with entredeux. (Fig. 46) The yoke placket is double lace insertion. (Fig. 47) The yoke is edged with a lace ruffle.

The skirt has four lace bands, two tucked bands, and one embroidered band. The skirt is edged with a ruffle embellished with tucks and lace.

The embroidered band should be french seamed into a circle before the embroidery design is drawn on the fabric. Roll and whip each side of the strip before you do the embroidery. (Fig. 48)

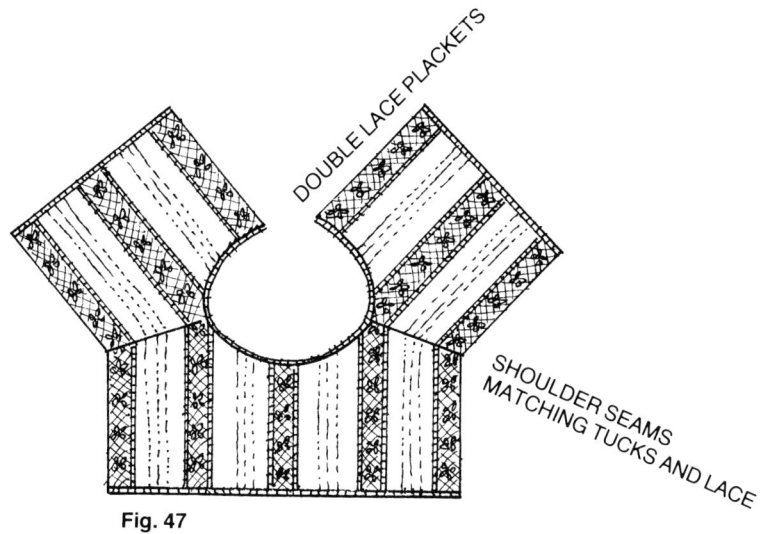

Fig. 47

YOKE BLOCKS — LACE, ENTREDEUX, AND TUCKS

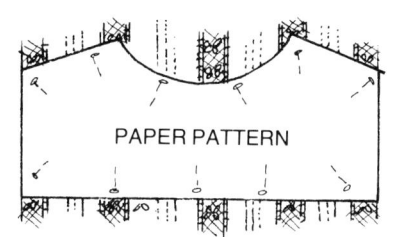

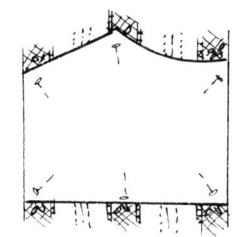

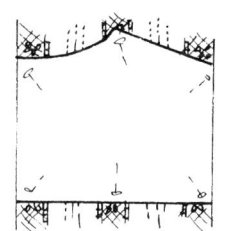

PAPER PATTERN

Fig. 46

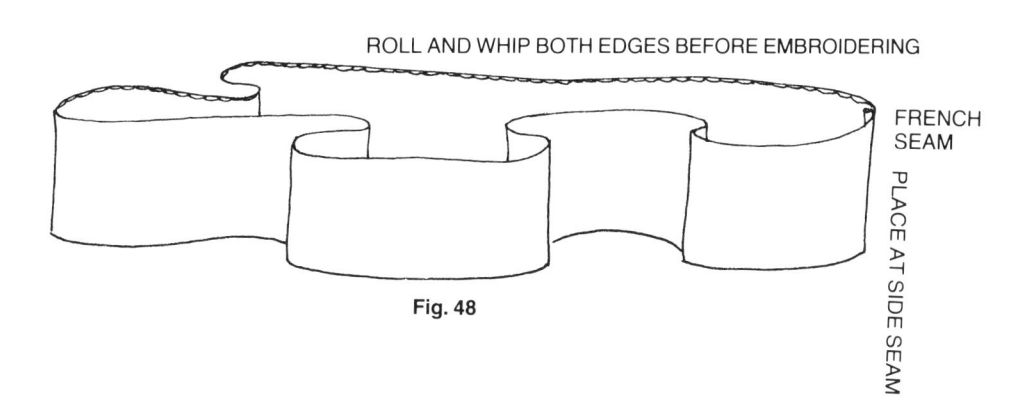

ROLL AND WHIP BOTH EDGES BEFORE EMBROIDERING

FRENCH SEAM

PLACE AT SIDE SEAM

Fig. 48

USE THIS DAISY FOR THE REPEAT
IN ORDER TO EXTEND THE EMBROIDERY
DESIGN TO THE SIDE SEAMS

EMBROIDERY DESIGN FOR TUCKED YOKE AND BANDS CHRISTENING DRESS

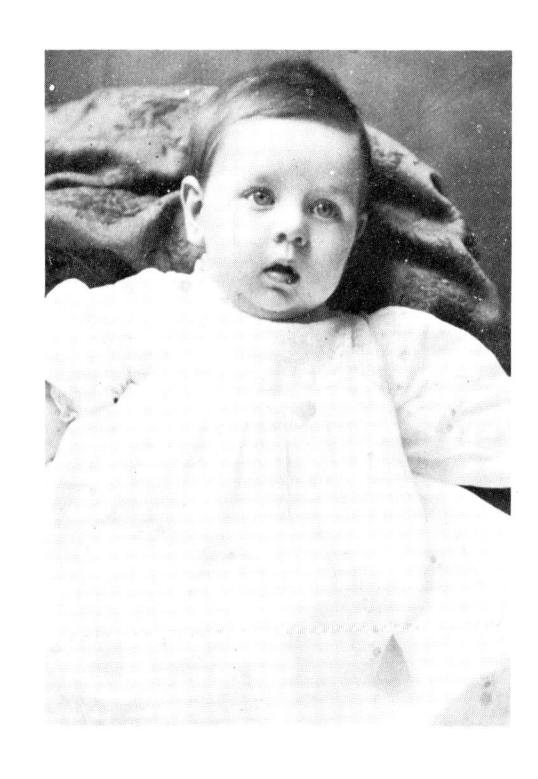

CENTER FRONT
AND
CENTER BACK

Puffing Yoke and Panel

The yoke and skirt parts of this panel are one piece. The top of the panel starts with a lace band and the bottom of the panel ends with a puffing strip. (Fig. 49) A lace band edged with a ruffle encircles the bottom of the skirt. The lace and

BACK YOKE

39

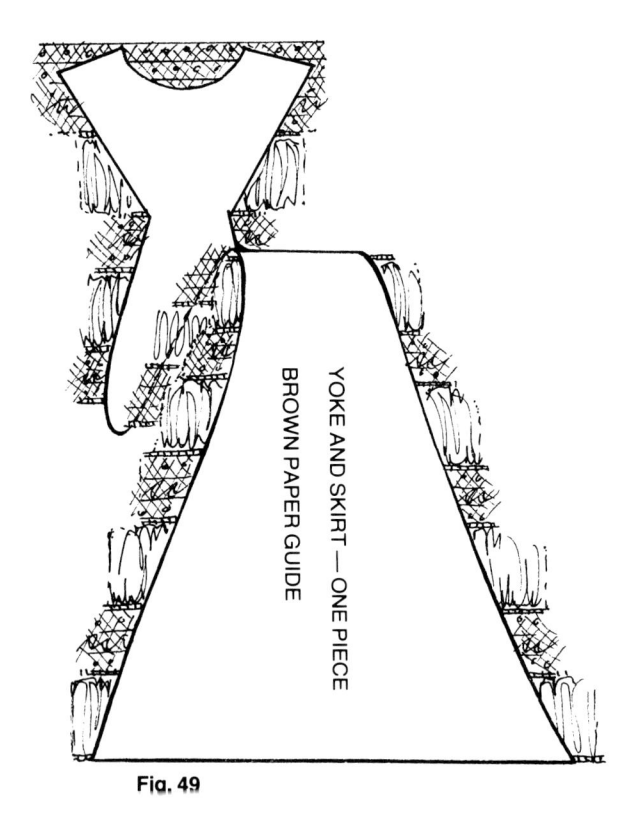

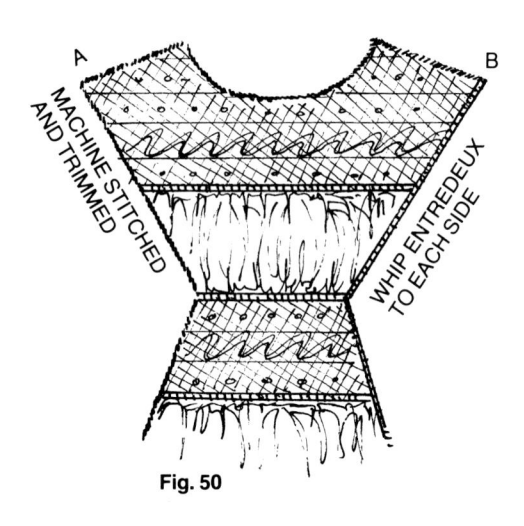

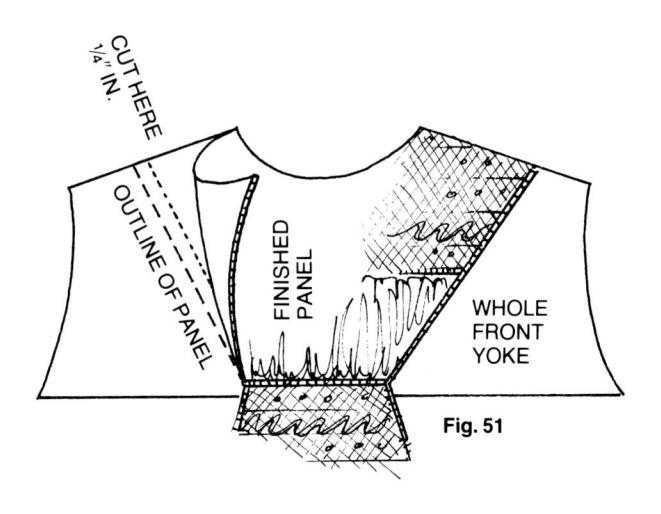

puffing bands should be made on brown paper guides. The yoke and panel as well as the sleeves are enhanced with a lace ruffle. Insertion and edging may be sewn together to form a lace ruffle if wide edging is not available.

Whip entredeux to each side of the panel using the machine stitching as a rolled edge. (Fig. 50, A and B)

Cut a whole front yoke. Lay the yoke part of the panel on the yoke and mark the sides with a pencil. Measure 1/4 inch toward the center and make another row of marks. Cut on the mark towards center. (Fig. 51) Roll and whip to the pencil mark. Roll and whip the bottom edge. (Fig. 52A) Whip entredeux to the rolled bottom edge. (Fig. 52B)

Cut the front skirt length, which should be 1/2 inch longer than the skirt panel. NOTE: (1/4 inch at top and bottom). Lay the skirt panel on the skirt front and mark the edge of the panel with pencil marks. Measure in 1/4 inch toward center and make another row of marks. Cut on the inside marks. Roll and whip and pull as if to gather and then release gathers. This will keep the bias edge from stretching. (Fig. 53)

Whip the sides of the yoke strips and the shaped sides of the skirt to the entredeux on each side of the panel, leaving the 1/4 inch at the top of the skirt above the entredeux at the bottom of the yoke. (Fig. 54A) Cut armholes in the top of the skirt front. (Fig. 54B) Roll and whip and gather the top of the skirt front and whip to the entredeux on the bottom of the front yoke. (Fig. 54C)

Split the back yokes and insert entredeux at the same angle as on the front. (Fig. 55) Turn the

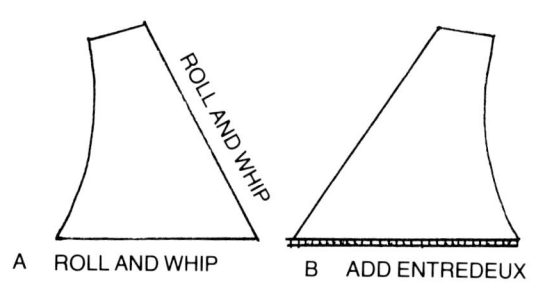

¼" LONGER

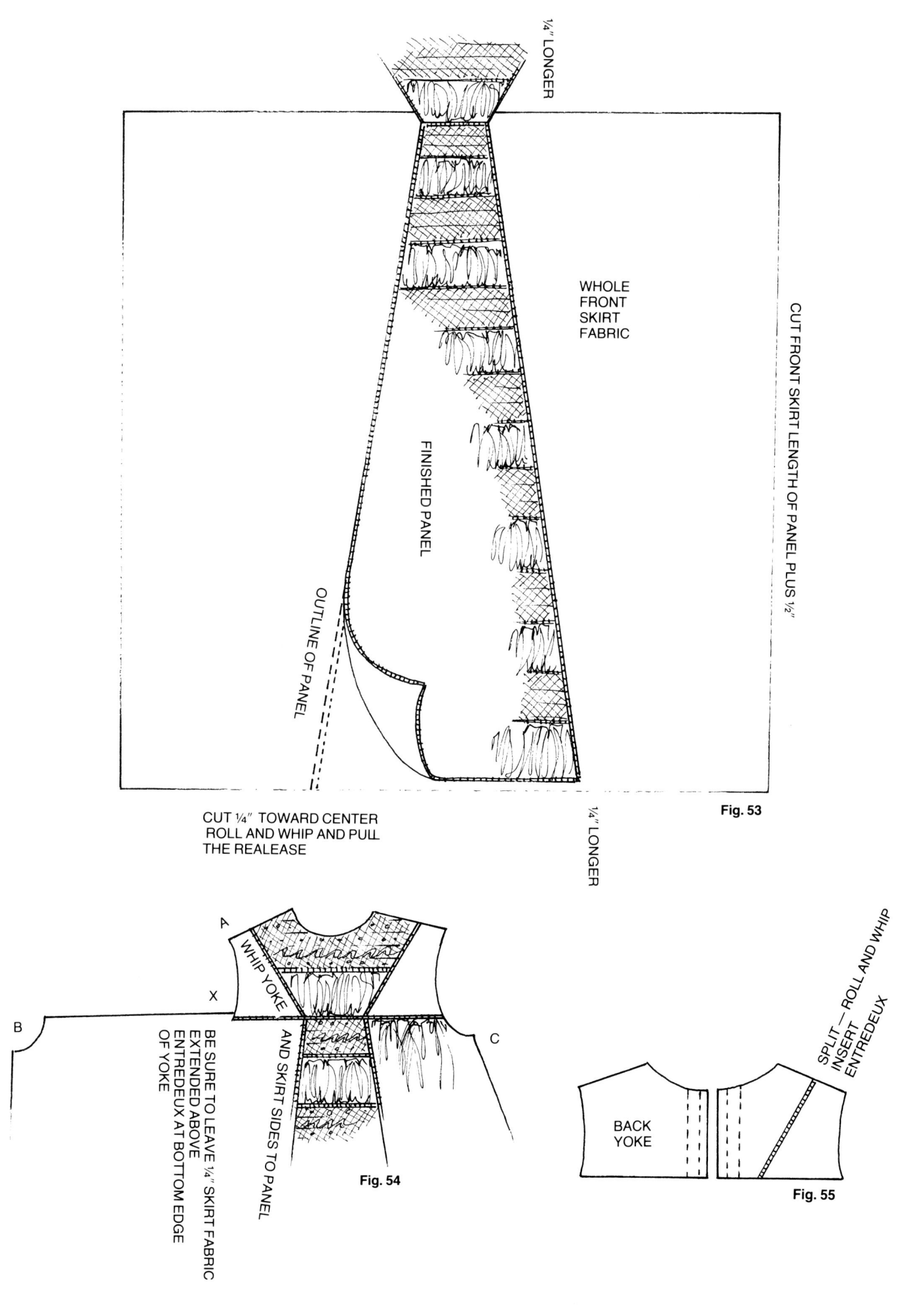

WHOLE FRONT SKIRT FABRIC

CUT FRONT SKIRT LENGTH OF PANEL PLUS ½"

FINISHED PANEL

OUTLINE OF PANEL

CUT ¼" TOWARD CENTER
ROLL AND WHIP AND PULL
THE REALEASE

¼" LONGER

Fig. 53

WHIP YOKE

BE SURE TO LEAVE ¼" SKIRT FABRIC EXTENDED ABOVE ENTREDEUX AT BOTTOM EDGE OF YOKE

AND SKIRT SIDES TO PANEL

Fig. 54

SPLIT — ROLL AND WHIP INSERT ENTREDEUX

BACK YOKE

Fig. 55

41

back plackets on fold line. Turn the raw edge under enough to finish 1/2 inch wide. Roll and whip the bottom edge of the back yokes. Whip entredeux to the rolled edge. (Fig. 56) French seam the shoulder seams of the yoke (front to back). Roll and whip the neck. Whip entredeux to the rolled neck edge. Whip gathered lace edging to the entredeux. (Fig. 57)

Cut the back skirt the same length as the front. Cut armholes in the top of the back skirt. Put a continuous placket in the top center back. Roll and whip and gather the top of the skirt to fit the entredeux on the bottom of the back yokes. French seam the side seams. Roll and whip the bottom edge of the skirt. Add entredeux to the skirt edge, joining it to the entredeux at the panel edge. (Fig. 58) Join the lace band and ruffle to the entredeux at the bottom edge of the skirt.

Whip gathered lace edging to the outer edge of the panel extending across the shoulders and back yoke edge.

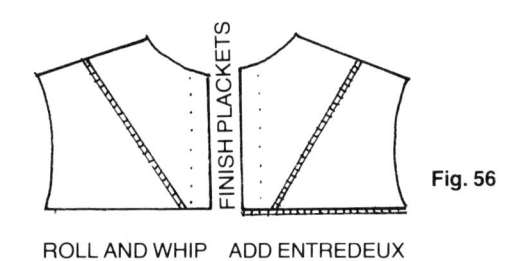

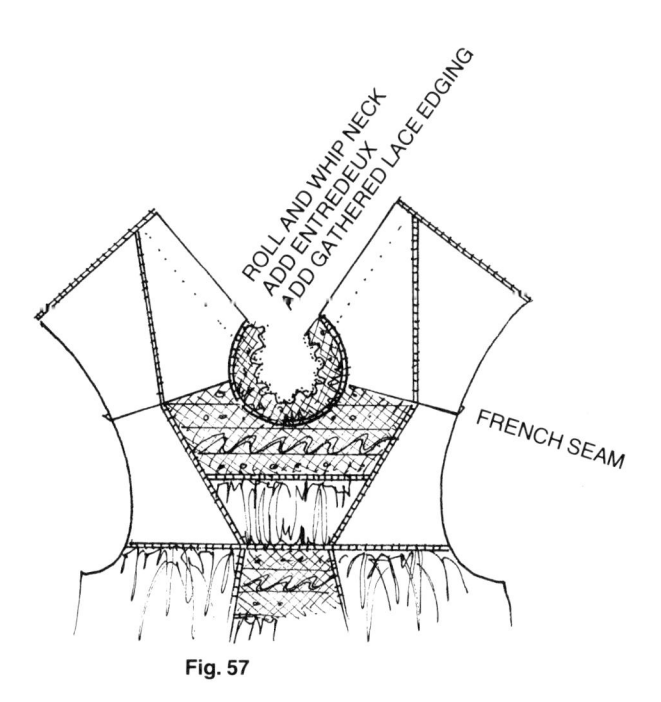

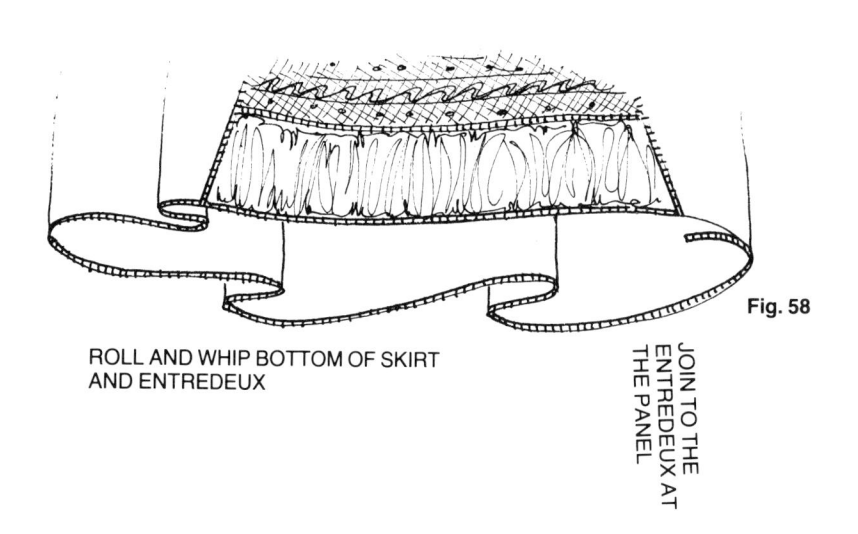

Tatted Butterfly Panel

The square yoke is cut from a tucked block of material (front and back). (Fig. 59) The bottom of the yoke is trimmed with entredeux and tatted insertion.

TUCKED BLOCK OF MATERIAL

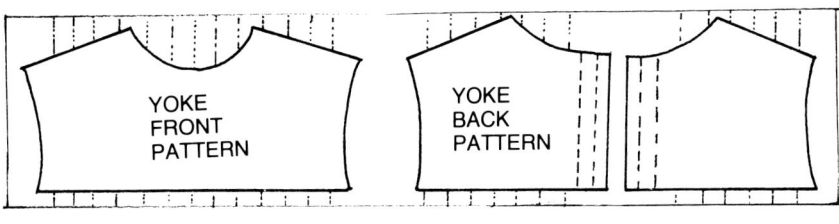

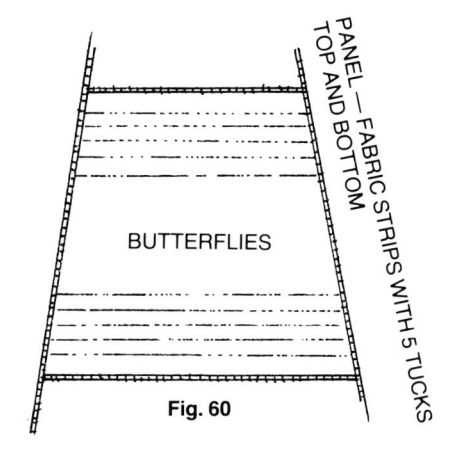

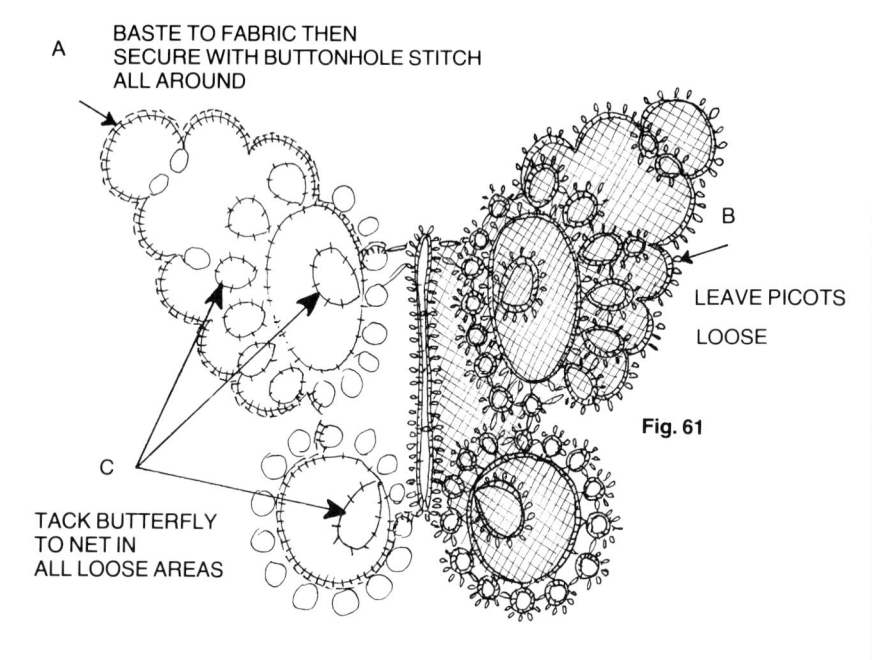

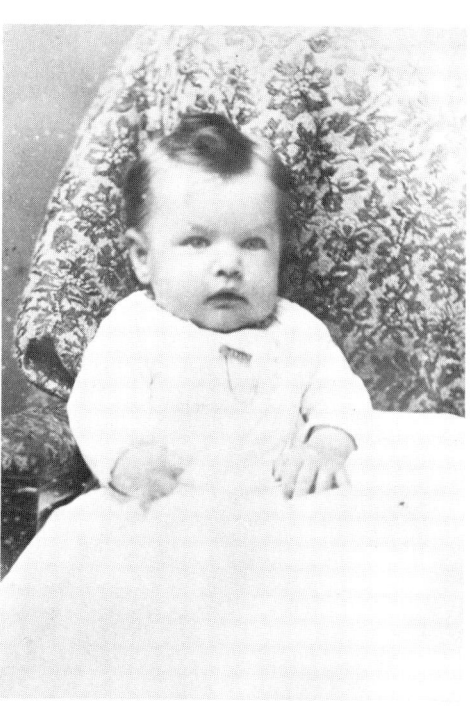

YOKE FRONT PATTERN

YOKE BACK PATTERN

Fig. 59

PANEL — FABRIC STRIPS WITH 5 TUCKS TOP AND BOTTOM

BUTTERFLIES

Fig. 60

A — BASTE TO FABRIC THEN SECURE WITH BUTTONHOLE STITCH ALL AROUND

B — LEAVE PICOTS LOOSE

Fig. 61

C — TACK BUTTERFLY TO NET IN ALL LOOSE AREAS

44

The panel is made up of fabric strips, each with five tucks at the top and bottom edge and tatted butterflies and embroidery placed between the tucks. (Fig. 60) The butterflies are basted to the panel and secured with a buttonhole stitch all around. (Fig. 61A) Leave the picots loose. (Fig. 61B) The fabric is trimmed away from behind (Fig. 62) and cotton net is applied under the butterfly. (Fig. 63) Then tack the butterfly to the net from the top side. (See Figure 61C)

The bottom edge of the skirt is tucked to match the tucks on the bottom strip of the panel. Tucks fill the space on the skirt where the butterflies and embroidery are used on the bottom section of the panel. The bottom is edged with wide tatted edging. (Fig. 64)

The slip is made to match the dress. The person I designed this dress for has never forgiven me for all the tucks I put on the slip. After many years, she still insists that she could put sleeves in the slip and it would make a beautiful dress. Don't believe her! The slip should be lovely enough to compliment the dress.

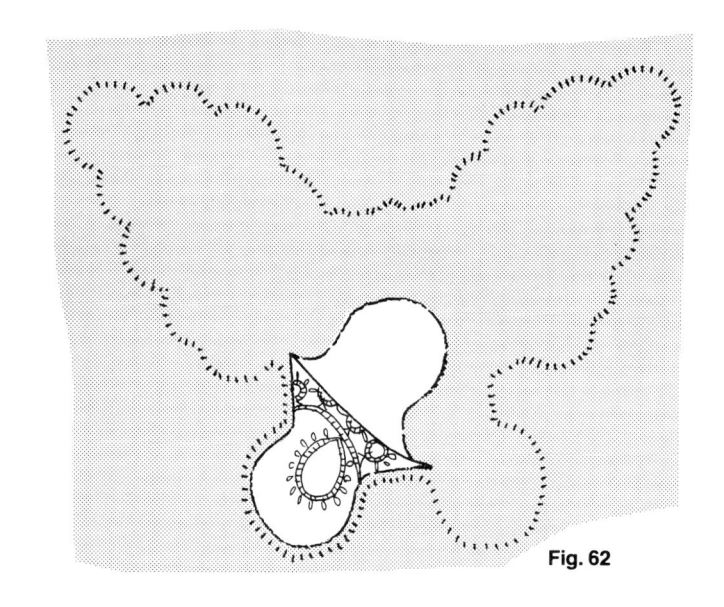

Fig. 62

TRIM FABRIC FROM BEHIND BUTTERFLY

TACK COTTON NET TO BUTTONHOLE STITCHING

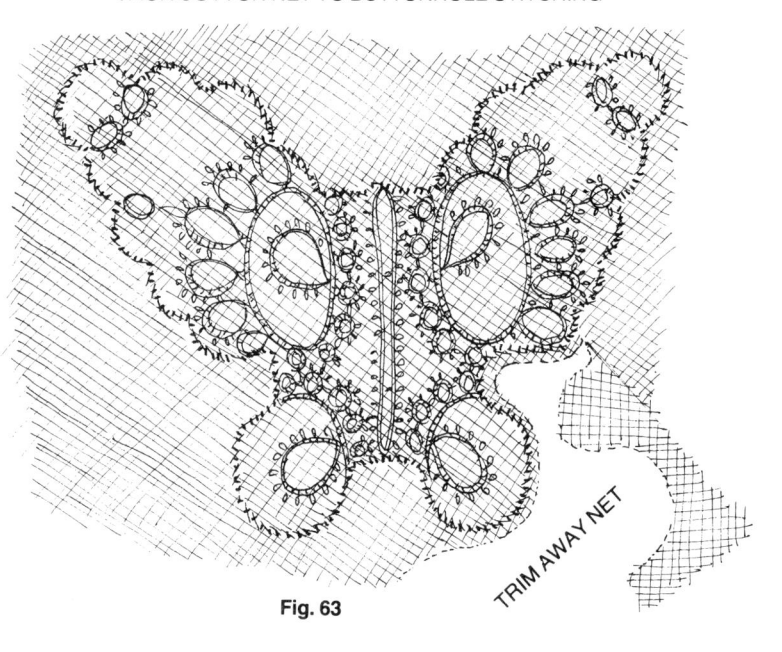

Fig. 63

TRIM AWAY NET

TUCK SKIRT TO MATCH BOTTOM PANEL

TUCKS FILL THIS SPACE

ENTREDEUX ADD TATTED EDGING

Fig. 64

SECTION 1A

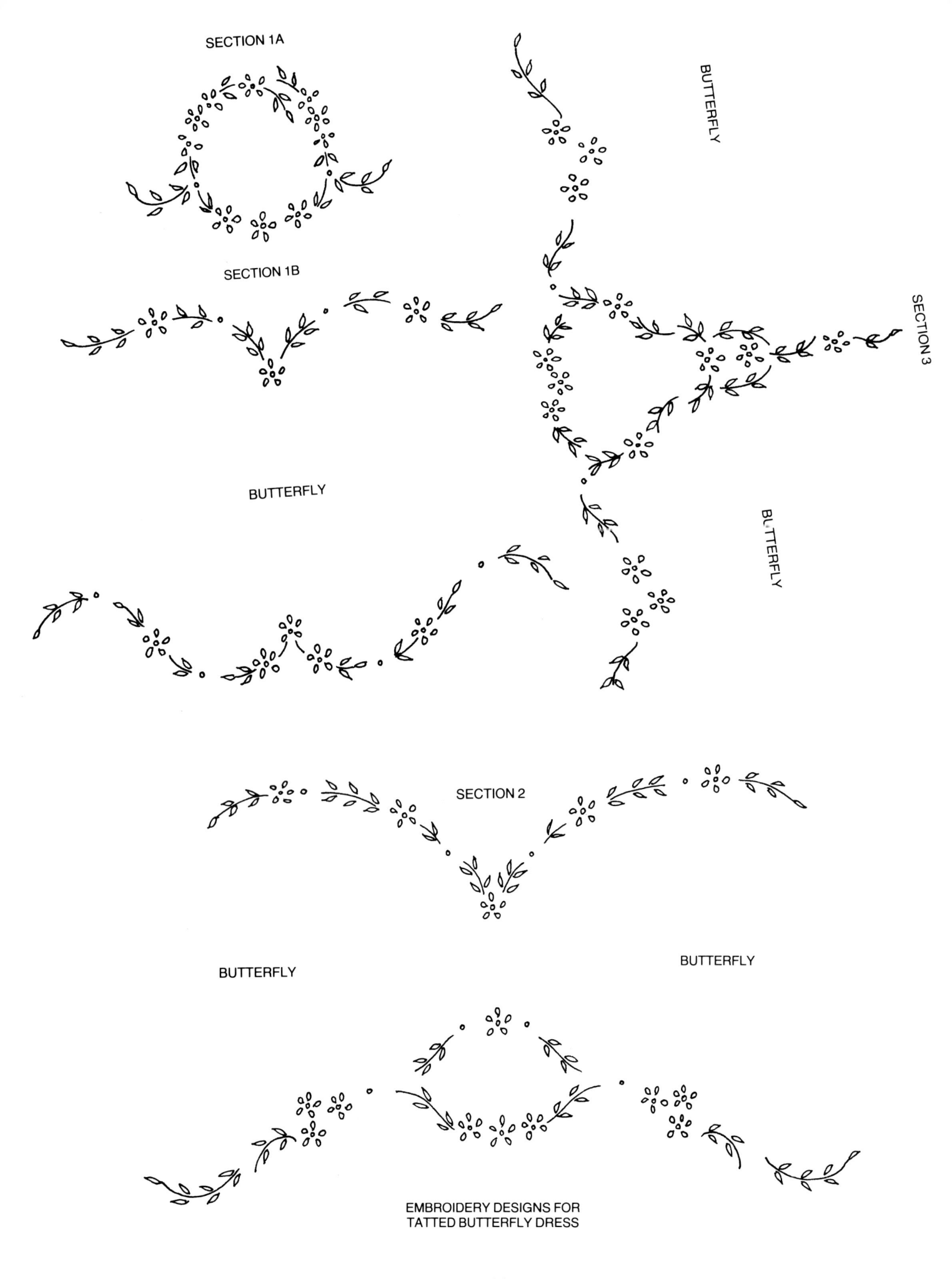

SECTION 1B

BUTTERFLY

BUTTERFLY

BUTTERFLY

SECTION 3

BUTTERFLY

SECTION 2

BUTTERFLY

EMBROIDERY DESIGNS FOR
TATTED BUTTERFLY DRESS

46

SECTION 4

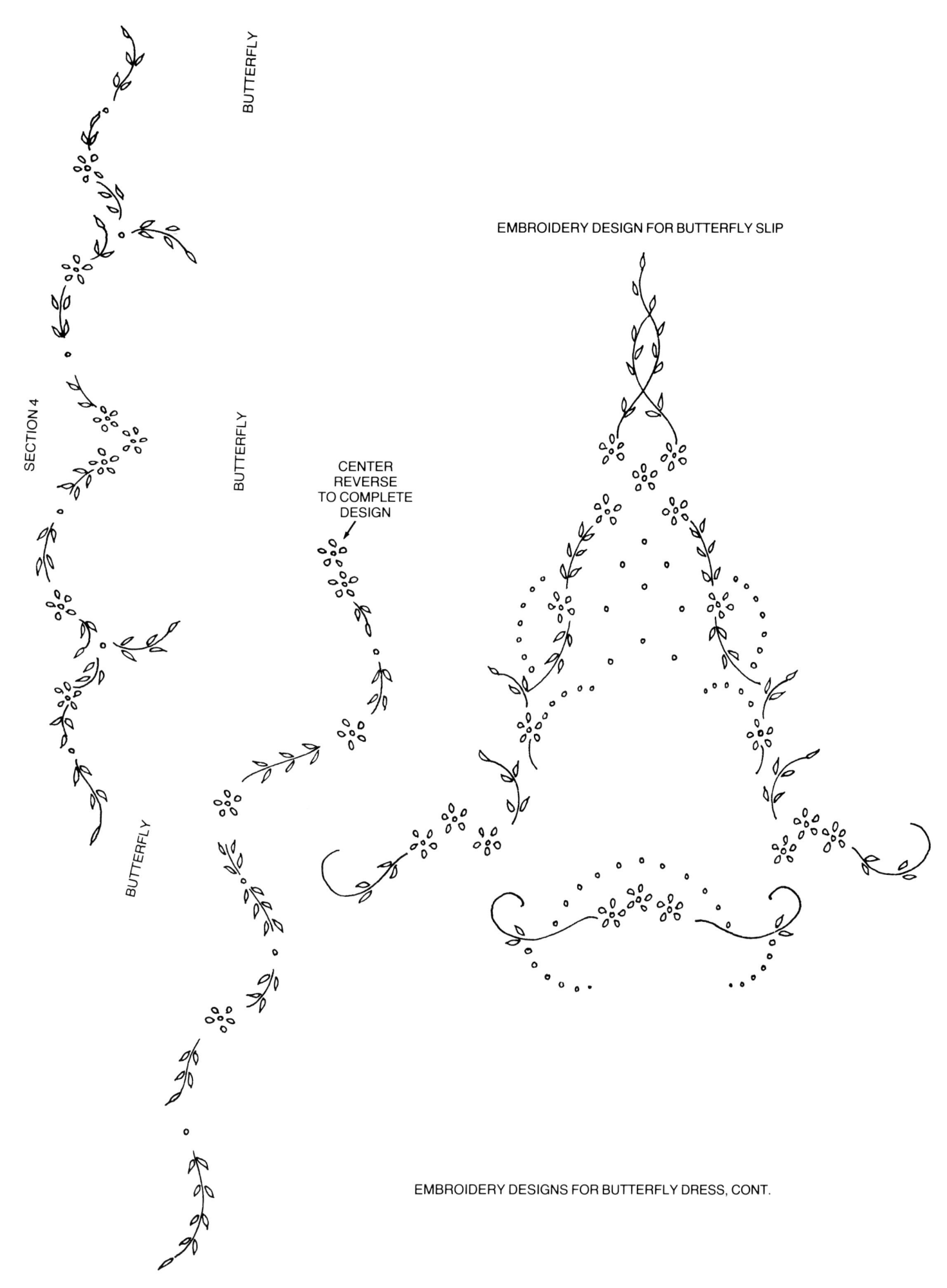

BUTTERFLY

BUTTERFLY

BUTTERFLY

CENTER REVERSE TO COMPLETE DESIGN

EMBROIDERY DESIGN FOR BUTTERFLY SLIP

EMBROIDERY DESIGNS FOR BUTTERFLY DRESS, CONT.

Basic Construction of Square Yoke Dress in Nine Steps

1. Make a yoke of your choice. (Fig. 65)
2. Make sleeves of your choice. (Fig. 66)
3. Make skirt. (For rounded (A) or pointed (B) yoke, skirt must be shaped.) (Fig. 67)
4. Cut armholes by armhole guide. (Fig. 67C)
5. Put continuous placket in top center back of skirt. (Fig. 68)
6. Roll and whip and gather top of skirt to fit entredeux on bottom of yokes. Whip to entredeux. (Fig. 69)
7. Roll and whip armhole. (Start at underarm seam.)
8. Whip entredeux to armhole.
9. Roll and whip and gather top of sleeve in equal 1/2's to fit entredeux in armhole. (Do not put gathers in skirt part of armhole.) Whip to entredeux.

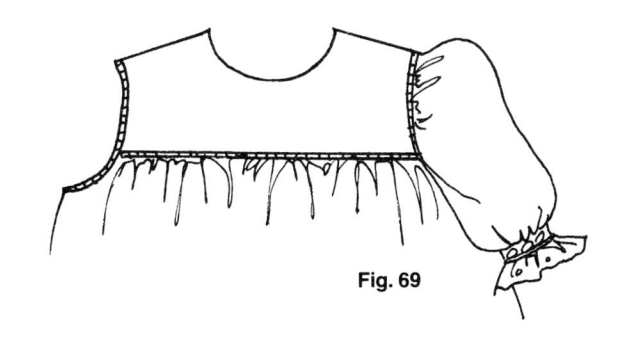

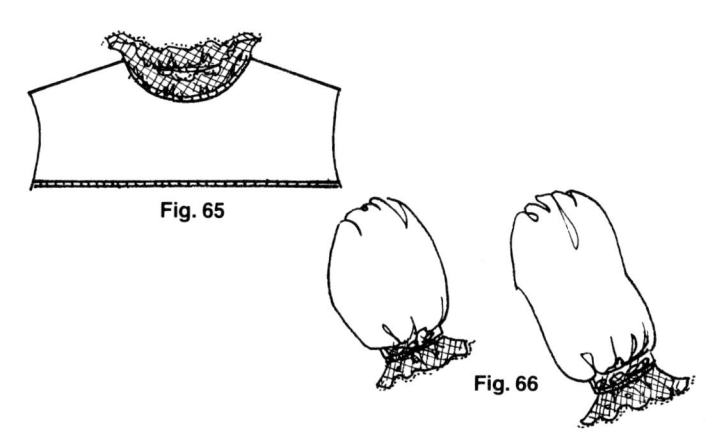

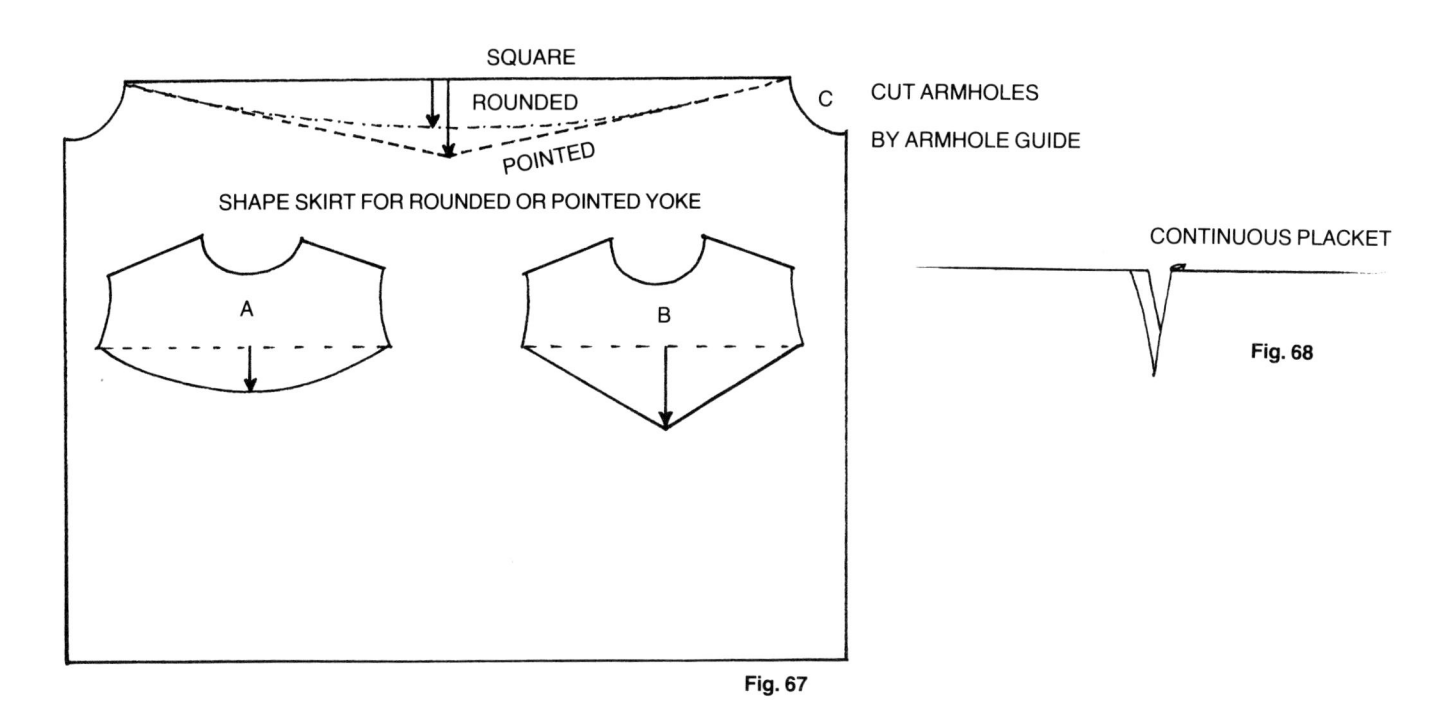

Fig. 69

Fig. 65

Fig. 66

SQUARE
ROUNDED
POINTED
SHAPE SKIRT FOR ROUNDED OR POINTED YOKE

C CUT ARMHOLES BY ARMHOLE GUIDE

CONTINUOUS PLACKET

Fig. 68

Fig. 67

EMPIRE DRESSES

Lace and Eyelet Yoke and Panel

Begin this dress by constructing the bodice. Make a horizontal block of lace and eyelet insertion for the bib front and make two blocks for the bib back. The paper guide for the bib front should

SLIP WITH SLEEVES

FINISHED DRESS
BACK VIEW

SLIP WITH FULL LENGTH SLEEVES ENDING IN LACE

DRESS WITH BELL SLEEVES ENDING IN EYELET

OPTIONAL — FABRIC SASH

be 3¾ inches at the top and 2⅞ inches at the bottom. Angle the paper guide from the widest width at the top to the narrowest width at the bottom and trim the paper guide on this angle line. This completes the front bib pattern. Make two bib patterns for the back. Including the placket allowance, each bib back pattern should be 3½ inches at the top and 2¾ inches at the bottom. (Fig. 70)

Lay the patterns for the bibs on the horizontal

blocks of trim. Pin to secure. Machine stitch with a tiny zigzag as close to the paper as possible. Trim excess away (Fig. 71A)

Whip entredeux to the top edge and to each side edge of the bib front. (Fig. 71B)

Make four lace strips (two for the front and two for the back). Make them long enough to set at an angle to the bibs as shown, and to extend 1/4 inch beyond the bottom edge of the bodice front and back. (Fig. 72)

Whip one vertical lace band to each side of the bib front. NOTE: Leave 1/4 inch extending beyond the bottom edge. Zigzag across the bottom of the lace band even with the bottom of the bib. Trim excess away. (Fig. 73)

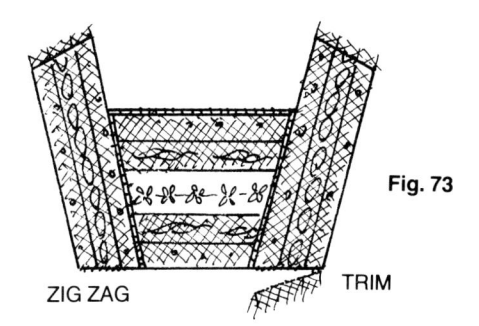

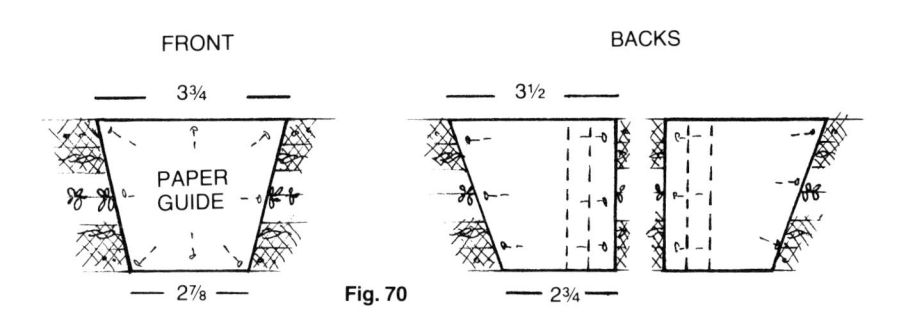

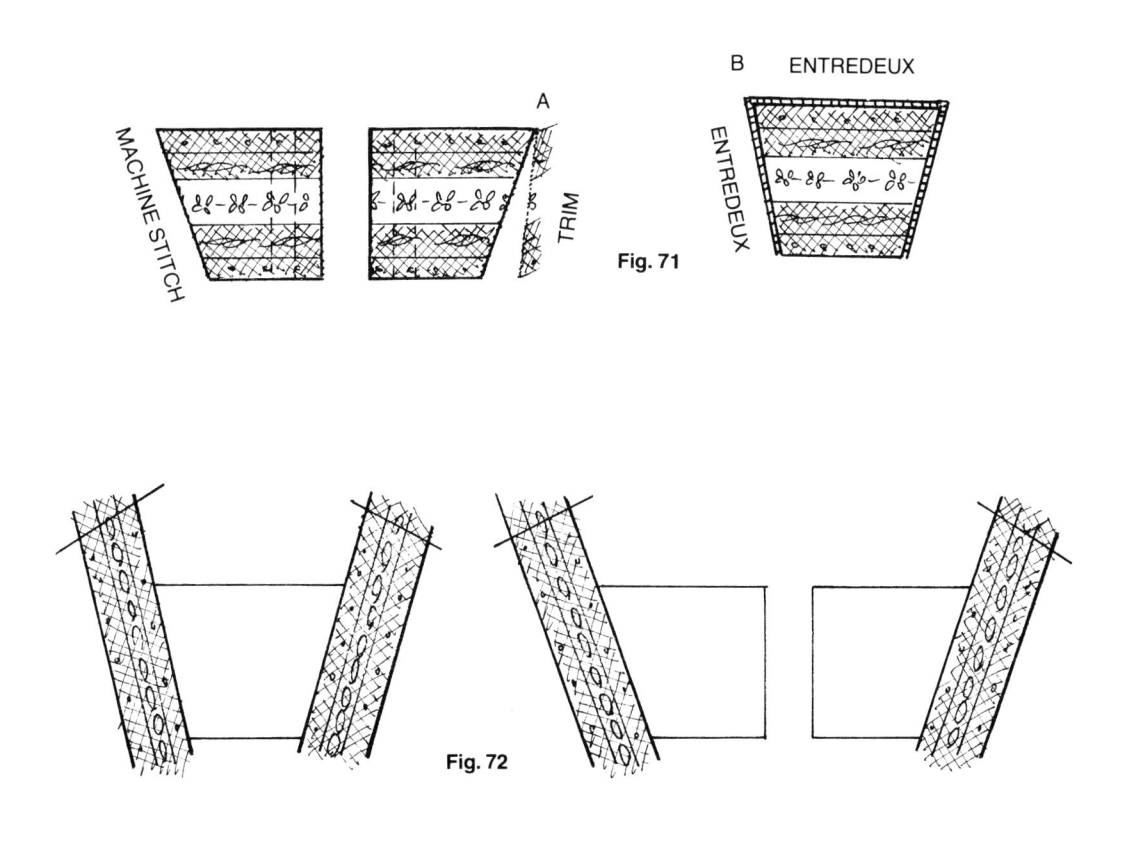

Fig. 73

Fig. 70

FRONT — 3¾ — 2⅞ — PAPER GUIDE

BACKS — 3½ — 2¾ —

Fig. 71

A — MACHINE STITCH — TRIM

B — ENTREDEUX

Fig. 72

51

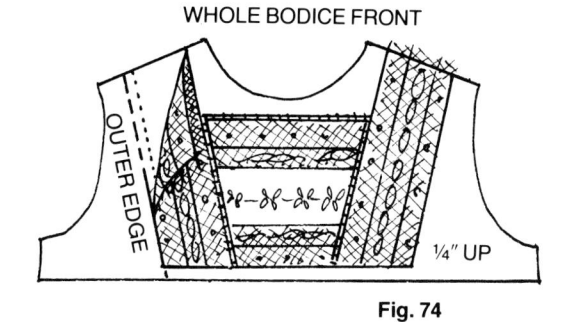

Cut a whole bodice front out of batiste. Lay the bib front on top of the bodice 1/4 inch from the bottom edge. Mark with a pencil at the outer edge of the vertical lace band. Take the bib front off the bodice and make pencil marks 1/4 inch from the original marks toward the center. (Fig. 74) Cut on these inner pencil lines and roll and whip to the first pencil lines. (Fig. 75A) Whip entredeux to the rolled edge (Fig. 75B) and join the vertical lace on the bib to the entredeux on the side of the bodice strip. (Fig. 75ABC)

Make each side of the bodice back in the same way in which you made the front. NOTE: Do not whip entredeux to the top of the bib until the placket has been finished. Turn the back placket of the bib on the fold line. Turn the raw edge under enough to finish 1/2 inch wide. Blind stitch to secure. Whip entredeux to the top edge of back bib. (Fig. 76)

French seam shoulder seams, matching laces. French seam the underarm seams. (Fig. 77A)

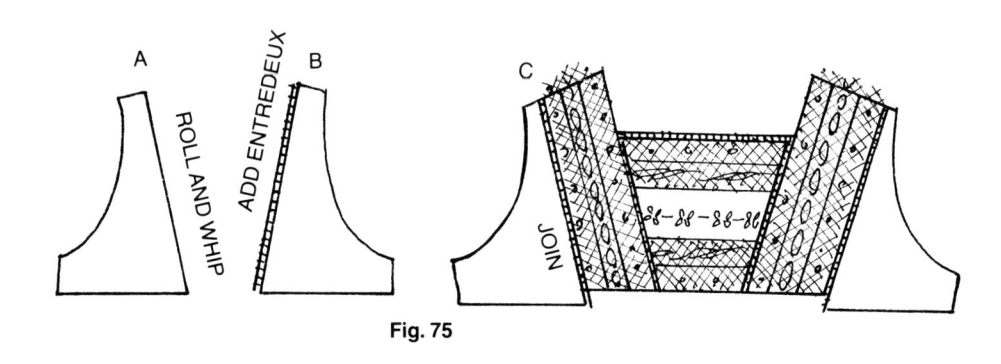

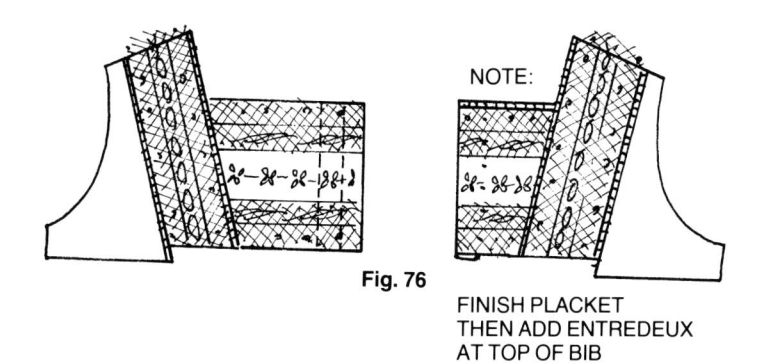

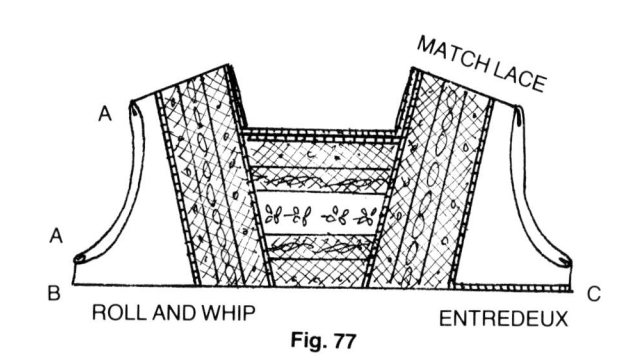

Fig. 74 — WHOLE BODICE FRONT / OUTER EDGE / 1/4" UP

Fig. 75 — A ROLL AND WHIP / B ADD ENTREDEUX / C JOIN

Fig. 76 — FINISH PLACKET THEN ADD ENTREDEUX AT TOP OF BIB

Fig. 77 — MATCH LACE / A / A / B ROLL AND WHIP / C ENTREDEUX

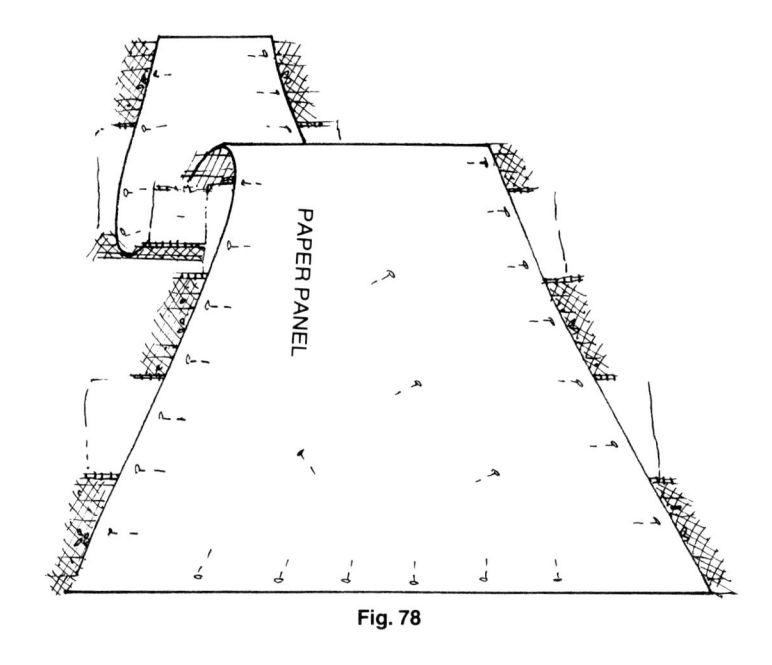

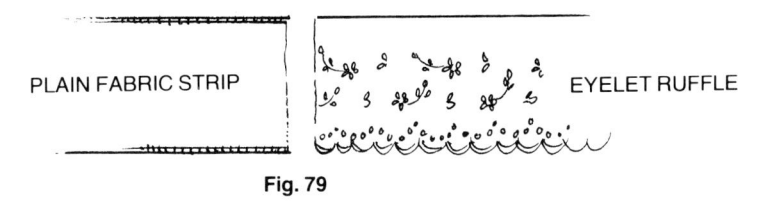

Roll and whip the fabric edge of the bodice that is extending 1/4 inch below the bib. (Fig. 77B) Whip entredeux to the bottom of the bodice, excluding the lace on the front bib. (Fig. 77C)

To construct the skirt, make a brown paper panel as wide at the top as the bottom of the bib front, including the vertical lace bands, to 18 to 20 inches across the bottom edge. Make as many lace bands as you need for the panel (one at the top edge, one at the bottom edge, and as many as you need equally spaced between). Pin to secure. Fill the space between the lace bands with plain fabric strips that have been rolled and whipped, with entredeux attached to both sides. Pin to secure. (Fig. 78) NOTE: The plain fabric strips should be the same width as the eyelet ruffles to be used on the panel. (Fig. 79)

Whip the lace bands to the entredeux on the plain strips, with the right side down on the paper and the wrong side facing you.

Roll and whip and slightly gather the eyelet edging and whip to the top of each plain fabric strip. (Follow the instructions for putting a ruffle to a finished edge.)

Machine stitch or zigzag the sides of the panel as close to the paper as possible. Trim the excess away. Whip entredeux to the sides of the panel, using the machine stitch as a rolled edge. (Fig. 80)

To construct the plain skirt, pull and cut two lengths of skirt fabric the length of the panel minus the bottom lace band plus 1/2 inch. French seam the side seams. (Fig. 81A) Roll and whip the bottom edge of the skirt. (82B) Mark the bottom width

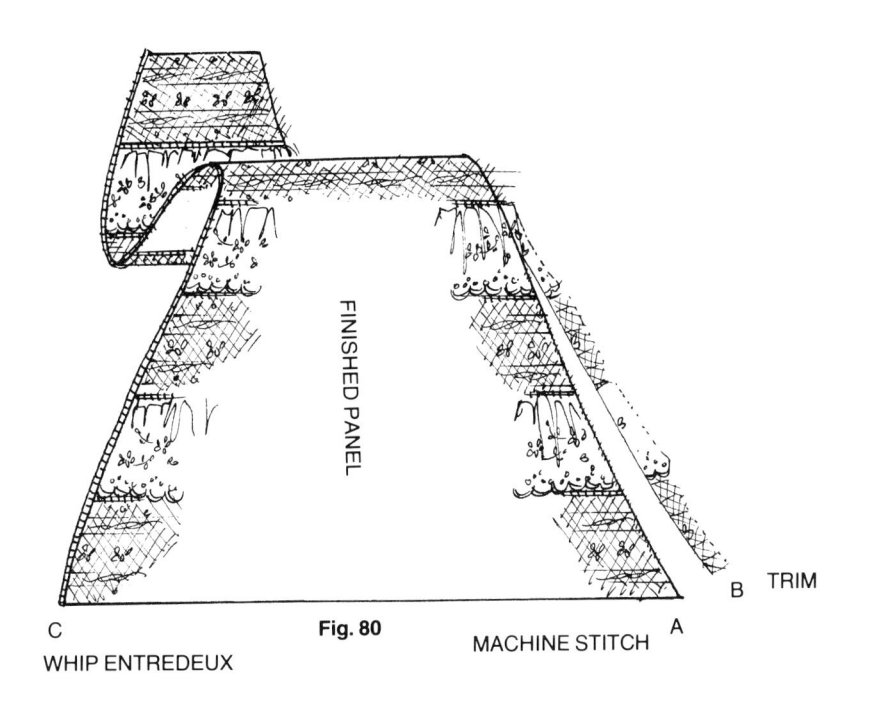

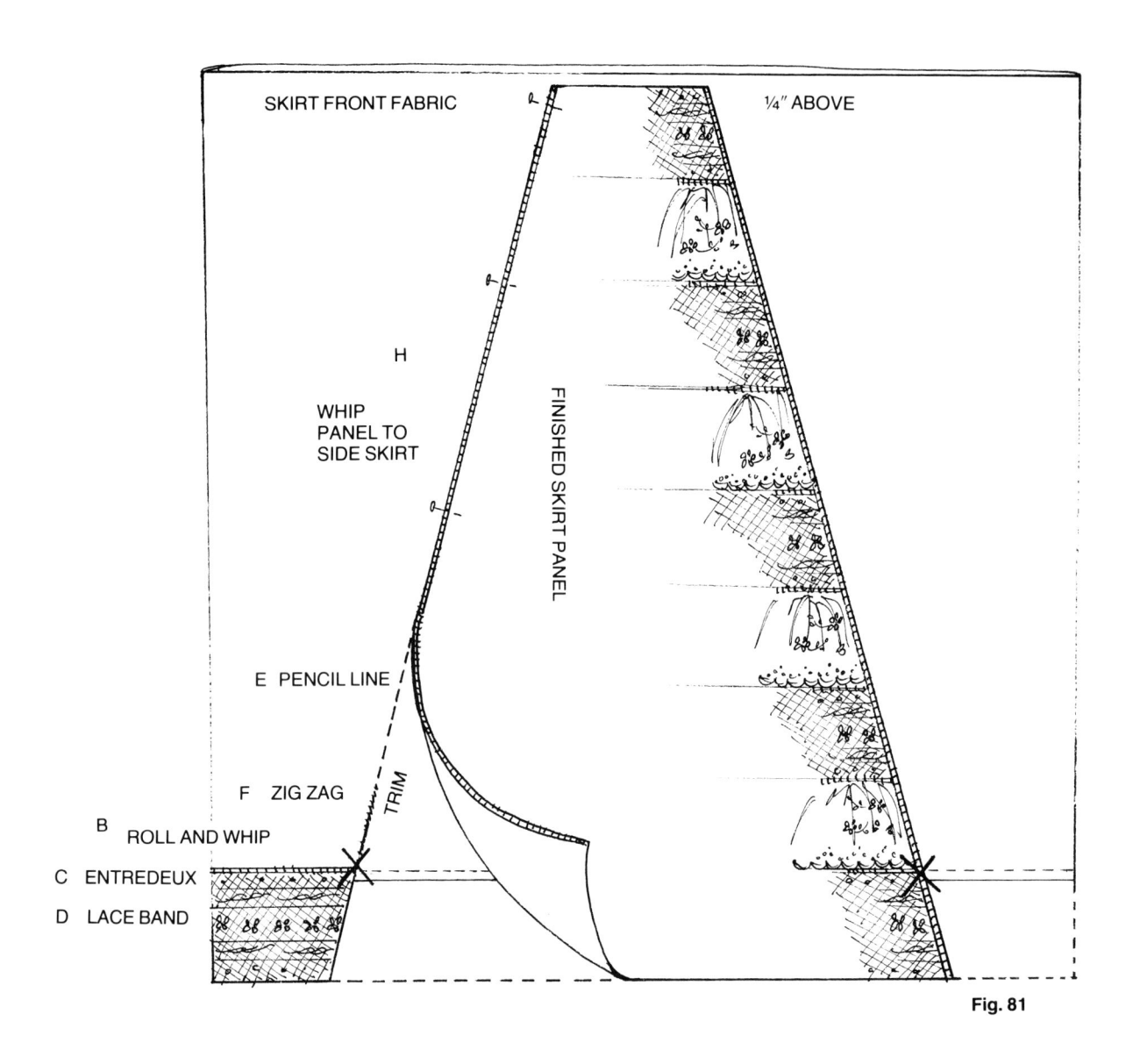

SKIRT FRONT FABRIC ¼" ABOVE

H WHIP PANEL TO SIDE SKIRT

FINISHED SKIRT PANEL

TRIM

E PENCIL LINE

F ZIG ZAG

B ROLL AND WHIP
C ENTREDEUX
D LACE BAND

Fig. 81

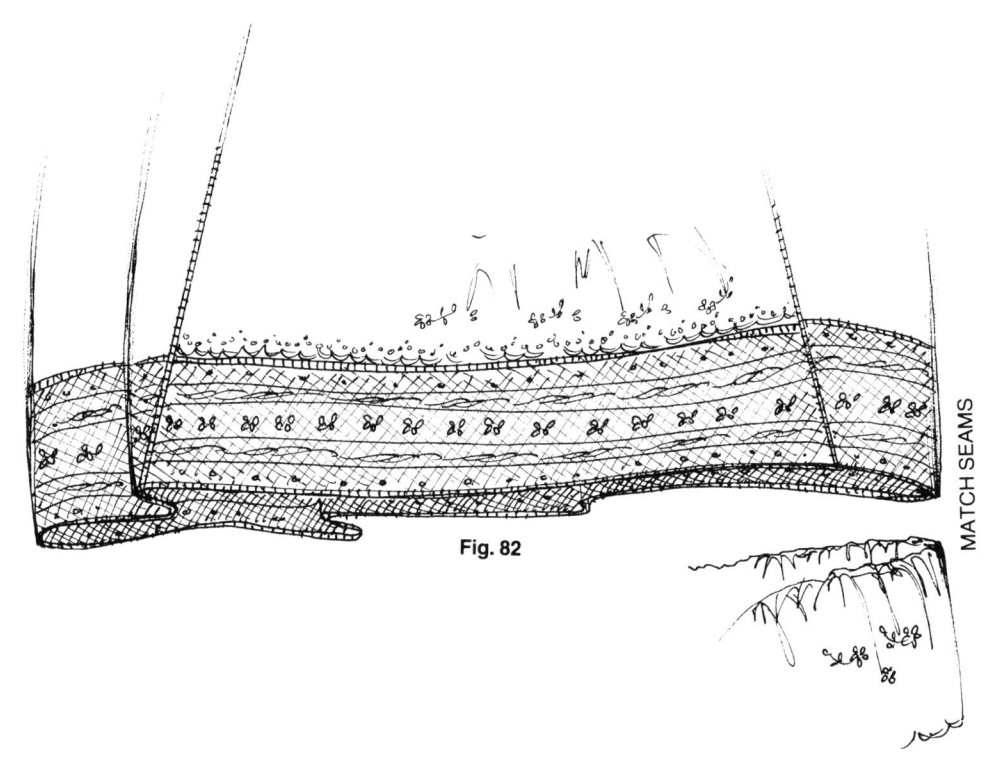

Fig. 82

MATCH SEAMS

54

of the panel on the center skirt front with X's. From X to X, whip entredeux to the rolled edge, excluding the space between the X's where the panel will go. Make a lace band (length needed) like the bands on the panel. Whip the lace band to the entredeux on the bottom of the skirt. (Fig. 81)

Lay the panel on the skirt front. NOTE: Leave 1/4 inch fabric extending above the panel. Mark the sides of the panel next to the entredeux with a pencil. Remove the panel from the plain skirt and zigzag on the pencil lines. Trim the center of the plain skirt away close to the stitching line and use the stitching line as a rolled edge when inserting the panel. Whip the entredeux on the panel to the machine-stitched edge of the skirt, making sure to pin in place at each end, in the middle, and equally spaced between. NOTE: This pinning keeps the panel in line with the skirt. Whip entredeux to the bottom of the lace band. Roll and whip and gather the wide eyelet edging to the entredeux on the skirt in equal 1/4's. Let the side seam of the ruffle match one side seam of the skirt. (Fig. 82)

Put a continuous placket in the top of the skirt back.

To join the skirt and bodice, whip the top lace band on the front skirt panel to the bottom of the bib front (lace to lace). Roll and whip and gather the top of the skirt to fit the entredeux on the bottom of the bodice (Fig. 83A); whip to the entredeux. (Fig. 83B)

To construct the sleeves, roll and whip the armhole in the bodice. Whip entredeux to the rolled edge. Make a straight sleeve with a band of lace and eyelet insertion on the bottom. Edge the band with entredeux and flat eyelet edging. Roll and whip and ease the top of the sleeve (in equal 1/2's) to fit the entredeux in the armhole. Whip the rolled edge to the entredeux. (Fig. 84)

To finish the dress, whip a lace ruffle to the outer edge of the bib back, bib front, and skirt panel. (83C) Attach ribbons or sash at the waist. The long baby sleeve is part of the slip. The sleeve is edged with eyelet beading and a lace ruffle.

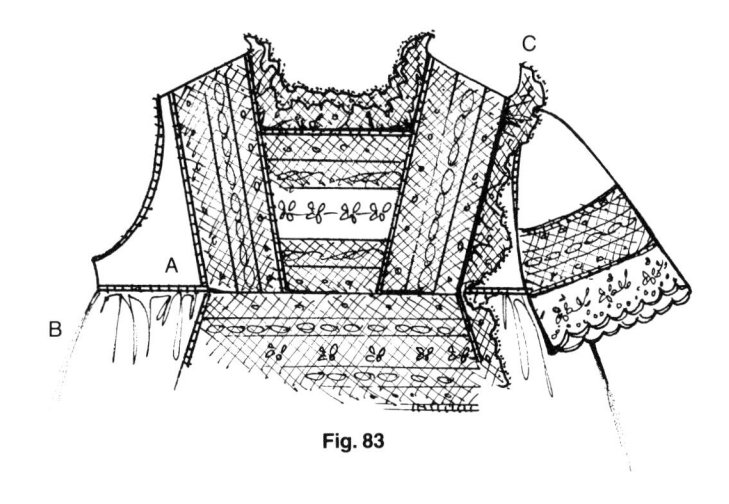

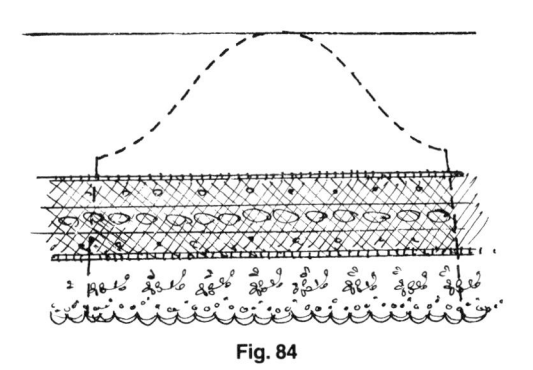

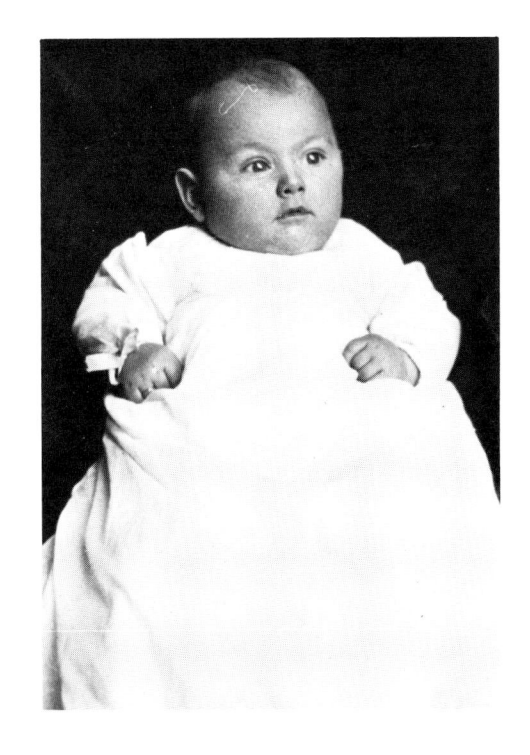

Fig. 83

Fig. 84

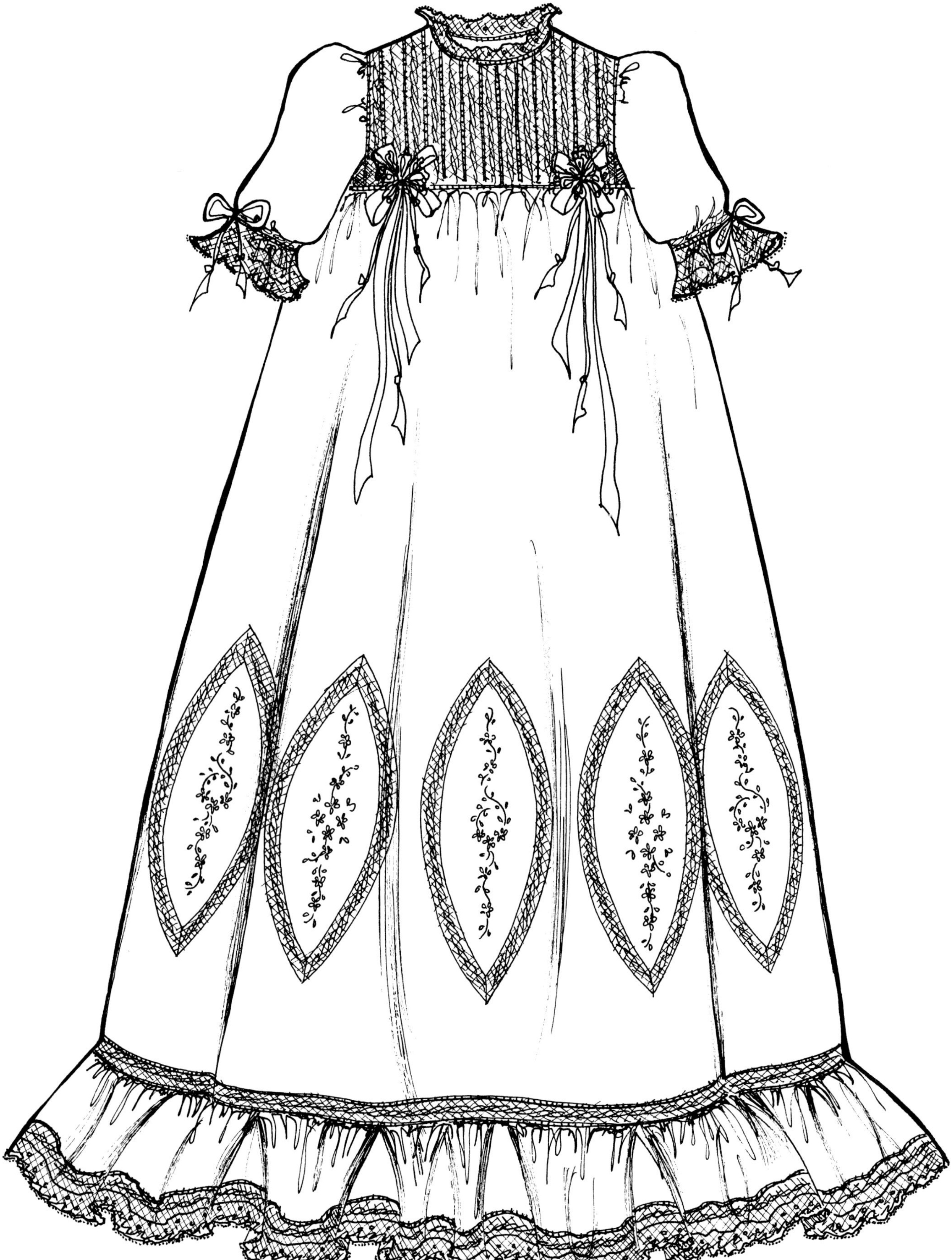

Lace Yoke and Skirt Ovals

The bodice of this dress drops about 1/2 inch under the arm. The entire armhole is in the bodice, and the top of the skirt is straight and gathered to the bottom of the bodice. (Fig. 85) The bodice is made entirely of lace insertion and entredeux. The back placket is double lace insertion.

The ovals for the skirt are drawn on a strip of fabric, and the embroidery design is transferred onto the fabric with a No. 2 lead pencil.

Hand baste the outline of the ovals with a pastel thread. Complete the embroidery before washing and ironing the fabric strip. (Fig. 86A)

Outline the ovals with lace insertion starting at the bottom edge. NOTE: Leave enough lace extending beyond the starting point to miter. You must pull a thread in the heavy line of the lace on the inside so that it will ease on the curve without puckering on the outer edge. (Fig. 86B) Miter the

STRAIGHT SKIRT

NO ARMHOLE CURVE   GATHER TO FIT BODICE

Fig. 85

STRIP OF FABRIC

A

HANDBASTE OUTLINE   EMBROIDER

B   OUTLINE OVALS WITH LACE

LEAVE ENOUGH LACE TO MITER

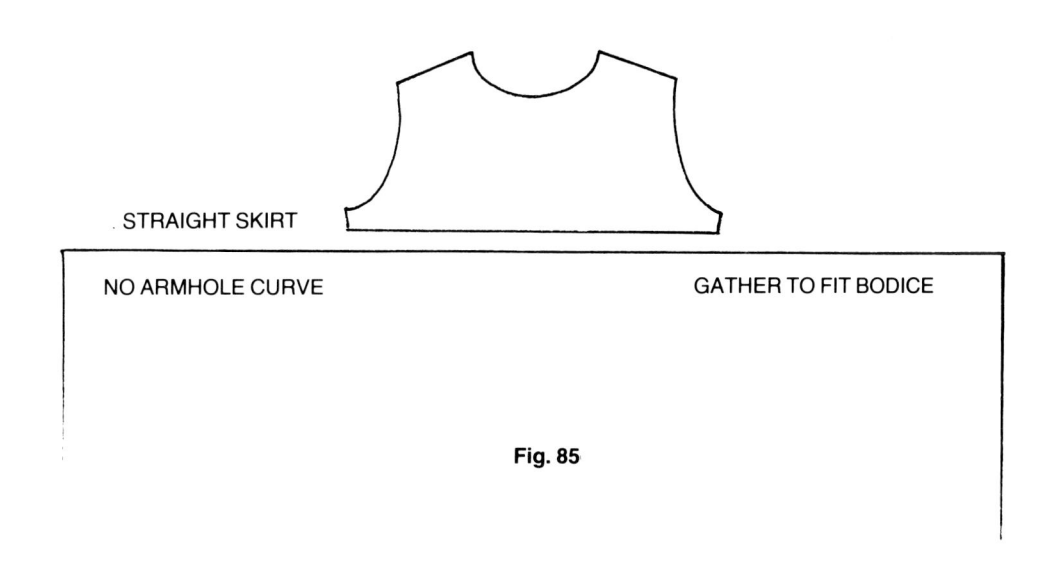

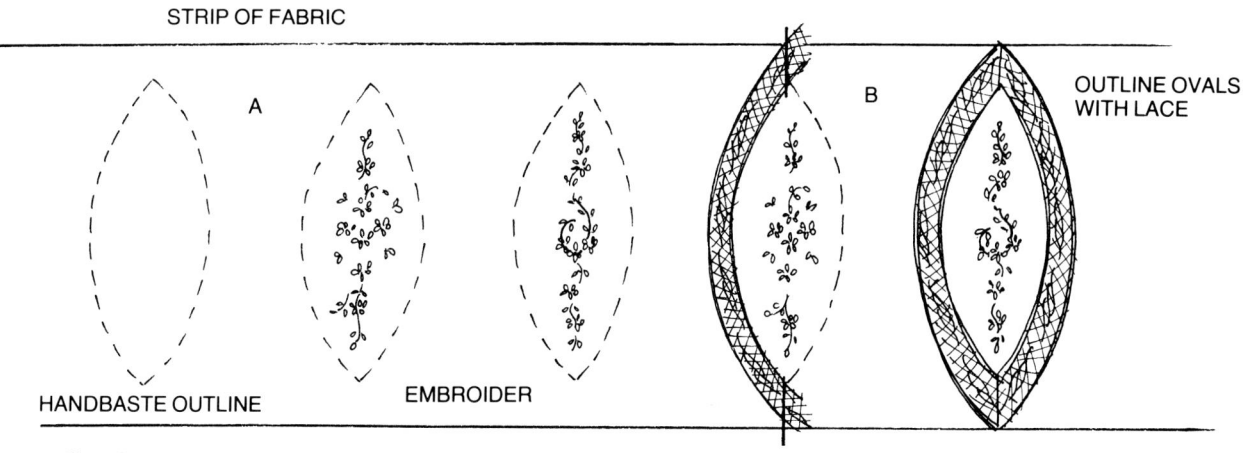

Fig. 86

top and bottom points. Tiny baste the lace to the fabric on the inside edge. Secure lace with buttonhole, satin, pin, or zigzag stitch. (Fig. 87) Cut each oval away from the fabric strip within 1/8 inch of inside stitching line. (Fig. 88)

Place the ovals on the skirt and secure the outer edges of the ovals to the skirt in the same manner in which the inside was done. (Fig. 89) Trim plain fabric of the skirt from behind the oval within 1/8 inch of the stitching line. (Fig. 90)

NOTE: The embroidery designs for this dress are shown on page 60.

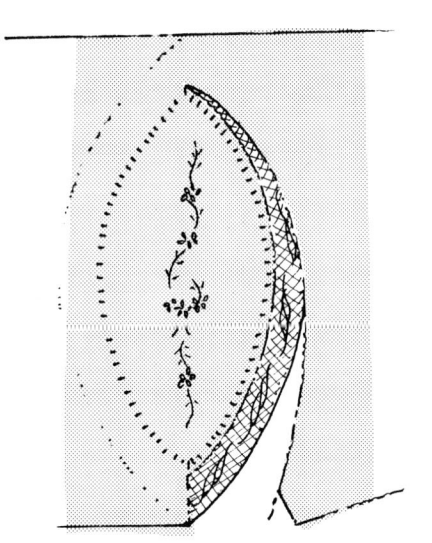

Fig. 87 TINY BASTE BUTTONHOLE, PIN, SATIN STITCH, OR ZIG ZAG

Fig. 88 TRIM WITHIN ⅛" OF STITCHING LINE

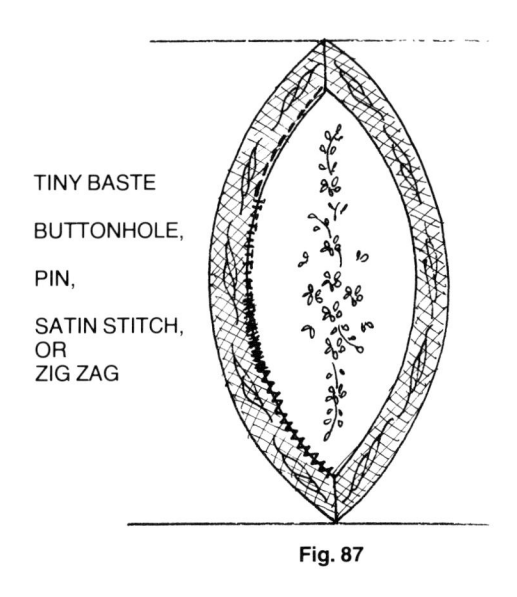

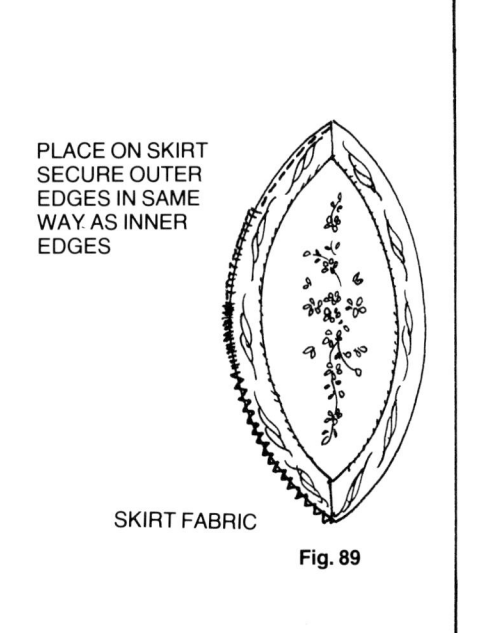

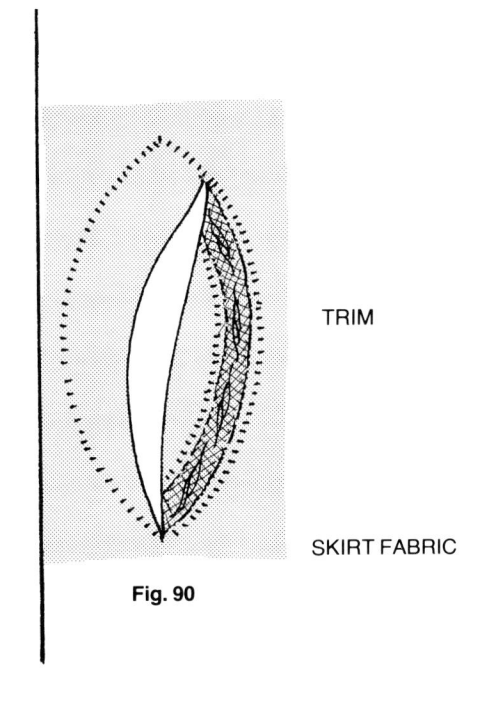

Fig. 89 PLACE ON SKIRT SECURE OUTER EDGES IN SAME WAY AS INNER EDGES — SKIRT FABRIC

Fig. 90 TRIM — SKIRT FABRIC

Basic Construction of Empire Dress in Ten Steps

1. Make a bodice of your choice. (Fig. 91A)
2. Make sleeves of your choice. (91B)
3. Make a skirt of your choice. (91C)
4. Roll and whip armhole. (91D)
5. Whip entredeux to armhole. (91E)
6. Roll and whip and gather top of sleeve in equal 1/2's to fit entredeux in armhole. (Do not put gathers in the bottom part of the armhole.) (91F)
7. Whip to entredeux. (91G)
8. Put a continuous placket in top center back of skirt. (91H)
9. Roll and whip and gather skirt in equal 1/4's, matching side seams, center front, and placket. (91I)
10. Whip to entredeux on bottom of yoke. (91J)

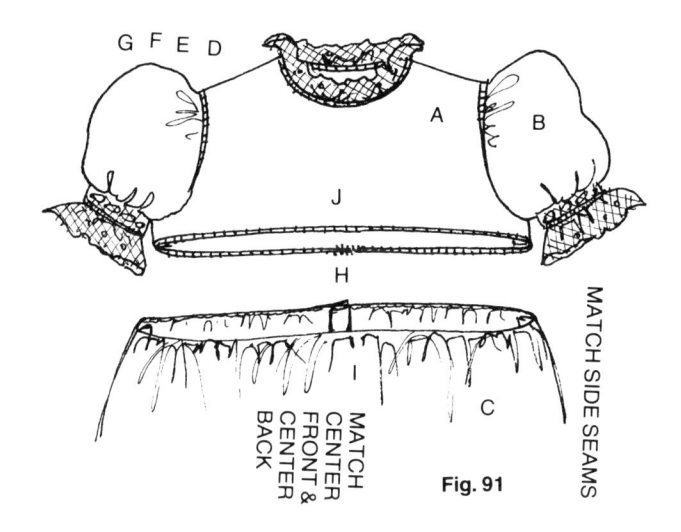

Fig. 91

CENTER FRONT AND BACK

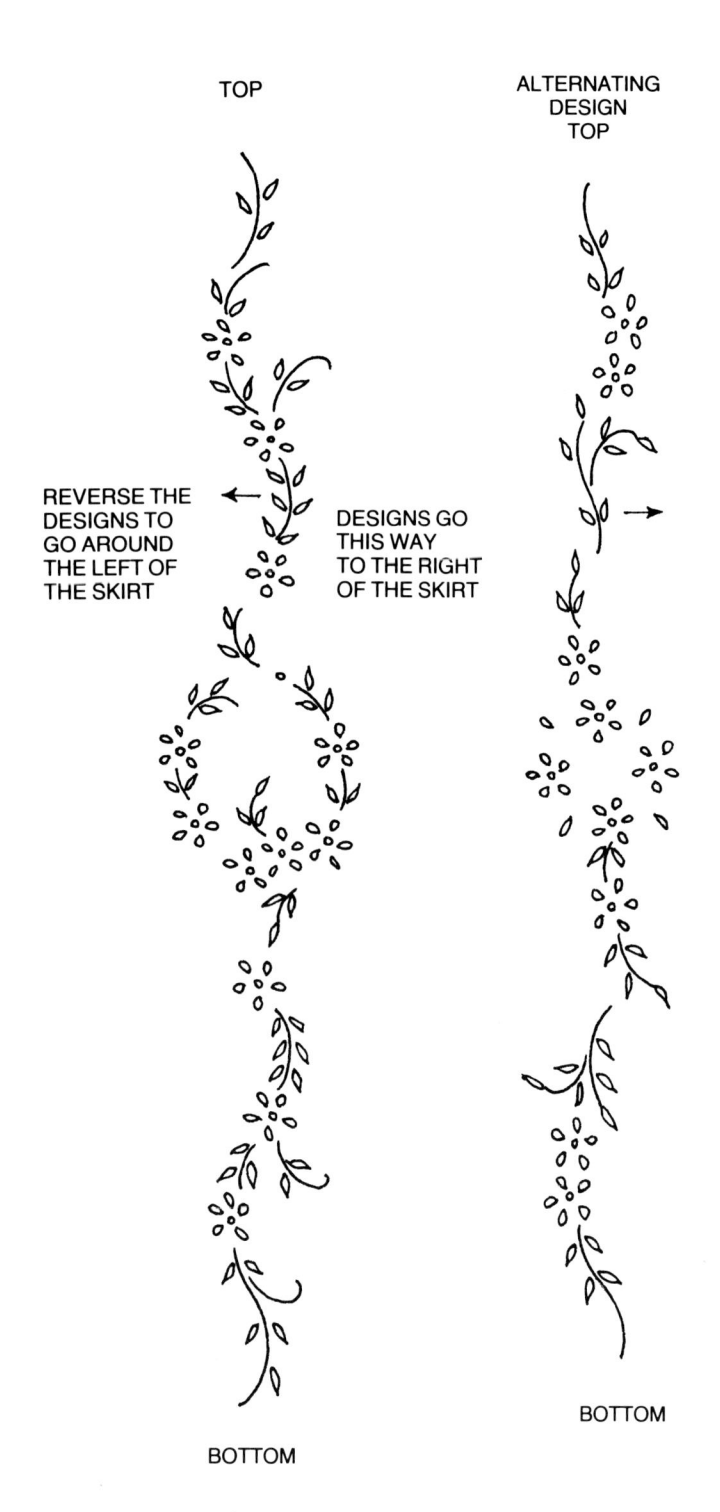

TOP　　　　　ALTERNATING
　　　　　　　　DESIGN
　　　　　　　　　TOP

REVERSE THE
DESIGNS TO
GO AROUND
THE LEFT OF
THE SKIRT

DESIGNS GO
THIS WAY
TO THE RIGHT
OF THE SKIRT

BOTTOM　　　　BOTTOM

60

A Special Gift

One of the most celebrated christening gowns I have designed was made as a gift for the first grandchild of President and Mrs. Lyndon B. Johnson.

To honor the birth of Patrick Lyndon Nugent, my sewing group, The Sew and Sews, of Montgomery, Alabama, stitched the christening gown, slip (at left), and bonnet shown. The ensemble was completed by a tiny pair of tatted shoes. The First Lady learned of this ongoing project through rela-

61

tives in the area. She sent along the slip (shown on page 61, at right) from the christening ensemble worn by the baby's mother, Luci Johnson Nugent, first worn by the President himself, so that it might be embroidered and monogrammed by the group.

To complete the work on the christening gown and accessories, seventeen members of the group worked eight hours a day for seven weeks. In all, they used thirty packages of needles, thirty spools of waxed thread, forty-five yards of insertion, fifteen yards of edging, ten yards of satin ribbon, and countless yards of embroidery thread!

The Sew and Sews were delighted to learn that Patrick Nugent wore the bonnet, embroidered slip, and tatted shoes as part of his christening ensemble. Later, the child of the Johnsons' daughter Lynda wore the full ensemble of christening gown and accessories.

EMBROIDERY DESIGN FOR JOHNSON DRESS

Slips

Slips are made to enhance the beauty of the dress. Choose the style slip that fits best under the dress you have made. The illustrations will

NO GATHERS FOR PANEL DRESSES

SLIPS FOR ROUND YOKE DRESSES

SOME SLIP YOKE VARIATIONS

Fig. 92

give you some idea of the variety possible. (Figs. 92 and 97-99) Note that the same style slips may be used with the baby and Babette dresses, adjusting the length.

To adjust the yoke pattern to use for the slip, trim 1/2 inch out of the neck. (Figs. 93-95) Trim 1/4 inch from the shoulder part of the armhole to nothing at the bottom edge. (Figs. 94-96)

For a square neck, trim the neck 1/2 inch to match the neck of the dress. (Fig. 96)

Finish the bottom edge of the slip in the same way as you finish the edge of the dress. Make the slip 1 inch shorter than the dress.

The slip should come to the shortest point in the scallop when you have a dress with a scalloped bottom.

When making a slip for a dress with a panel, do not gather the front skirt under the panel. (Fig. 97)

With certain styles of dress, a liner may be substituted for a slip. (Fig. 100, 101, 102)

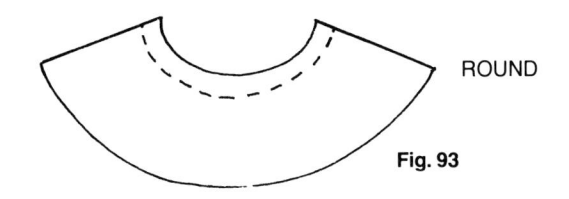

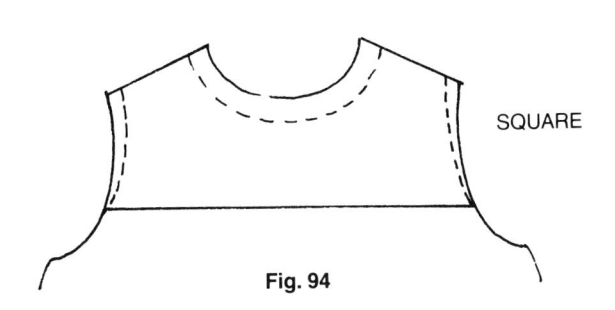

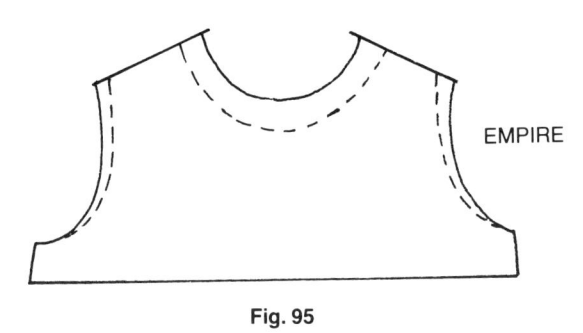

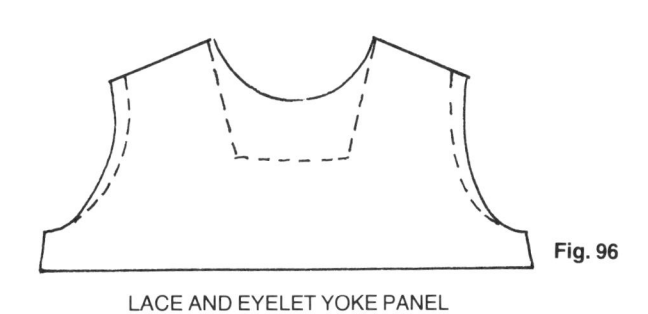

ROUND
Fig. 93

SQUARE
Fig. 94

EMPIRE
Fig. 95

Fig. 96
LACE AND EYELET YOKE PANEL

SLIPS FOR SQUARE YOKE DRESSES

NO GATHERS FOR PANEL DRESSES

SOME SLIP YOKE VARIATIONS

Fig. 97

SLIPS FOR EMPIRE DRESSES

NO GATHERS FOR PANEL DRESSES

Fig. 98

A-LINE SLIP

Fig. 99

LINERS

NOTE: THE EYELET LACE AND TUCKS DRESS IS AN EXCELLENT EXAMPLE OF A DRESS SUITABLE FOR A LINER, IN ORDER NOT TO DETRACT FROM THE LACE WORK IN THE YOKE, THE LINER SUFFICES AS THE SLIP.

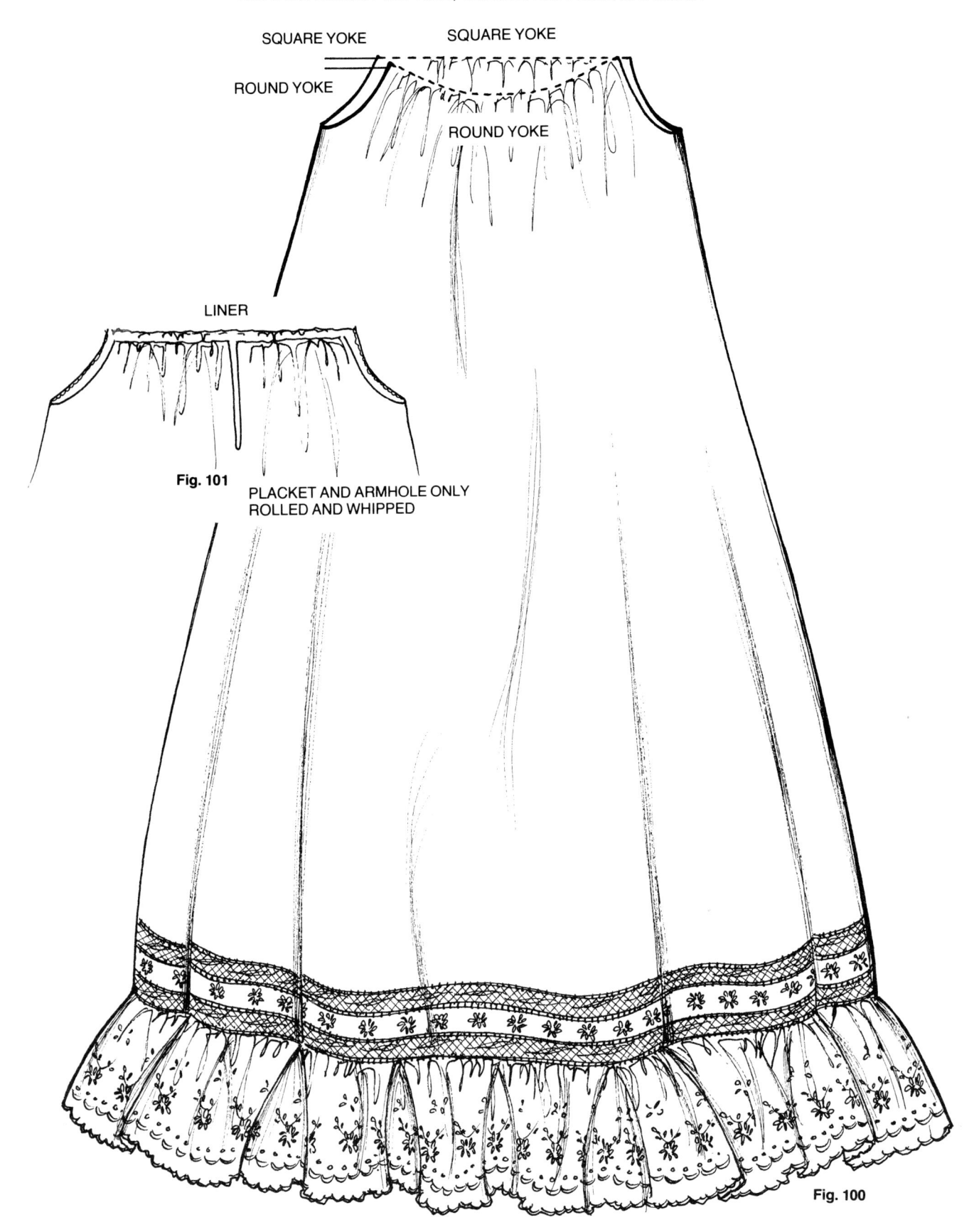

SQUARE YOKE

SQUARE YOKE

ROUND YOKE

ROUND YOKE

LINER

Fig. 101

PLACKET AND ARMHOLE ONLY ROLLED AND WHIPPED

Fig. 100

Fig. 102

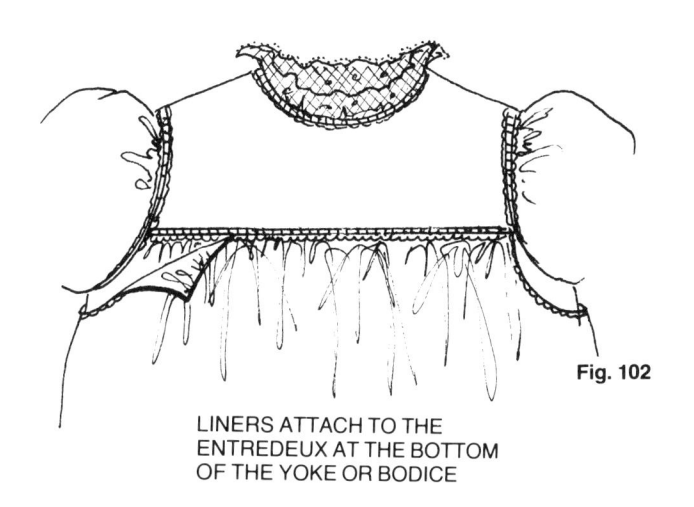

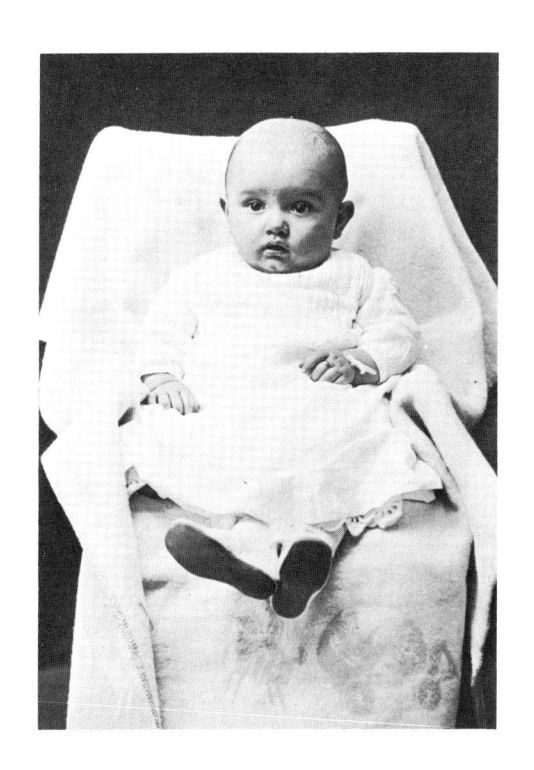

LINERS ATTACH TO THE
ENTREDEUX AT THE BOTTOM
OF THE YOKE OR BODICE

69

CAPS & BONNETS

Small Bonnet	73
Cap with Crown	77
Bonnet with Drawstring Back	79
T-Cap	81
Moppet Bonnet	85
Bonnet with Horseshoe Back	86

Right: Katherine Ingram
Daughter of Mr. & Mrs. Michael Ingram

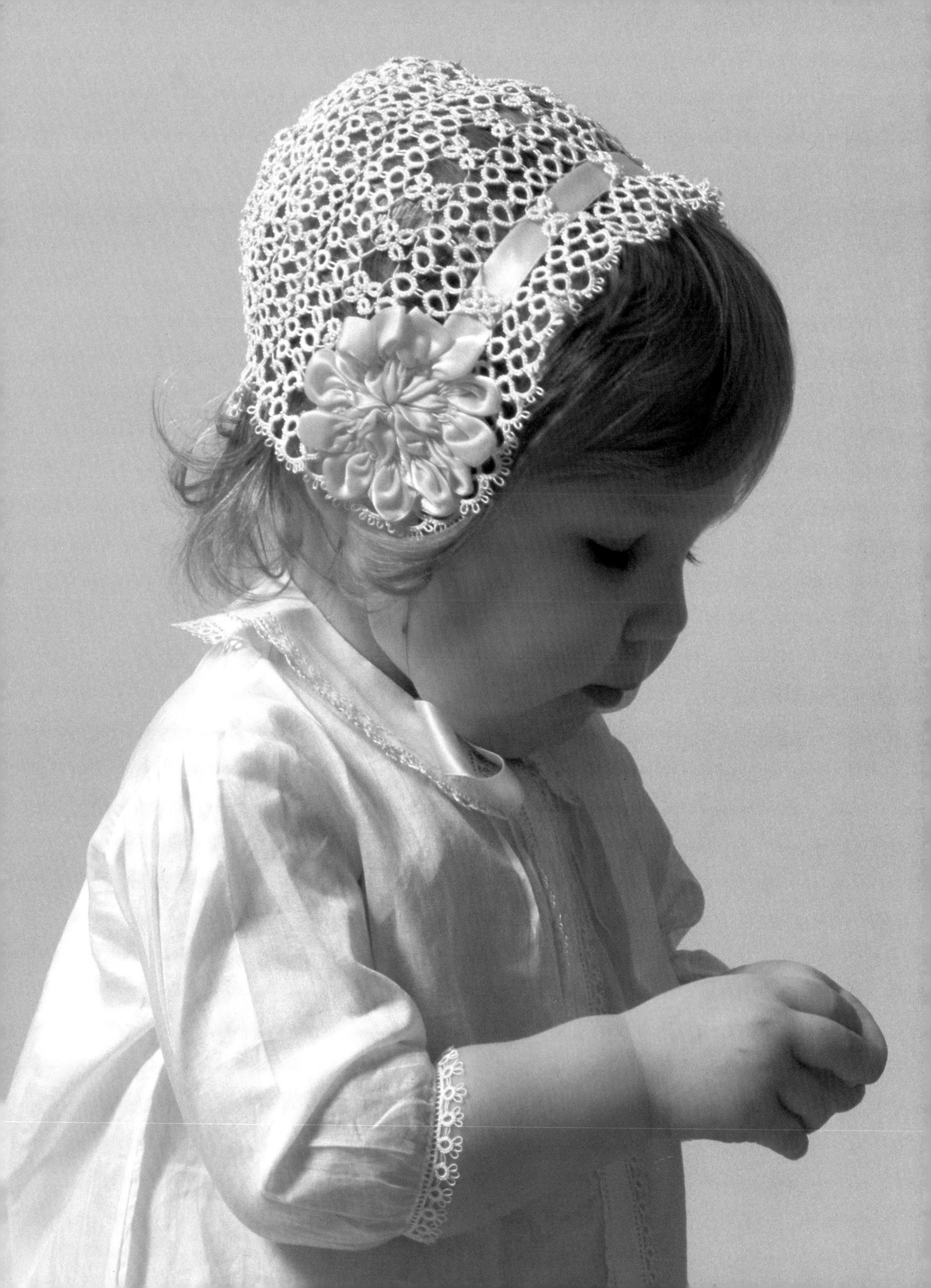

INTRODUCTION

Pretty caps and bonnets are made of batiste, silk, organdy, or challis, and there is no end to the hand work that you can put into these delicate creations. In this chapter, I will explore six different shapes, some more suitable for girls than boys, and give you numerous ideas for embellishing them. Caps and bonnets are fun to create and make lovely gifts.

Standard measurements for headbands are 11¾, 12, and 13 inches. It is always better to measure the child's head if possible. The measurement is taken from under the ear lobe, across the head where the band will fit, to under the other ear lobe. You will add 1/2 inch if the ends of the band are to be rolled and whipped. Any of the designs shown can be made larger or smaller.

Silk and challis caps are usually lined with china silk. Ribbon rosettes of different varieties may be used on any of the styles.

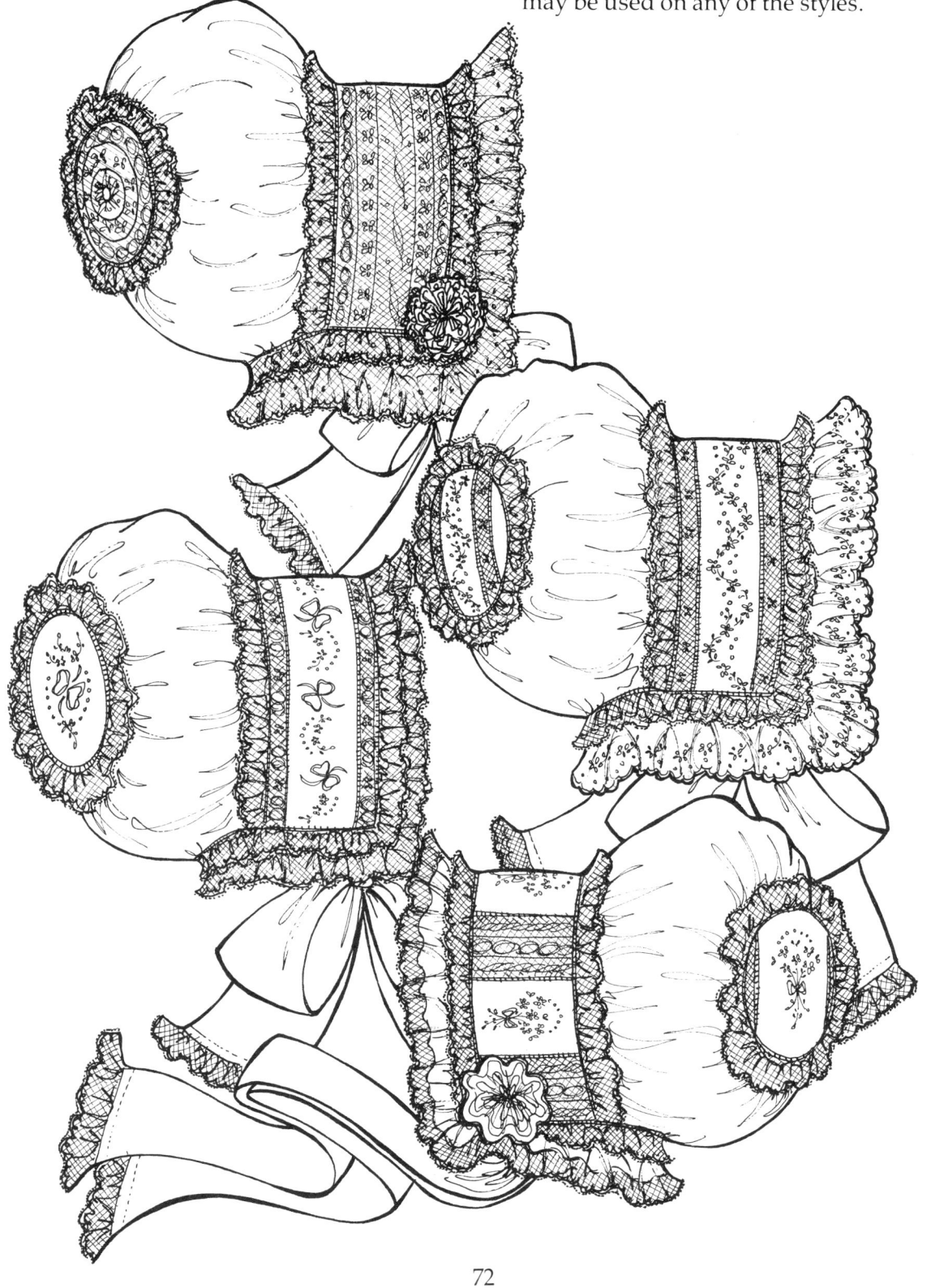

Small Bonnet

This style makes a lovely christening bonnet for a little girl and is equally suitable for wear with the baby and Babette dresses. The bonnet may be made on a plain headband with a fancy band placed on top. Make a crown that will go with a variety of fancy bands and change them as often as you like. The ruffle around the outer edge may be made of fabric, lace, or eyelet edging. It should be 1 to 1½ inches wide and one and one-half to two times in length for fullness.

This bonnet may be made of batiste or organdy to be worn with dresses and is angelic made of silk or challis to wear with coats.

The fancy band is connected to the plain band down the long sides only, forming a casing through which you can run ribbon to add color. The ribbon is turned under 1/4 inch and whipped to the bottom of the plain band at each end.

The plain headband should be cut 2½ x 13½ inches to finish 2 x 13 inches. Roll and whip all four sides and whip entredeux to one long side which will be the back of the band. (Fig. 103)

The crown is 3 inches in diameter, finished. Whip entredeux to the outer edge. (Fig. 104)

BACK

PLAIN HEADBAND 2" x 13" FINISHED

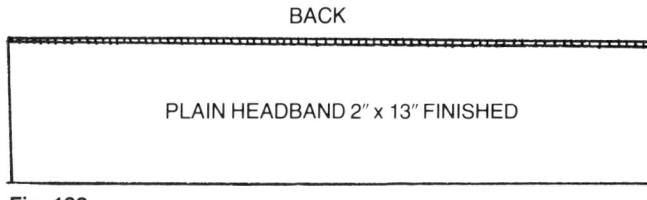

Fig. 103

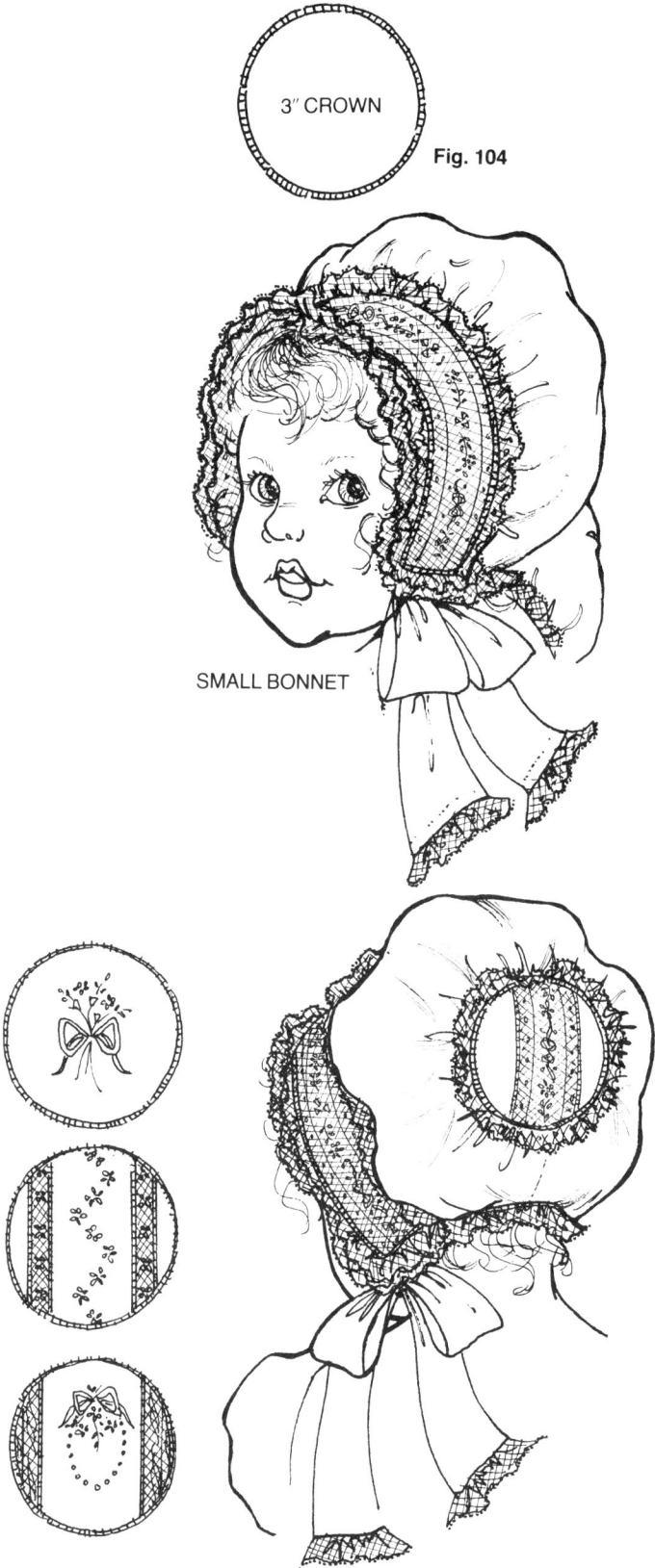

3" CROWN

Fig. 104

SMALL BONNET

SOME BAND AND CROWN VARIATIONS

EMBROIDERY

EYELET

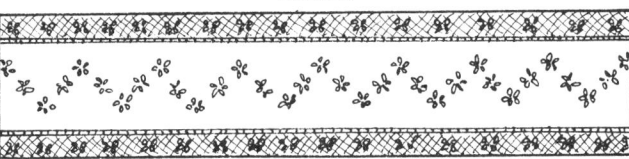

LACE AND EMBROIDERY

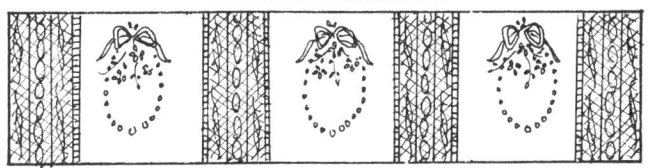

BACK

STREAMERS

Fig. 105

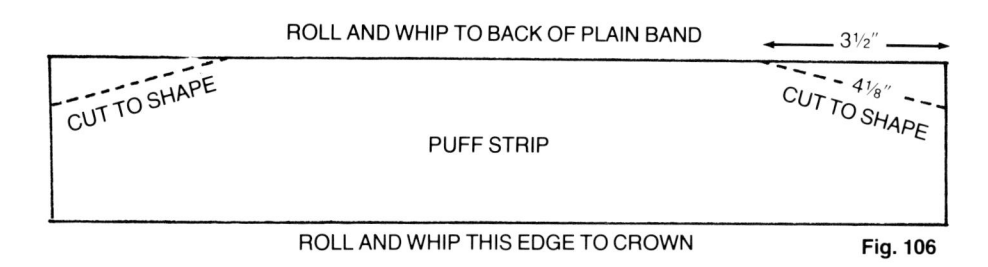

ROLL AND WHIP TO BACK OF PLAIN BAND — 3½"

CUT TO SHAPE — 4⅛" — CUT TO SHAPE

PUFF STRIP

ROLL AND WHIP THIS EDGE TO CROWN

Fig. 106

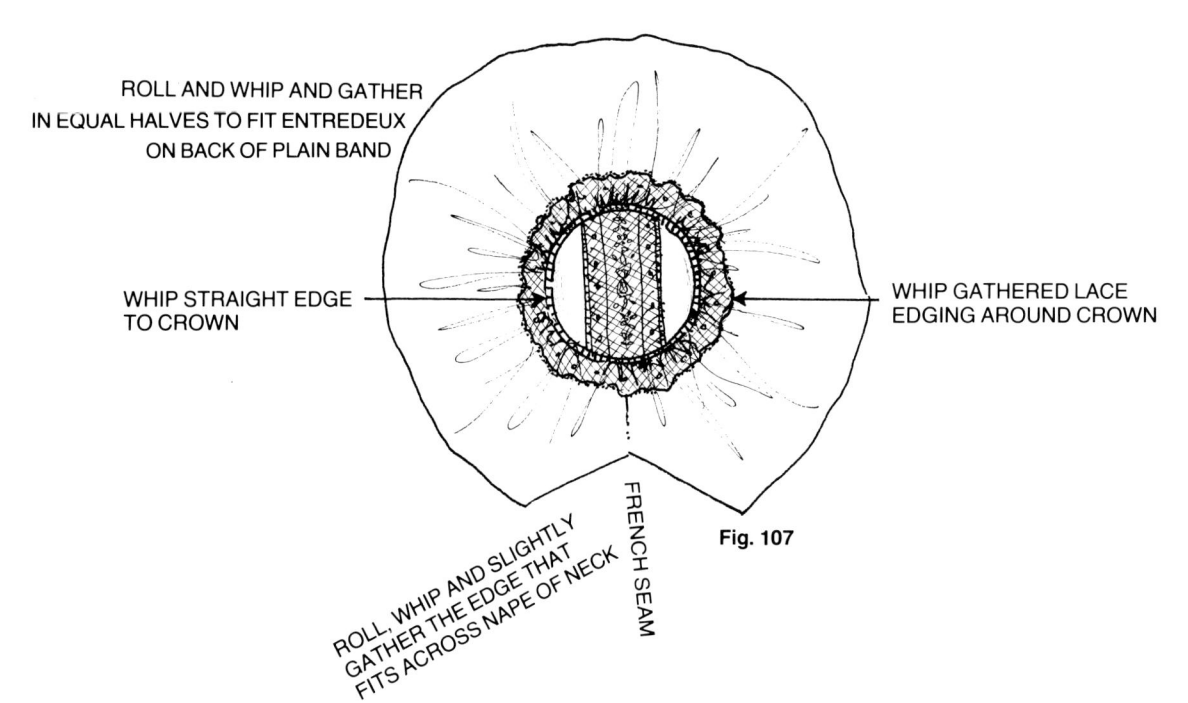

ROLL AND WHIP AND GATHER IN EQUAL HALVES TO FIT ENTREDEUX ON BACK OF PLAIN BAND

WHIP STRAIGHT EDGE TO CROWN

WHIP GATHERED LACE EDGING AROUND CROWN

ROLL, WHIP AND SLIGHTLY GATHER THE EDGE THAT FITS ACROSS NAPE OF NECK

FRENCH SEAM

Fig. 107

The streamers are 2 x 20 inches. Roll and whip the long sides of each strip. Put a tiny hem in one end of each strip. Whip gathered lace edging to the bottom of the hem. (Fig. 105)

The puff is a strip of fabric 4½ x 36 to 44 inches. Shape each end. (Fig. 106) French seam the ends together to form a circle. Roll and whip and gather the back edge of the puff in equal halves to fit the entredeux on the back of the plain band. Whip the rolled edge to the entredeux. Roll and whip and gather the other side of the puff in equal halves to fit the entredeux on the crown. Whip the rolled edge to the entredeux. Whip gathered lace edging around the crown. (Fig. 107)

Roll and whip and slightly gather the raw edge of the puff that fits across the nape of the neck.

Whip entredeux to the entire outer edge of the bonnet. (Fig. 108)

Divide the outer edge of the bonnet into equal fourths. Mark each fourth with pins or colored thread loops. Attach the ruffle (in equal fourths) to the entredeux around the outer edge. (Fig. 109)

Roll and whip and gather the raw ends of the streamers to 1 inch. Attach them to the plain band at the front bottom edge.

Make the fancy band the same width and length as the plain band, finished. Whip entredeux to all four sides. Whip gathered lace edging to the entredeux.

Lay the fancy band on top of the plain band and join entredeux to entredeux down the long sides. (Fig. 110)

Run ribbon under the fancy band, if you desire. Rosettes may be used at each end of the band.

If needed, put one tie inside the bonnet to hold its shape. Use a 7-inch length of 6-strand embroidery floss for tie. Place tie in center top of crown. Knot the ends of the floss to keep them secure. Tie floss together to make the bonnet fit properly. (Fig. 111) Untie to wash and iron.

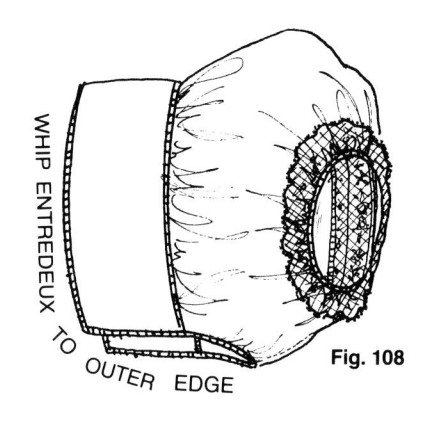

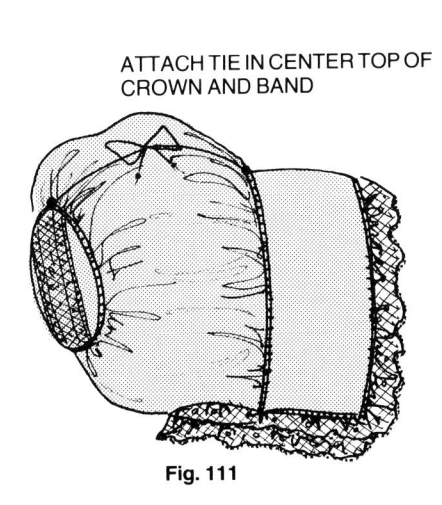

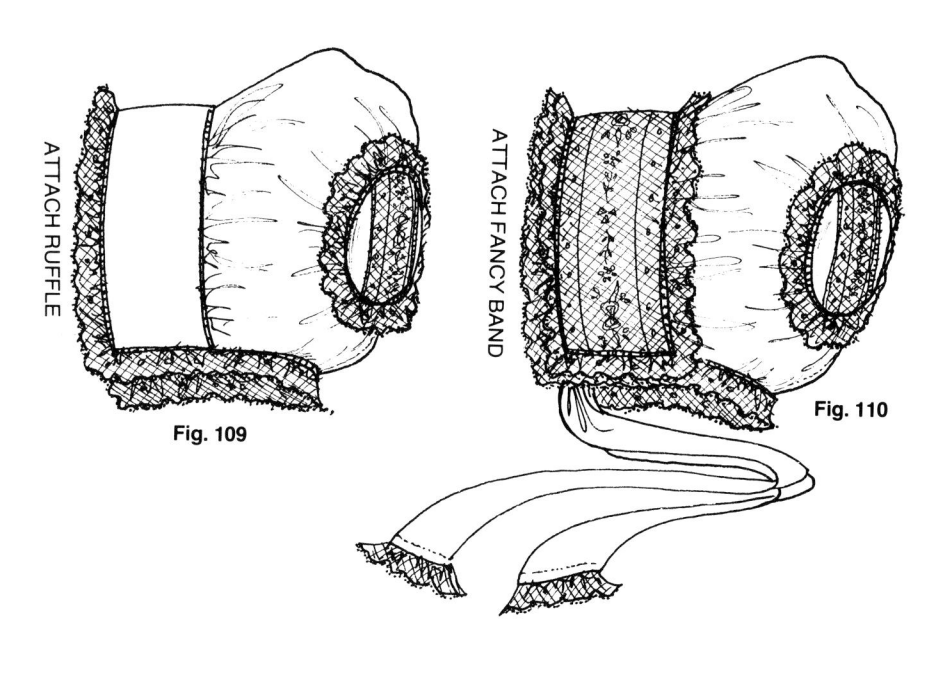

Fig. 108 WHIP ENTREDEUX TO OUTER EDGE

Fig. 109 ATTACH RUFFLE

Fig. 110 ATTACH FANCY BAND

Fig. 111 ATTACH TIE IN CENTER TOP OF CROWN AND BAND

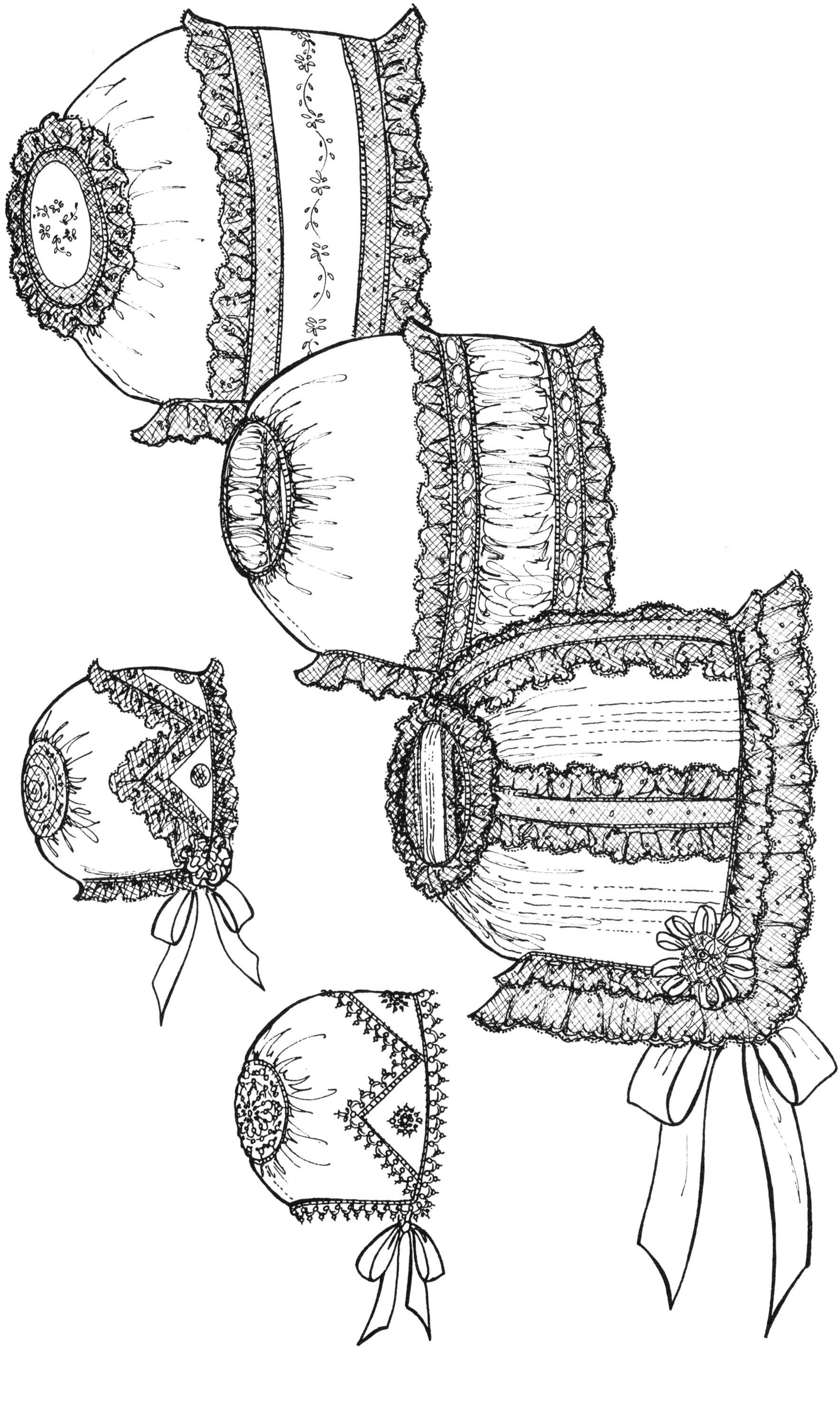

Cap with Crown

This cap may be easily adapted for boys or girls. There is no end to the creations you can make with this basic pattern. The body of the cap can be made fancy or made plain with a fancy band added to the top. I would suggest that you line it with china silk if you choose to make it in challis or silk.

For the infant size, the cap should be 12 inches from ear to ear, with a 3-inch crown; and for size 6 months, it should be 13 inches, with a 3½-inch crown. (These are finished measurements.) (Fig. 112) See 6-month size pattern on page 88.

The fancy band is sewn across the front edge and sides of the cap. (Fig. 113A, B) Lace edging may then be whipped to the entire outer edge and around the crown. Use satin ribbon for the ties, which should be ½ to 1 inch wide.

ROLL AND WHIP AND GATHER ACROSS TOP TO FIT CROWN

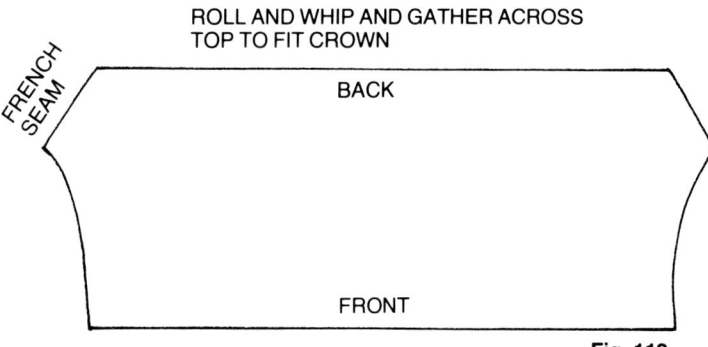

FRENCH SEAM

BACK

FRONT

Fig. 112

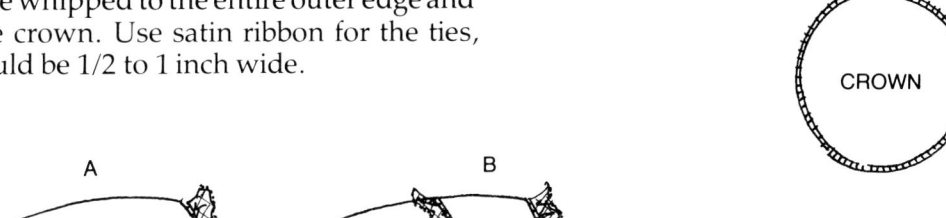

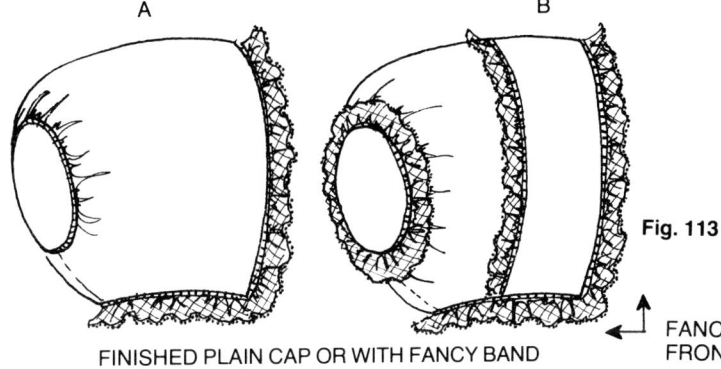

CROWN

Fig. 113

FINISHED PLAIN CAP OR WITH FANCY BAND

FANCY BAND IS SEWN ACROSS FRONT EDGE AND SIDE OF CAP

VARIATIONS OF CAP WITH CROWN

EYELET OR EMBROIDERY

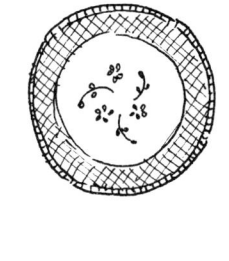

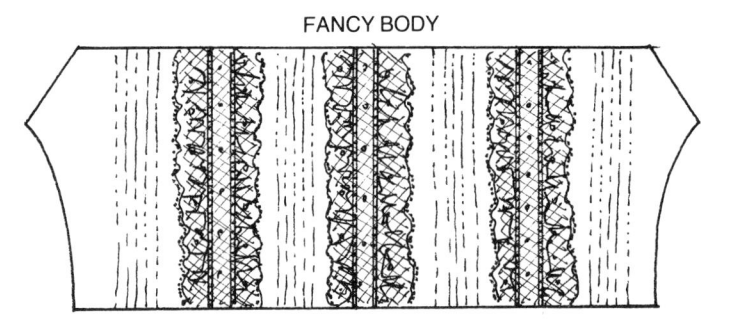

FANCY BAND

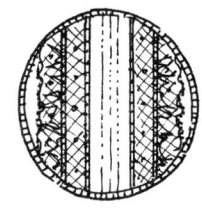

FANCY BODY

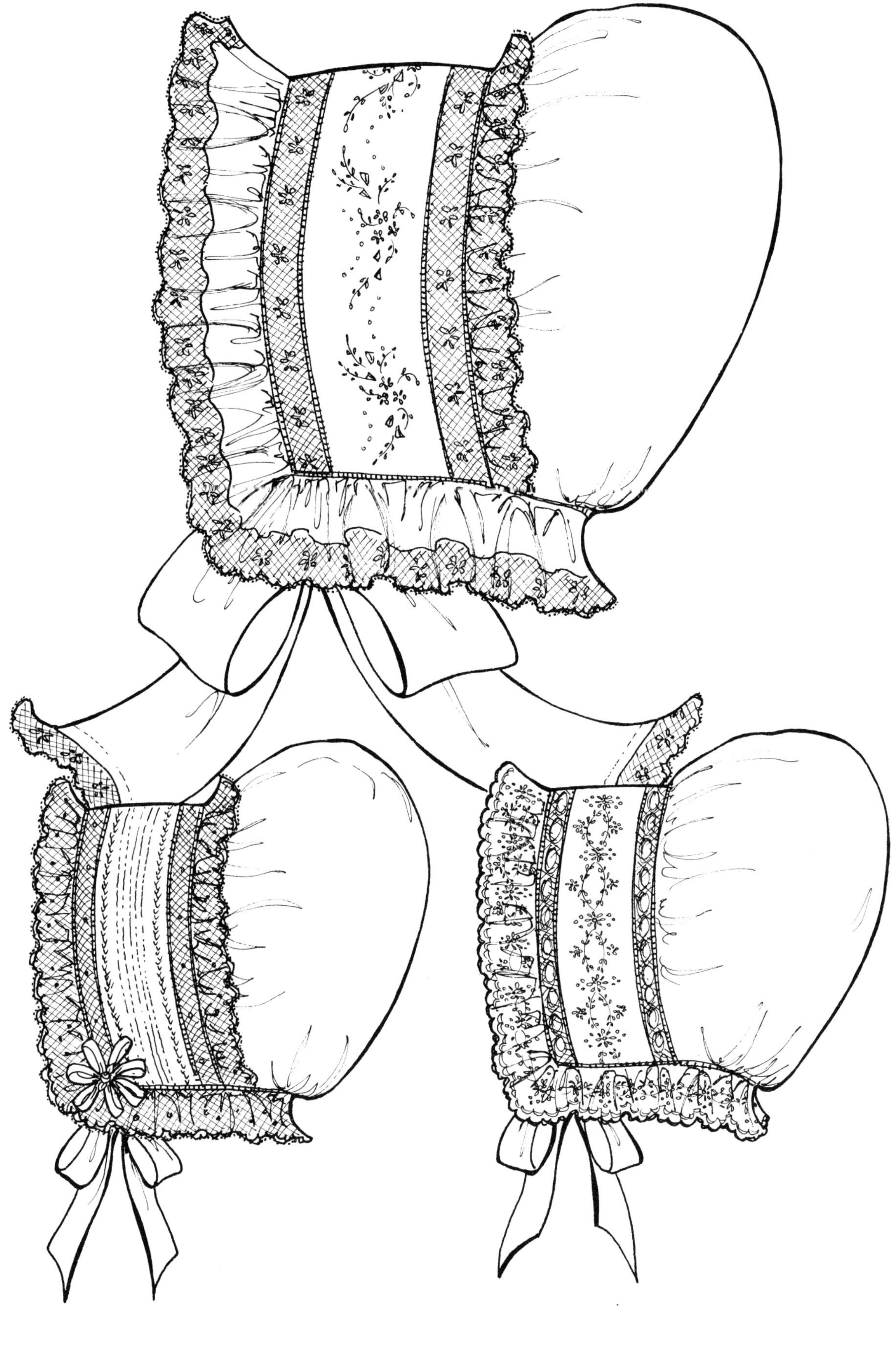

Bonnet with Drawstring Back (Infant Size)

Make a fancy head band 2 x 12 to 13 inches long finished. Whip entredeux to the entire outer edge of the band. (Fig. 114)

Cut a bonnet back (pattern on page 80) and make a casing on the nape of the neck. Fold the casing to the wrong side and turn the raw edge under 1/4 inch. Press in a crease. (Fig. 115A) Attach a 6-strand piece of embroidery floss or dental floss at each end of the casing to be used as a drawstring for the back. NOTE: I do not sew the casing down at this point because it is so easy to catch the drawstring while whipping the lace edging or ruffle to the back. (Fig. 115B)

Roll and whip and gather the back of the bonnet (gather between X's only), leaving 2 inches ungathered at each bottom edge. (Fig. 115C) Whip the rolled edge to the entredeux on the back of the headband. (Fig. 116A) Starting at the back of the band, whip gathered lace edging (gather 1½ for fullness) or a fabric, wide lace, or eyelet ruffle (1¼ yards long for fabric and eyelet and 1½ yards for wide lace) to the entire outer edge of the bonnet. Whip edging flat across casing fold. (Fig. 116B)

Sew the top of the casing with tiny running stitches, leaving a ½ inch opening in the center. (Fig. 117)

MAKE BAND — WHIP ENTREDEUX TO OUTER EDGE

Fig. 114

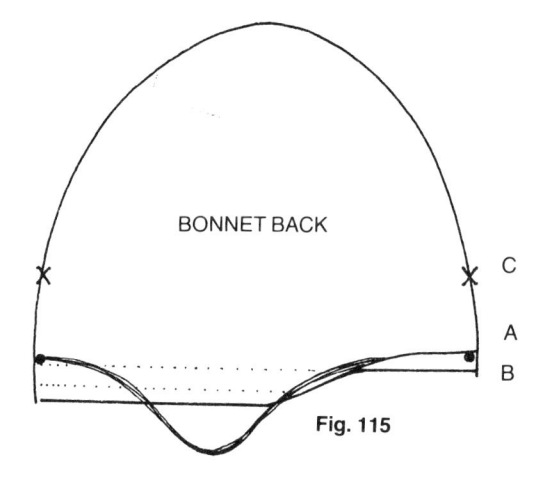

BONNET BACK

C ROLL, WHIP AND GATHER BETWEEN X'S
A MAKE A CASING — PRESS IN CREASE
B ATTACH DRAWSTRING

Fig. 115

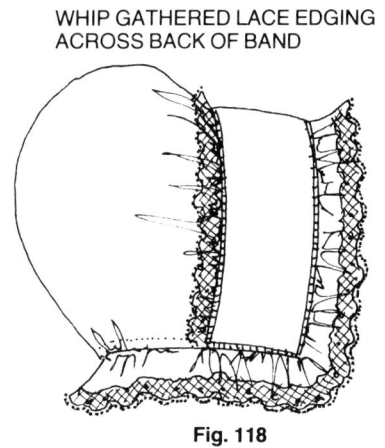

WHIP GATHERED LACE EDGING ACROSS BACK OF BAND

Fig. 118

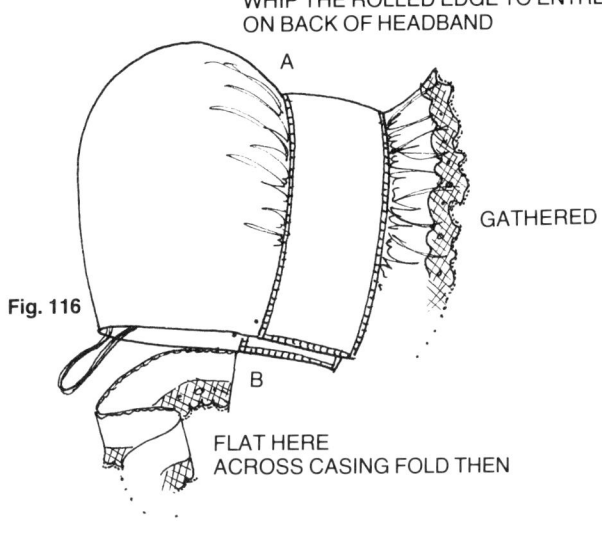

WHIP THE ROLLED EDGE TO ENTREDEUX ON BACK OF HEADBAND

A
GATHERED
B
FLAT HERE ACROSS CASING FOLD THEN

Fig. 116

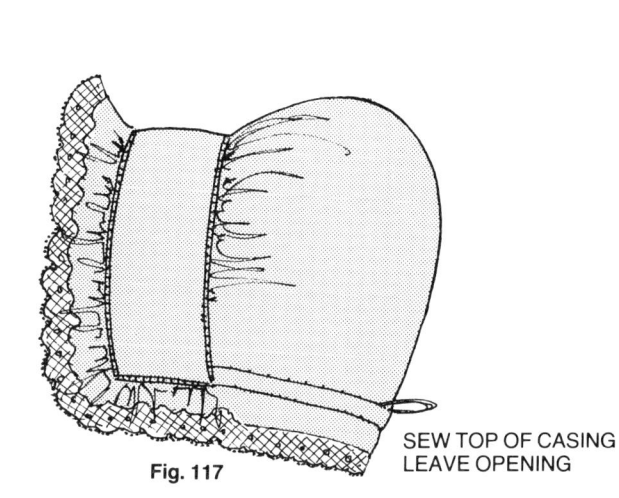

SEW TOP OF CASING LEAVE OPENING

Fig. 117

Whip gathered lace edging to the entredeux across the back of the band. Attach batiste or ribbon ties. Rosettes may be used if desired.

This bonnet may be enlarged by increasing the depth and length of the headband and increasing the width and depth of the back piece.

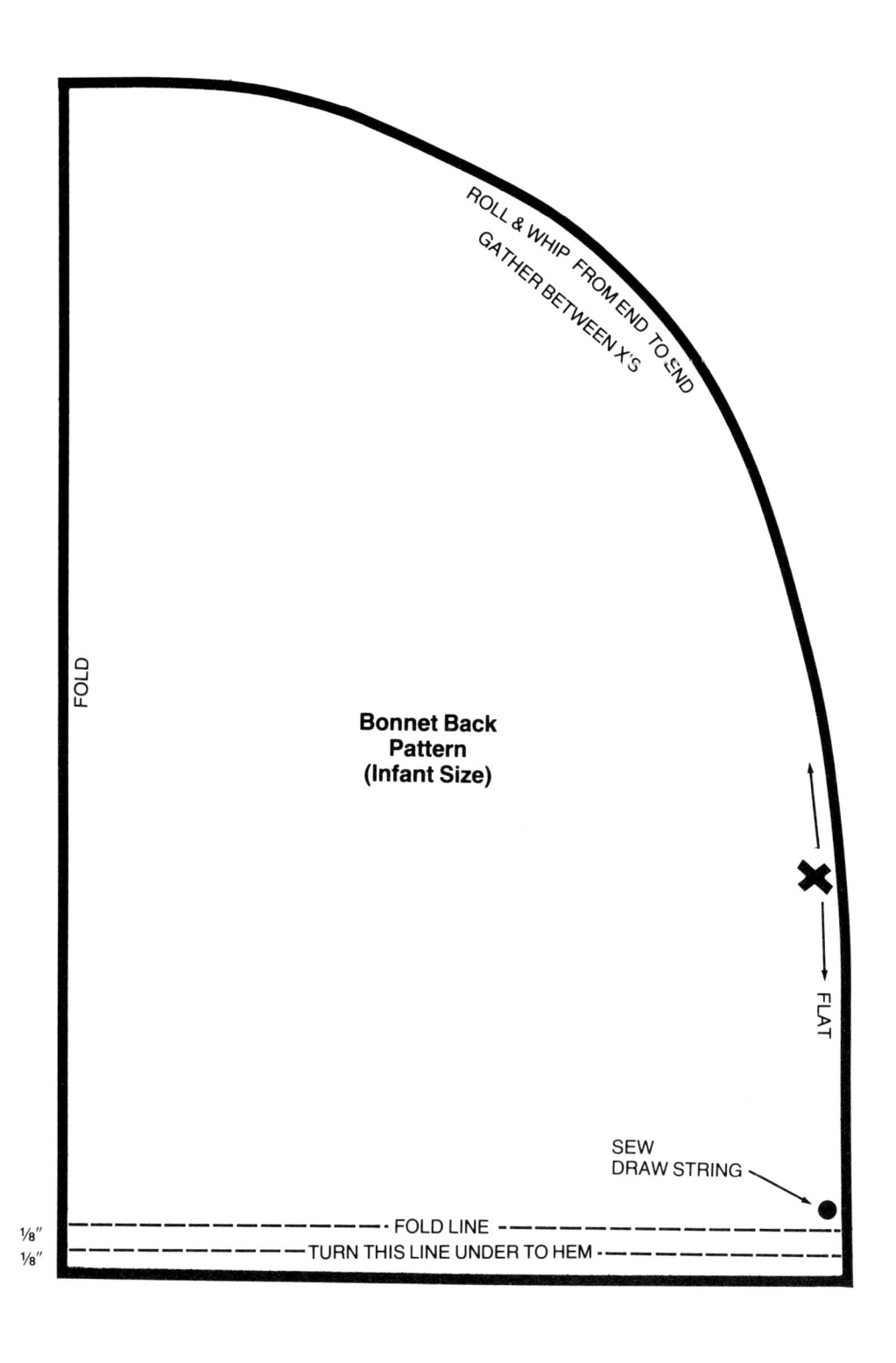

Bonnet Back Pattern (Infant Size)

ROLL & WHIP FROM END TO END
GATHER BETWEEN X'S

FOLD

FLAT

SEW DRAW STRING

1/8" — — — FOLD LINE — — —
1/8" — — — TURN THIS LINE UNDER TO HEM — — —

T-Cap

This cap is very nice for boys as well as girls. It fits well and can be made from a variety of trims. It can be edged with lace or with a fabric or wide lace ruffle.

Make a brown paper guide for the front band and back strip. It is always better to measure for size if possible, but if it is not, a standard measurement for an infant is 3½ x 12 inches (finished) for the top band and 2½ x 5¾ inches for the back strip.

Try to start and end with lace insertion and fill the space with tucks, puffing, embroidery, or more lace insertion. (Fig. 119) Roll and whip each raw end or zigzag by machine and use the machine stitching as a rolled edge. Whip entredeux to all four sides. Whip gathered lace edging

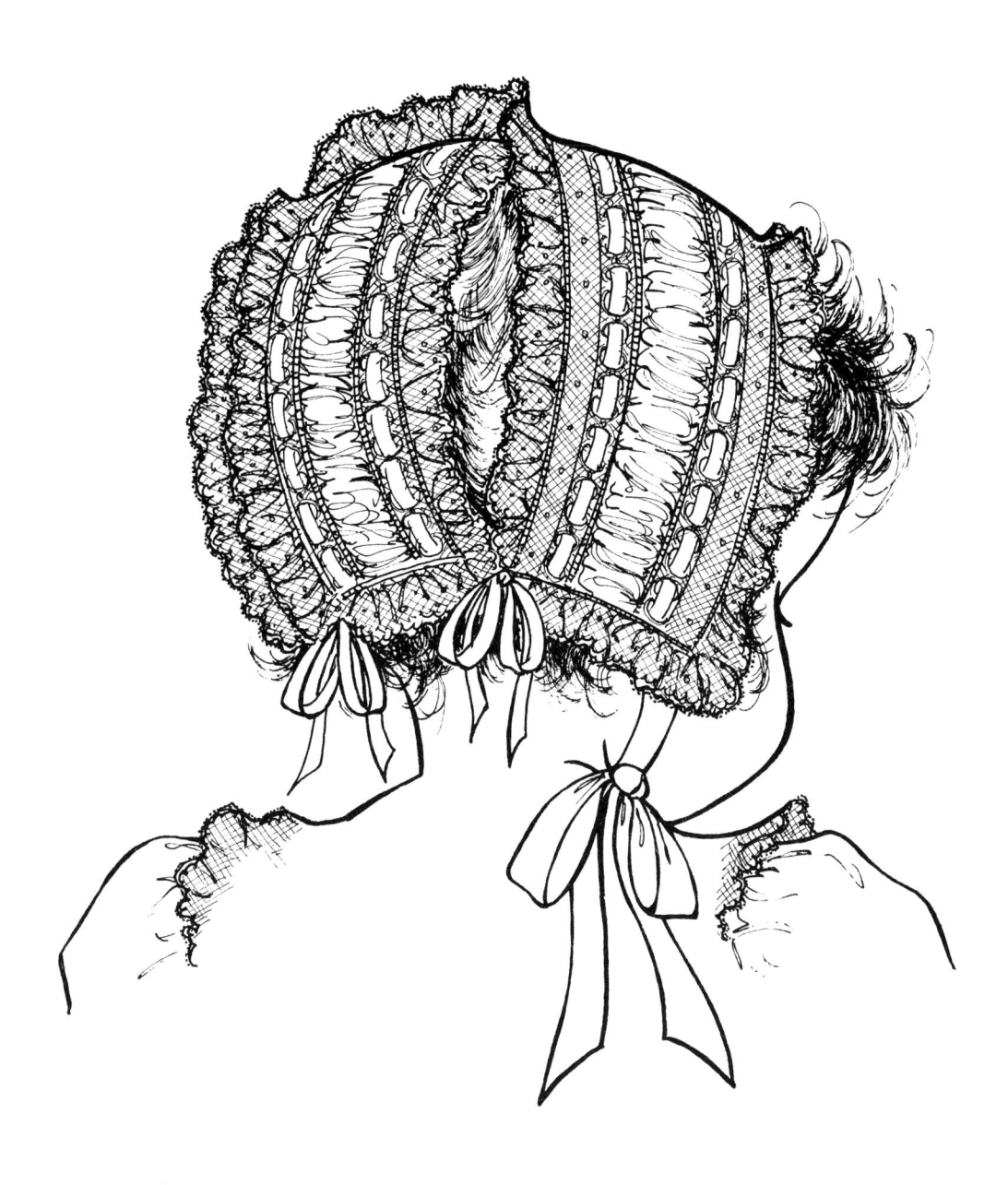

VARIATIONS FOR T-CAP

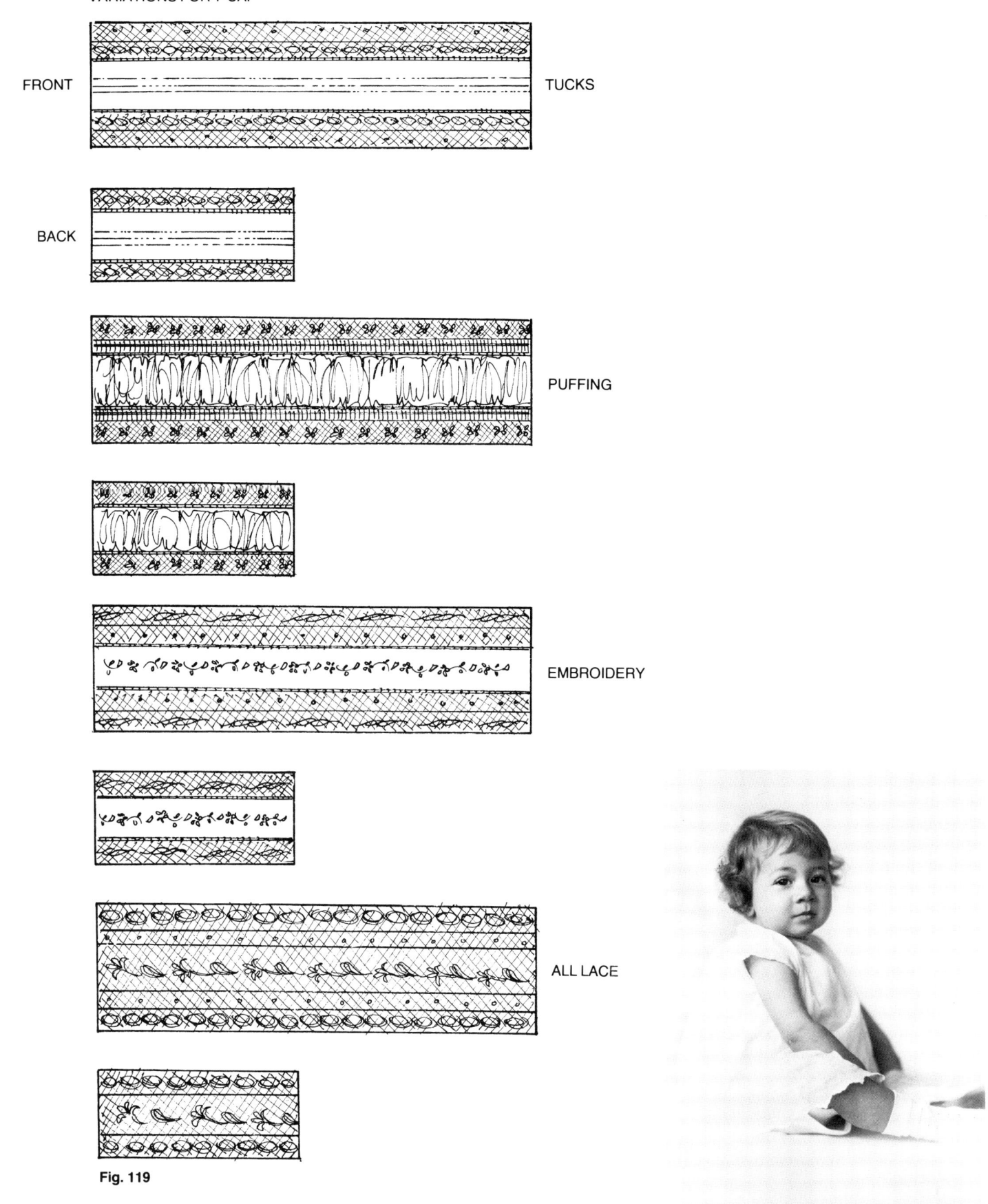

FRONT

TUCKS

BACK

PUFFING

EMBROIDERY

ALL LACE

Fig. 119

82

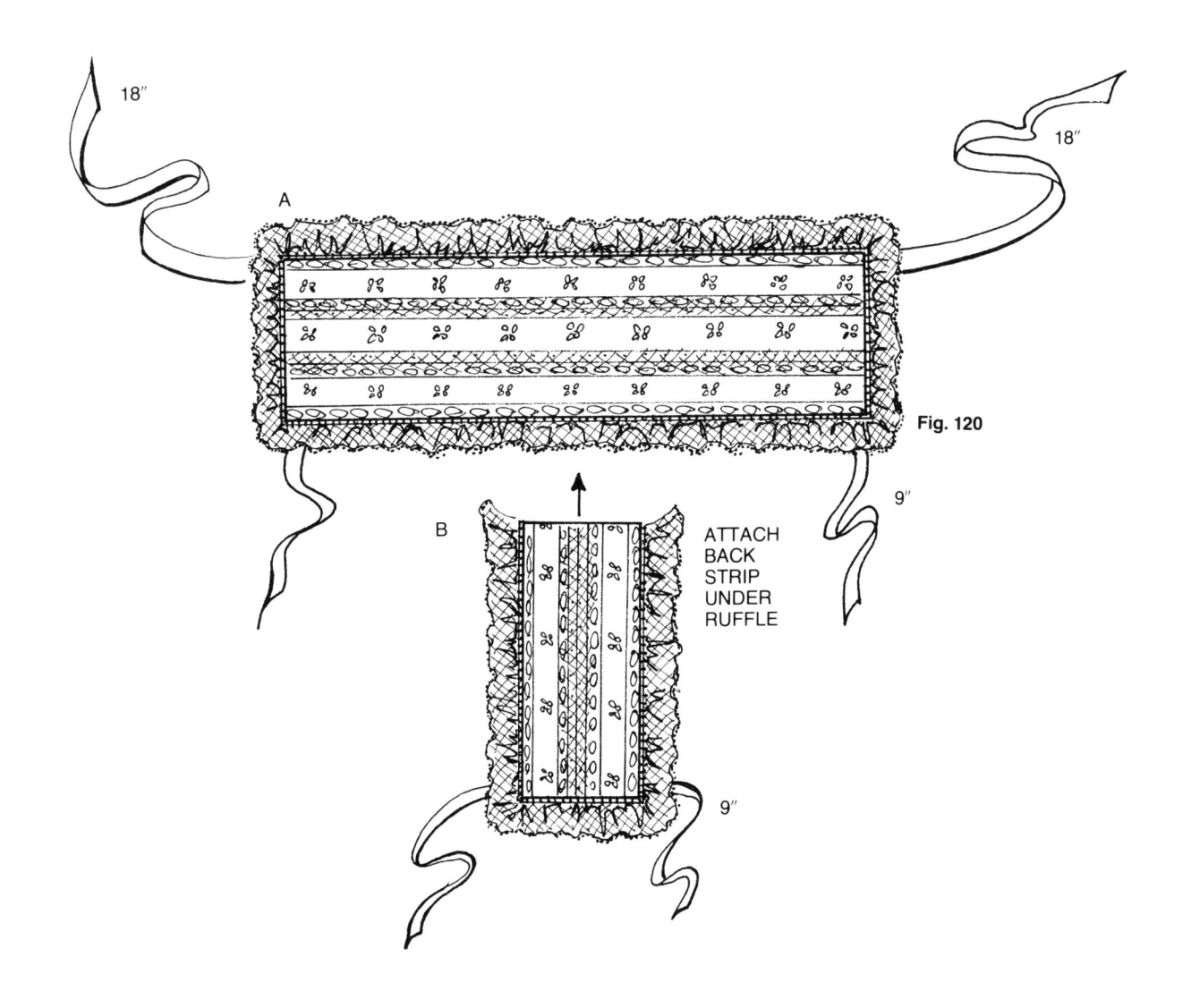

(1½ times for fullness) or a fabric ruffle (1 inch wide and 66 inches long) to the entredeux. (Fig. 120A)

Make the back strip in the same way as the top band, but whip entredeux to three sides (two long and one short), leaving one short end plain. Whip gathered lace edging or a fabric ruffle (1 x 33 inches) to the entredeux. (Fig. 120B)

Attach the plain top of the back strip to the entredeux at the center back of the headband under the lace or fabric ruffle.

Cut four strips of 1/4 inch double-face satin ribbon and whip to the bonnet under the edging. Sew two lengths of ribbon 18 inches long or make two fabric streamers 2 x 20 inches and attach at the front end of the headband. Rosettes add a finishing touch. Tie the 1/4 inch ribbon into bows. NOTE: When using a fabric ruffle, you may wish to tack the backs instead of using ribbon ties. (Fig. 121)

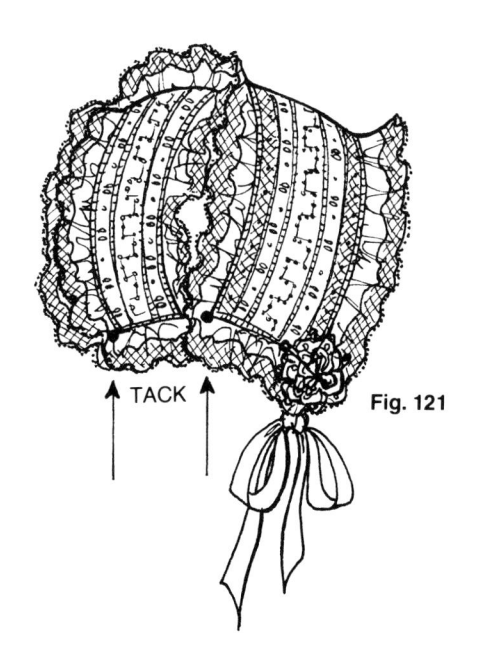

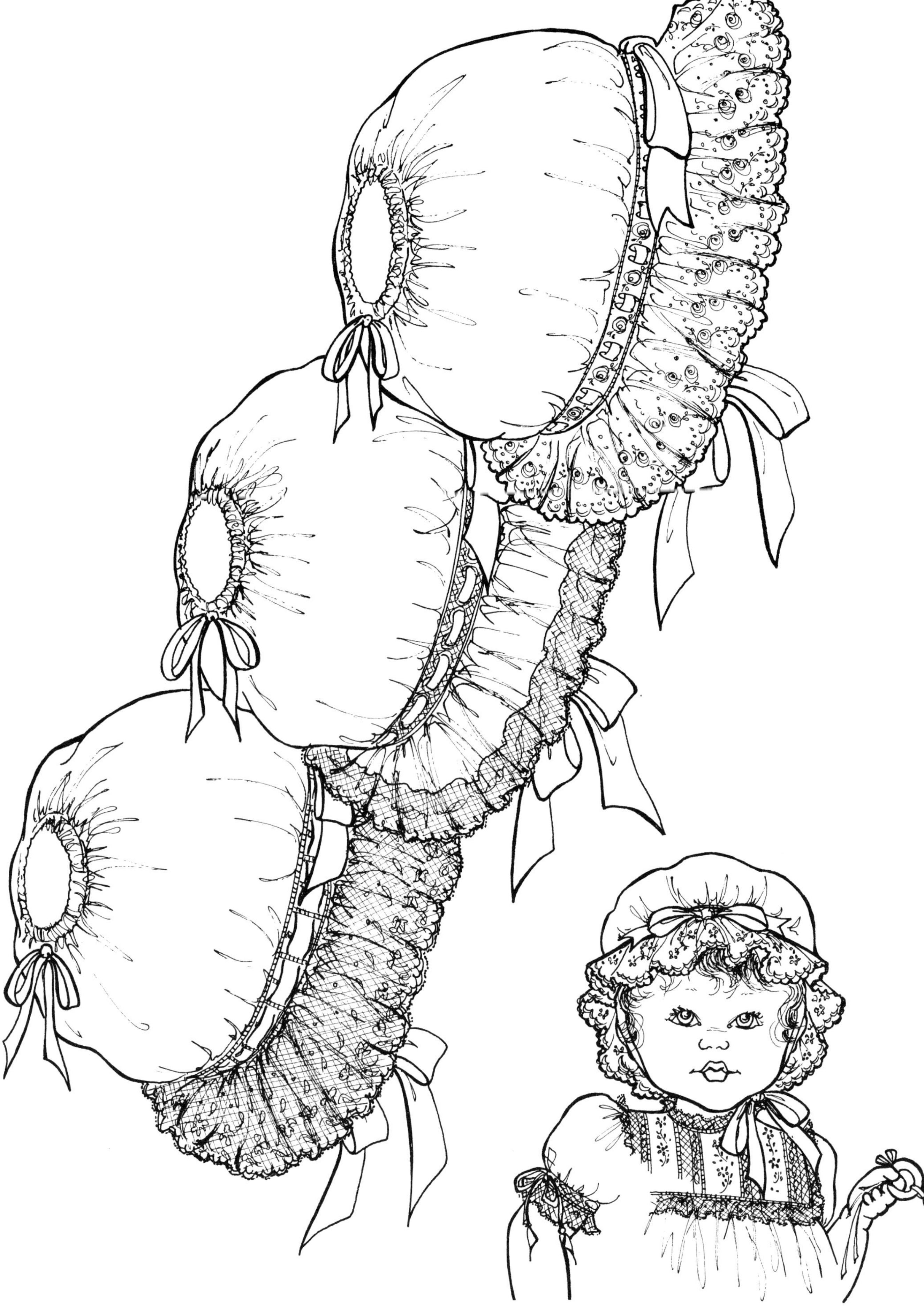

Moppet Bonnet
(Sizes Small, Medium, Large)

This precious cap is very easy to make. Use a strip of eyelet beading 1/2 to 3/4 inch wide for the headband. The strip should be 16½, 17½, or 18½ inches long, depending on the size you are making. This strip of beading is joined to form a circle. (Fig. 122A)

The ruffle for the front is 1¼ yards long for all sizes. It can measure up to 3 inches in width. You may use Swiss eyelet embroidery or make a batiste ruffle trimmed with lace or tatted edging. French seam the ruffle into a circle. Roll and whip and gather the raw edge in equal halves to fit one side of the beading. (Eyelet beading usually has entredeux on both sides. If not, you must add it.) Line all seams up, and this will be center back. (Fig. 122B)

Pull and cut one strip of batiste 7 inches deep and 36 or 44 inches long for the small and medium bonnet or 7½ x 44 inches for the large size. Shape each end as shown. French seam the strip to form a circle. Make a casing for 1/4 inch ribbon on the straight side. Roll and whip and gather the shaped side in equal halves to fit the other side of the beading. Whip the rolled edge to the entredeux. (Fig. 123)

Run ribbon through the beading; tack underneath at the back seam. Make a flat bow for the top of the band. The crown of the cap is formed by drawing up the 1/4 inch ribbon in the casing and tying a small bow at the bottom.

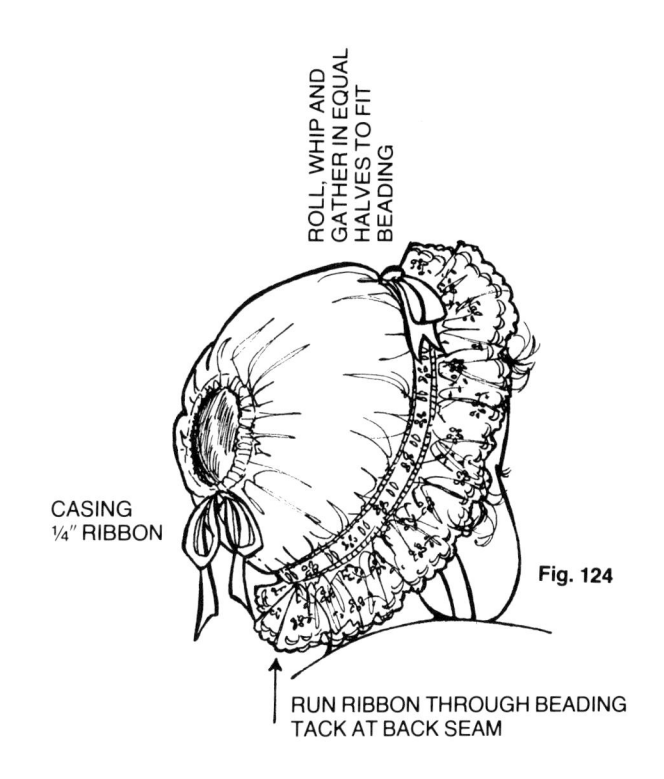

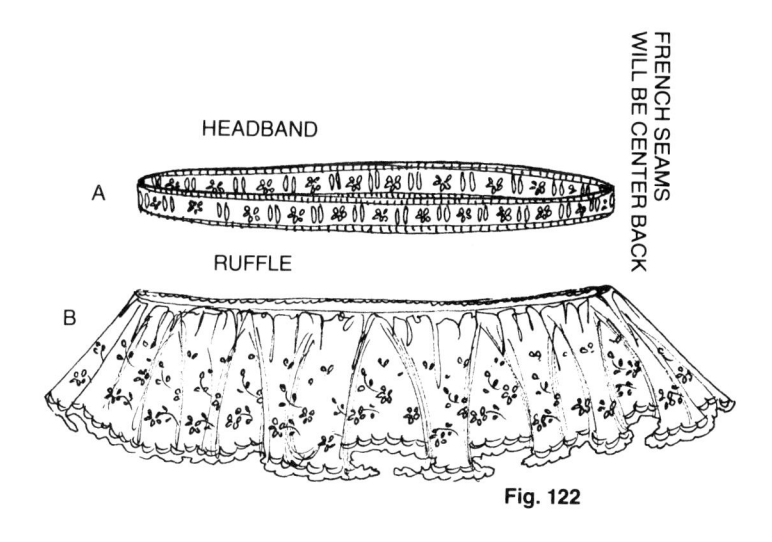

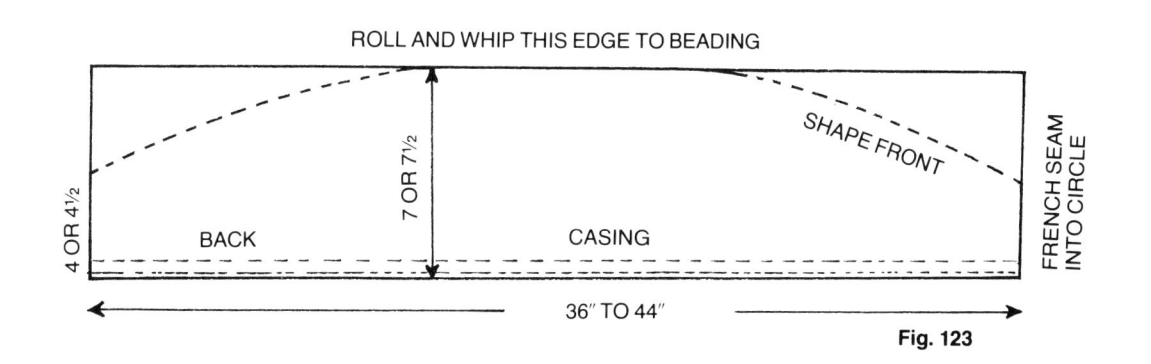

Fig. 124

Fig. 122

Fig. 123

Bonnet with Horseshoe Back

This bonnet is suitable for children from infants to seven years old. The flower girls on the cover of Volume I are wearing lace bonnets made from this pattern.

The design that I show here is a good learning project. It features lace, tucks, and puffing edged with a ruffle. The back of the bonnet has lace insertion applied to the edge, and the center is embroidered.

The top piece can be made from a wide eyelet edge. When eyelet is used, you can bind the bottom edge with fabric or ribbon, or you might choose to whip entredeux to the bottom edge and whip a gathered lace edging to the entire outer edge. Follow the scalloped edge on the eyelet, whipping the lace just under the scalloped outline and to the entredeux across the bottom.

Use satin ribbon or fabric ties.

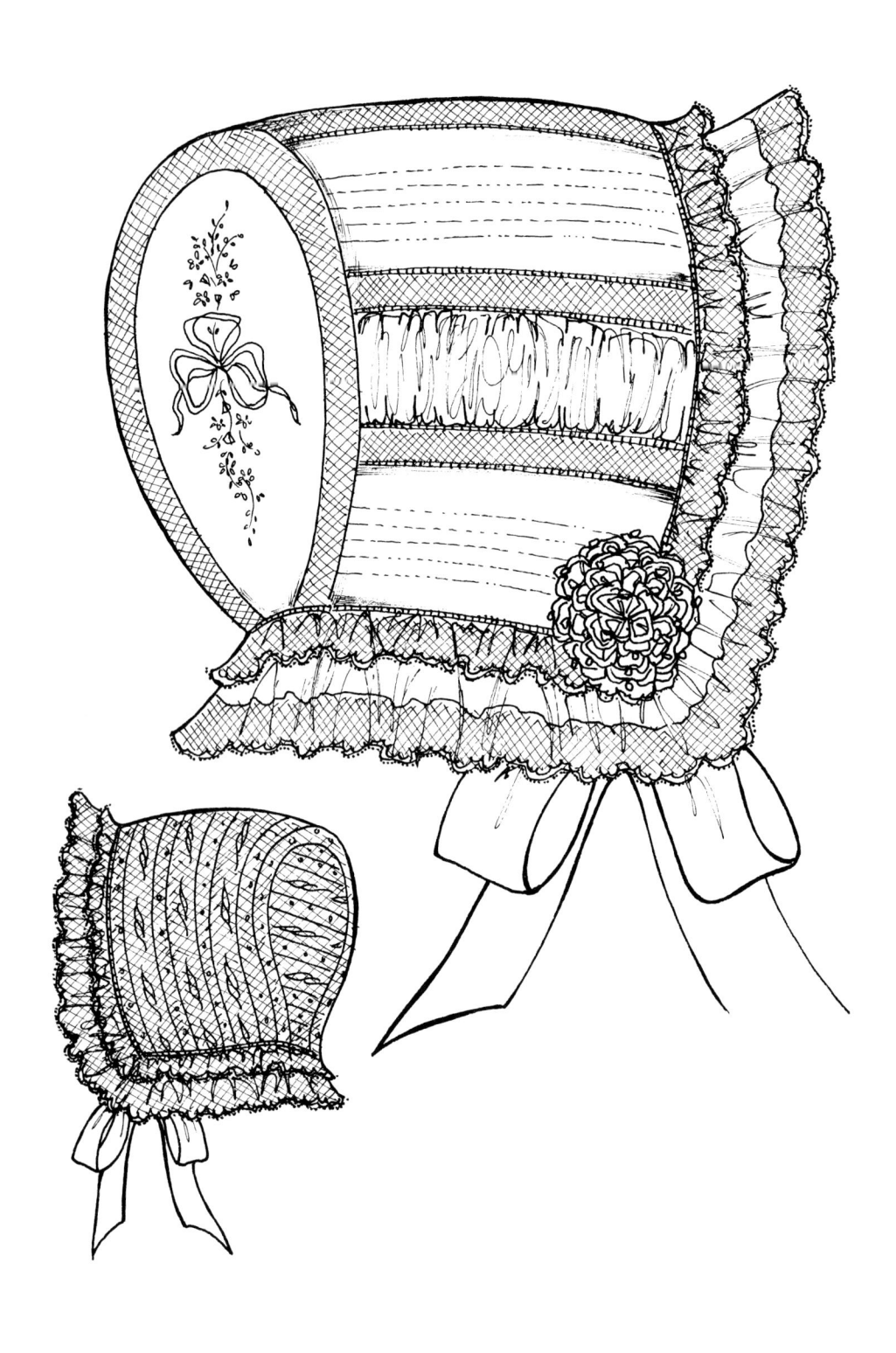

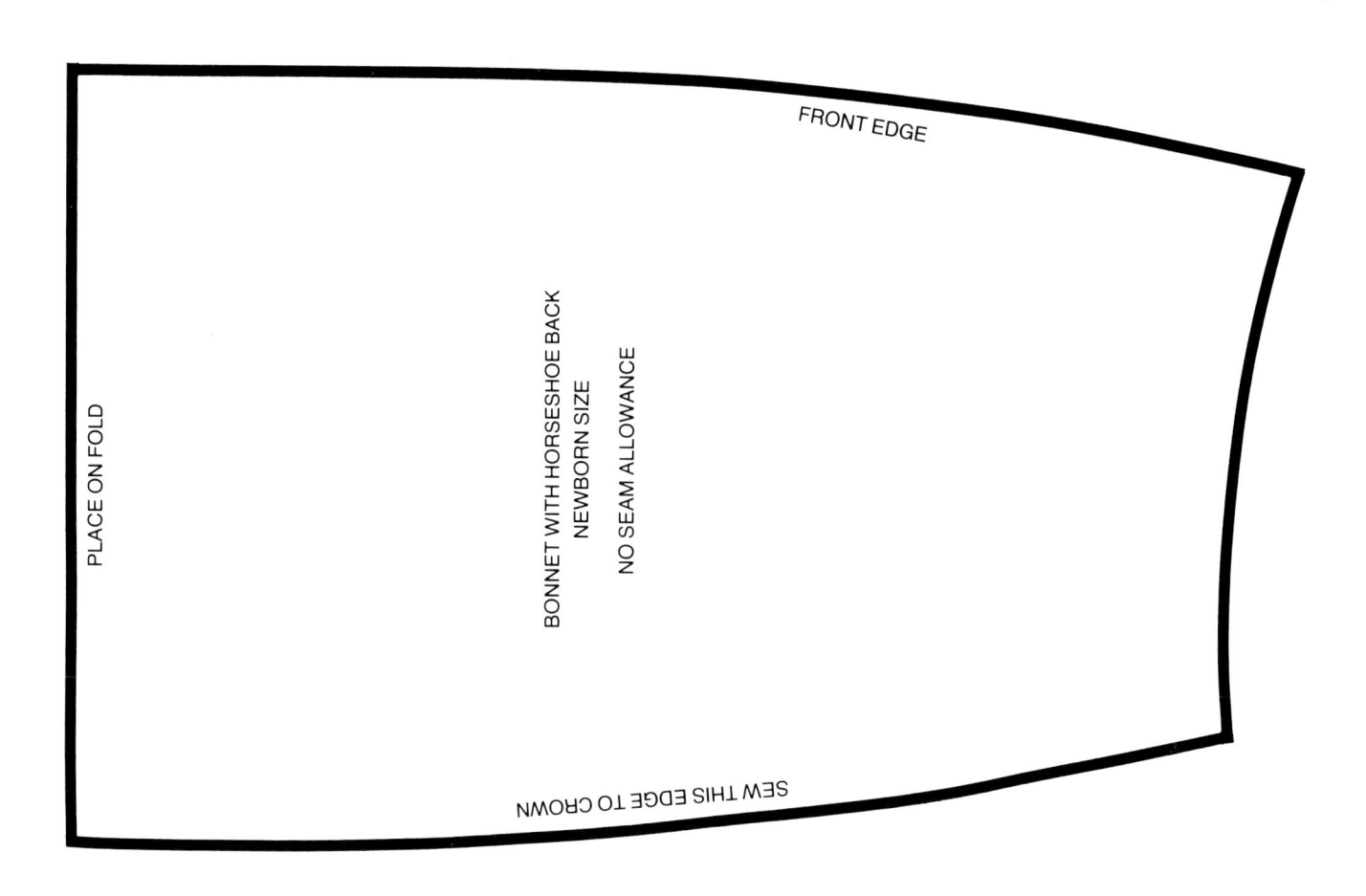

FRONT EDGE

PLACE ON FOLD

BONNET WITH HORSESHOE BACK
NEWBORN SIZE

NO SEAM ALLOWANCE

SEW THIS EDGE TO CROWN

NO SEAM ALLOWANCE

BONNET WITH HORSESHOE BACK
NEWBORN SIZE

PLACE ON FOLD

BONNET VARIATIONS

CORD

EYELET WITH LACE RUFFLE

FABRIC BINDING

FABRIC TIES

RIBBON TIES

RIBBON BINDING

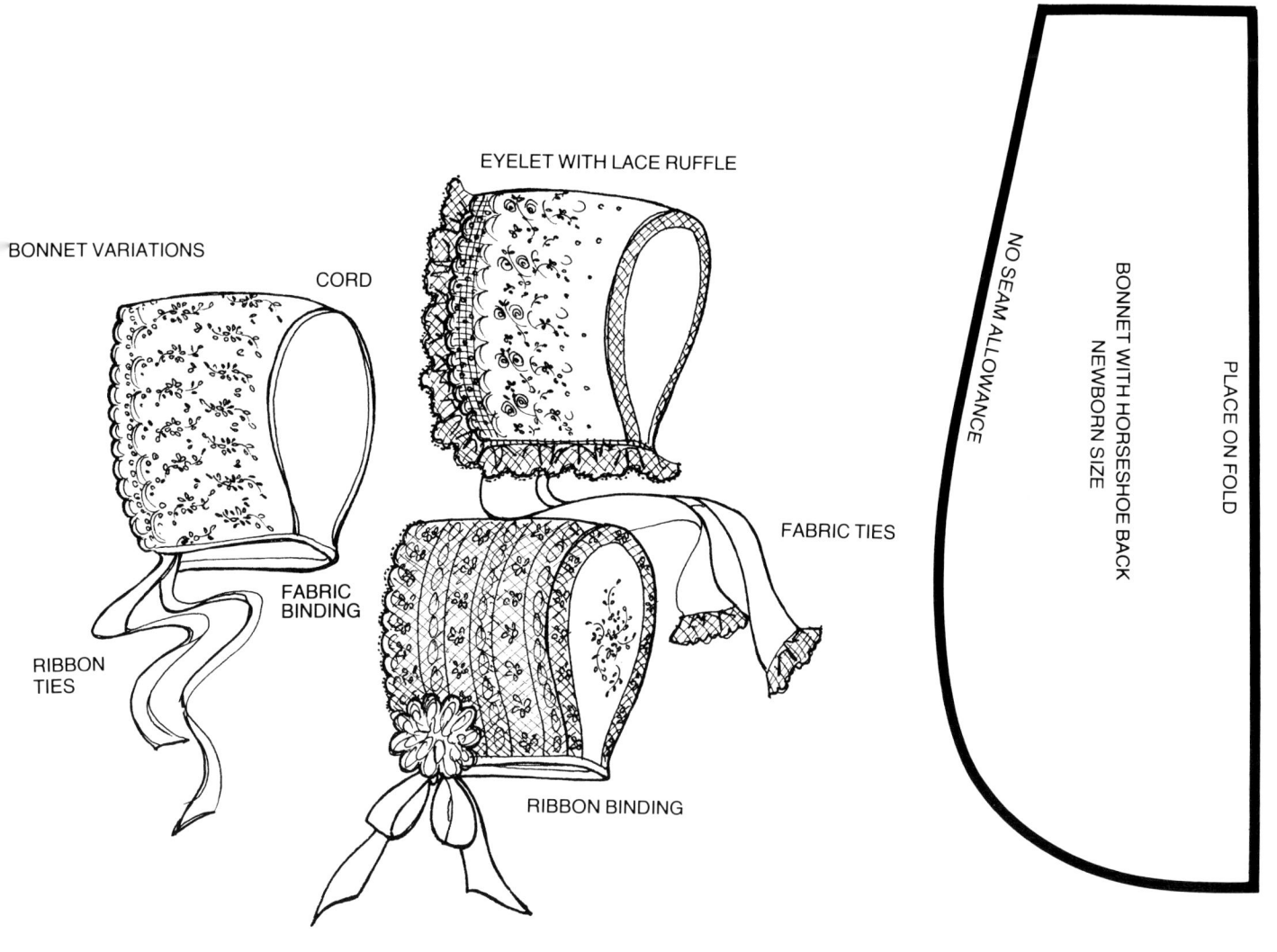

PATTERNS FOR CAP WITH CROWN (SIZE 6 MONTHS)

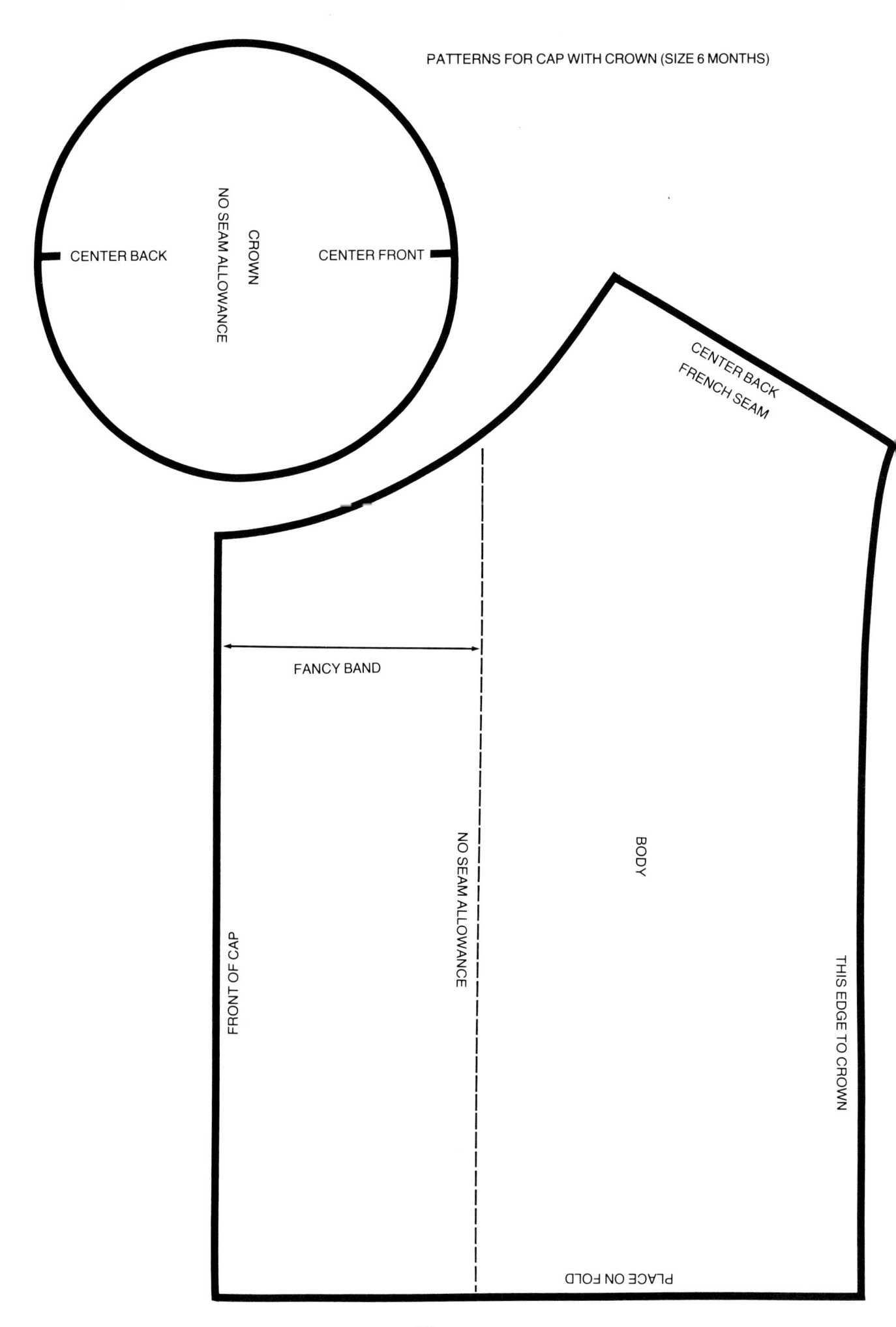

CROWN
NO SEAM ALLOWANCE
CENTER BACK
CENTER FRONT

CENTER BACK
FRENCH SEAM

FANCY BAND

NO SEAM ALLOWANCE

BODY

FRONT OF CAP

THIS EDGE TO CROWN

PLACE ON FOLD

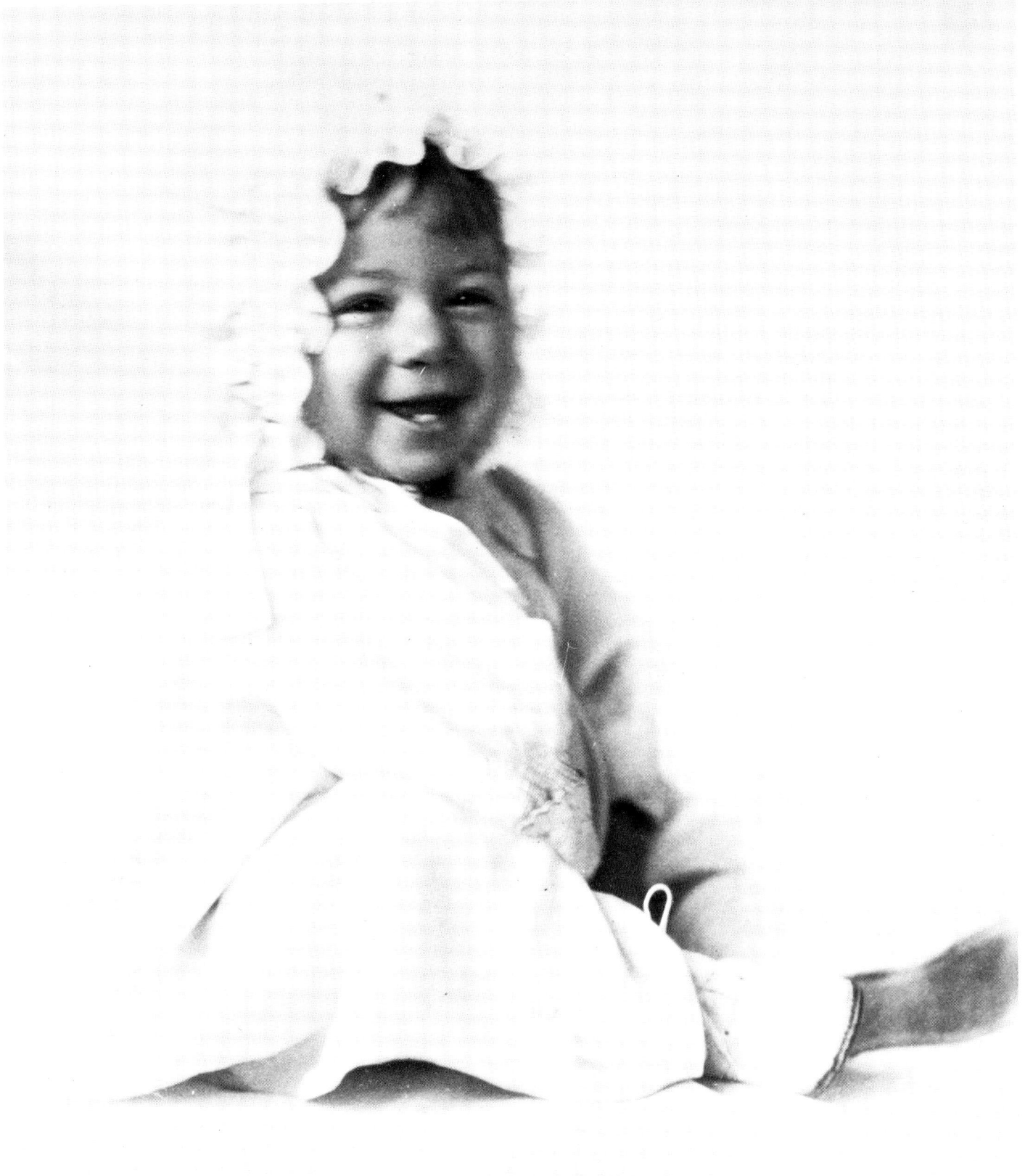

DAYGOWNS

Placket with Trim on Both Sides 92
False Placket. 93
Placket with Sewn Fabric Strip 95
Placket Trimmed with Ruffle 96
Gowns with Raglan Sleeves 99
Gowns with Set-In Sleeves 100
Gowns with Yokes 103
A-Line Gown with Back Opening 107

Right: Katherine Ingram

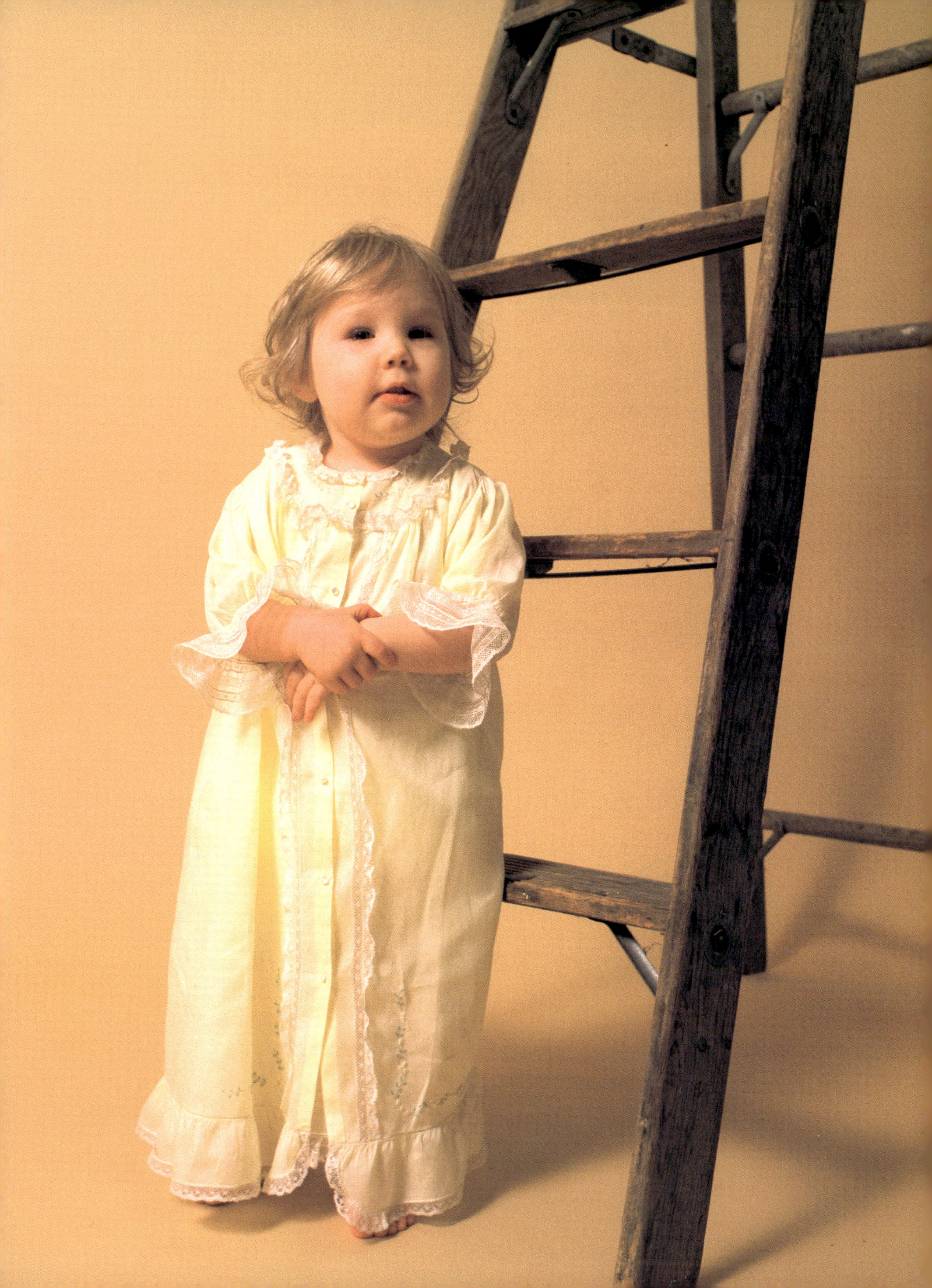

INTRODUCTION

Daygowns are the most practical item in a layette. They can be as elaborate or as simple as you like. Imported cotton or permanent-press batiste may be used depending on the style you choose. (Remember that permanent-press fabric does not roll and whip as well.) They vary in length from 22 to 27 inches. You may choose from several styles, such as the set-in or raglan sleeves, yoked daygown, or the round or square yoke. These basic patterns may be adapted to create other variations, such as the one in which tucks form the yoke. You may adorn the front with tiny tucks and gather the front. Do whatever you like, as long as the neck is 10½ inches from end to end before fastening.

Gowns can be opened down the front or back. There are four placket styles to choose from when the gown opens down the front. Sleeves may be finished with beading and ribbon or "Sarah's Sleeve Stitch." Collars can be used and are very appropriate for little boys. I personally do not use them because they seem to roll up rather than lie down as they should.

The bottom of the gown may be hemmed or finished with a ruffle. A-line slips compliment these lovely garments.

Placket With Trim On Both Sides

Turn the placket on the fold line to the right side. (Fig. 126)

Turn the raw edge under 1/4-inch. Press and whip entredeux to the crease. (Fig. 127A)

Whip gathered or flat lace edging or trim to the entredeux. (Fig. 127B)

Roll and whip the neck. (Gather where needed). The neck should be 10½-inches from end to end.

Whip entredeux to the outer edge of the placket and extend around the neck. (Fig. 128A)

Whip gathered lace edging or flat trim to the entredeux on the outer edge of the placket and continue around the neck edge. (Fig. 128B)

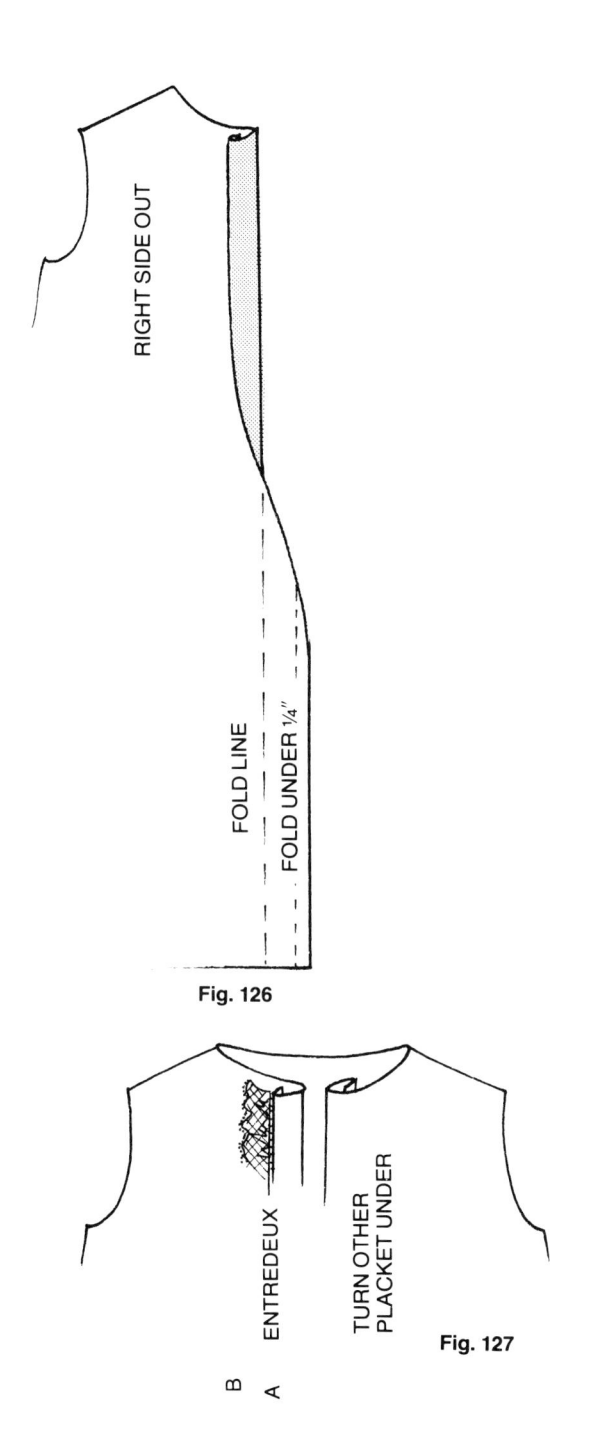

Fig. 126

Fig. 127

False Placket

A false placket may be a strip of handloomed embroidery, puffing or eyelet insertion. NOTE: Eyelet usually has entredeux on both sides. (Fig. 129)

Turn the placket of the gown on the fold line. Turn the raw edge under the desired placket width and blindstitch. This placket should be the same width as the false placket, so make this adjustment before cutting the gown front. (Fig. 130) (Buttonhole side only.) Work buttonholes in this placket, excluding the top buttonhole at the neck edge. NOTE: The top buttonhole is worked after the neck has been rolled and whipped and before the false placket is secured in place. Turn the other placket to the wrong side. Turn the raw edge under enough to finish width desired and blindstitch. (Fig. 131) Roll and whip the handloomed embroidery strip or make a puffing strip and attach the entredeux to both of the long sides.

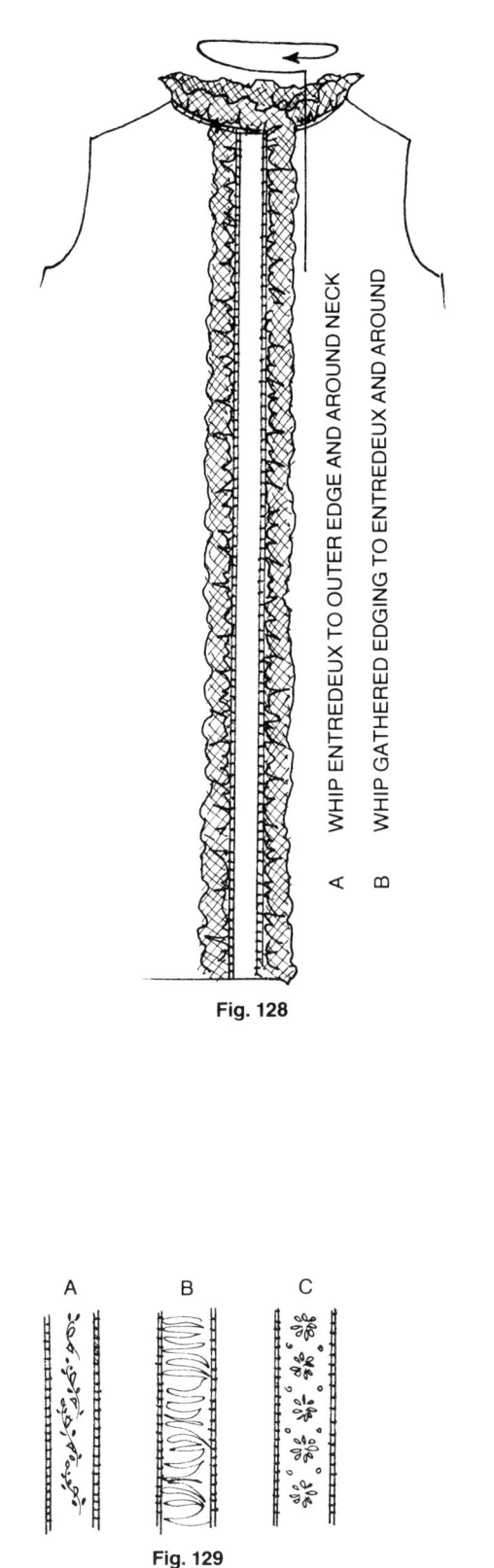

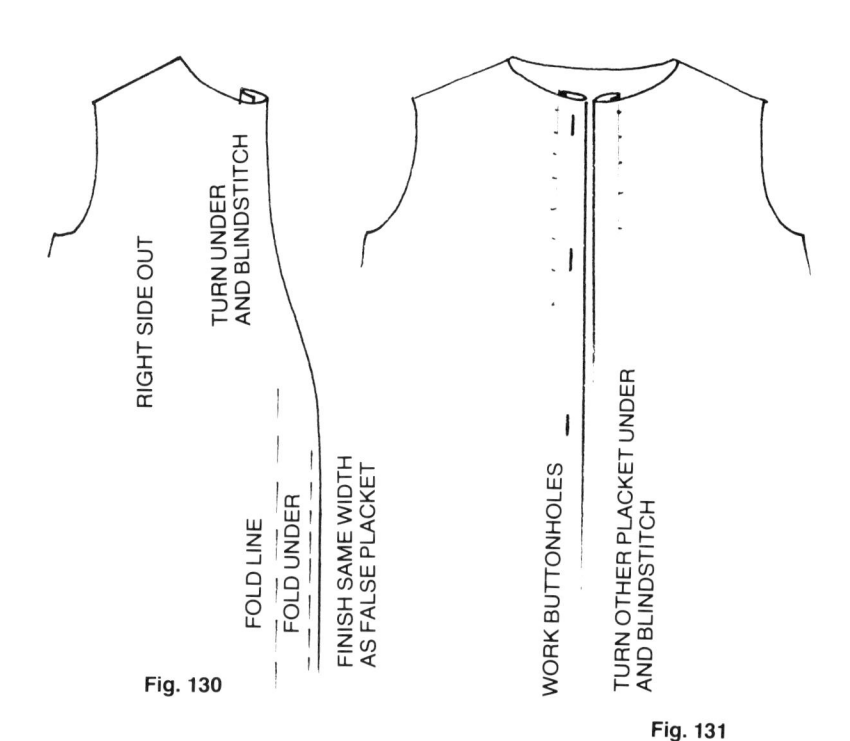

Attach edging to the inside entredeux. (Left side facing you.) (Fig. 132)

Place the fancy placket on top of the plain placket and stitch to secure across the top edge. (Fig. 133)

Roll and whip and gather (if necessary) the neck edge to 10½-inches. (Fig. 134)

Whip the entredeux to the other edge of the false placket and continue around the neck edge. (Fig. 135)

Whip edging to the entredeux on the outside (right side facing you) entredeux and continue around the neck edge. (Fig. 136)

Secure the placket half way between each buttonhole. This enables you to button the gown with ease. (Fig. 137)

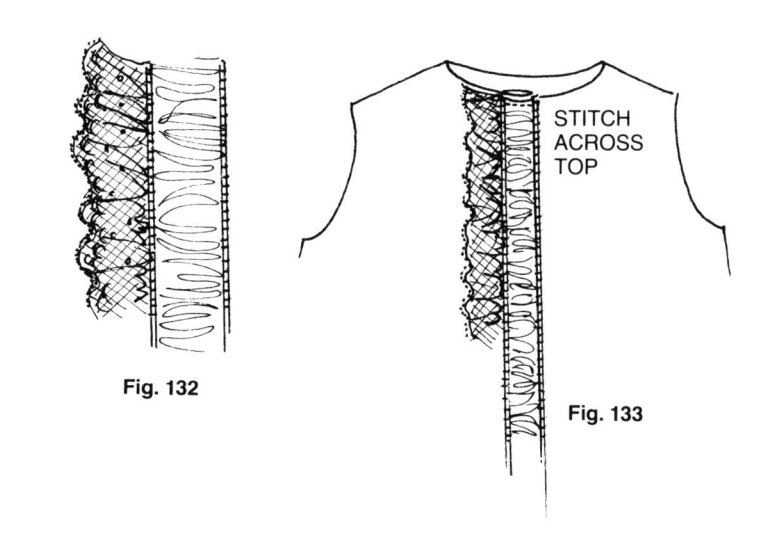

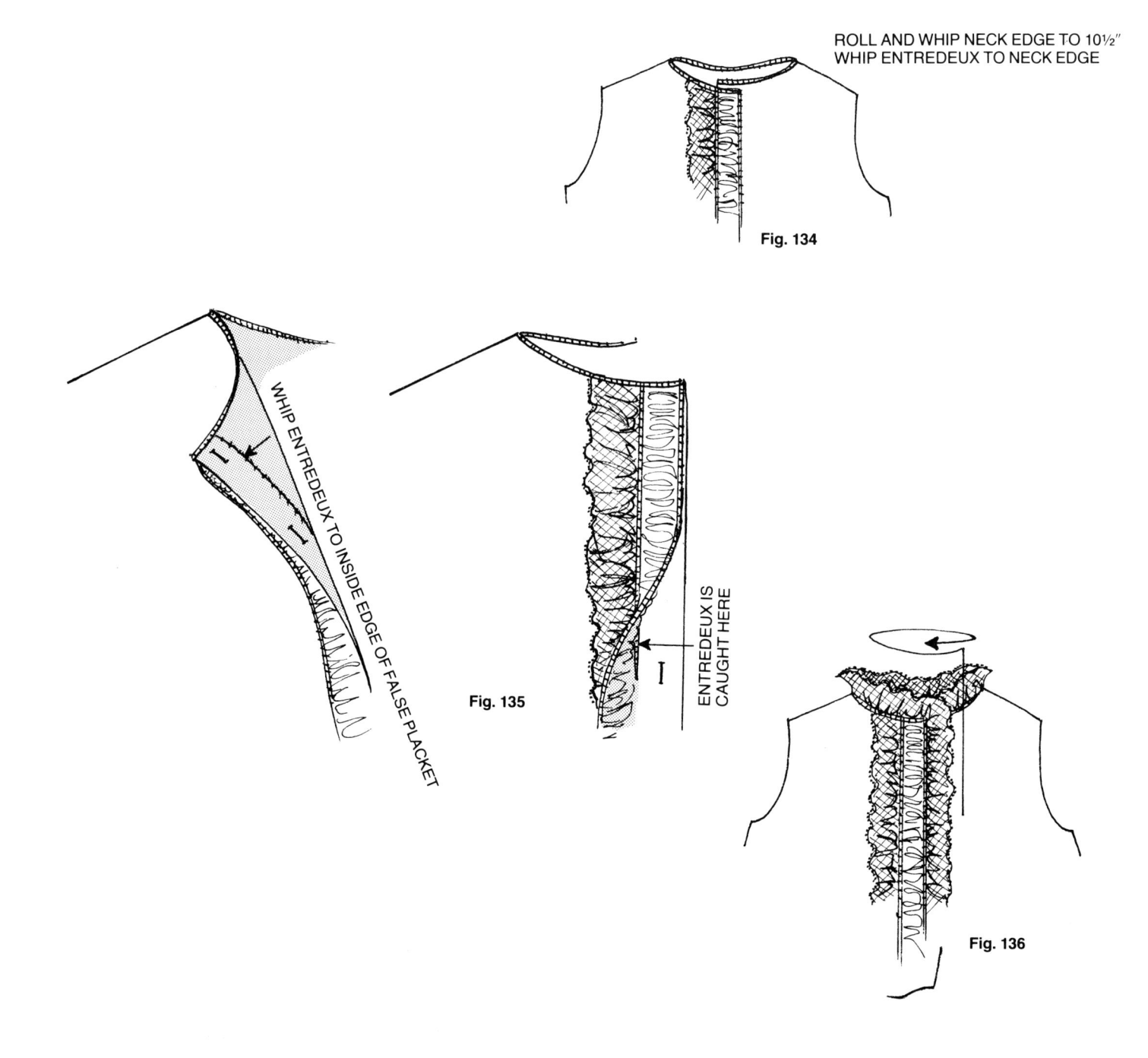

Fig. 132

STITCH ACROSS TOP

Fig. 133

ROLL AND WHIP NECK EDGE TO 10½"
WHIP ENTREDEUX TO NECK EDGE

Fig. 134

WHIP ENTREDEUX TO INSIDE EDGE OF FALSE PLACKET

Fig. 135

ENTREDEUX IS CAUGHT HERE

Fig. 136

Placket With Sewn Fabric Strip

This method is also used where the placket cannot be turned to the right side.

Trim the placket edge off of the buttonhole side of the gown leaving 1/8-inch beyond the fold line. (Fig. 138)

Cut a strip of fabric width x length needed to make the placket.

Lay the wrong side of the placket strip to the wrong side of the gown front (left side facing you) and sew with tiny running stitches or by machine 1/8-inch from the raw edge. (Fig. 140)

Turn the fabric (on stitching line) to the right side of the gown and follow the same directions as for the placket with trim on both sides.

SECURE PLACKET HALF WAY BETWEEN EACH BUTTONHOLE

Fig. 137

Fig. 138
TRIM 1/8" BEYOND FOLD LINE
FOLD LINE

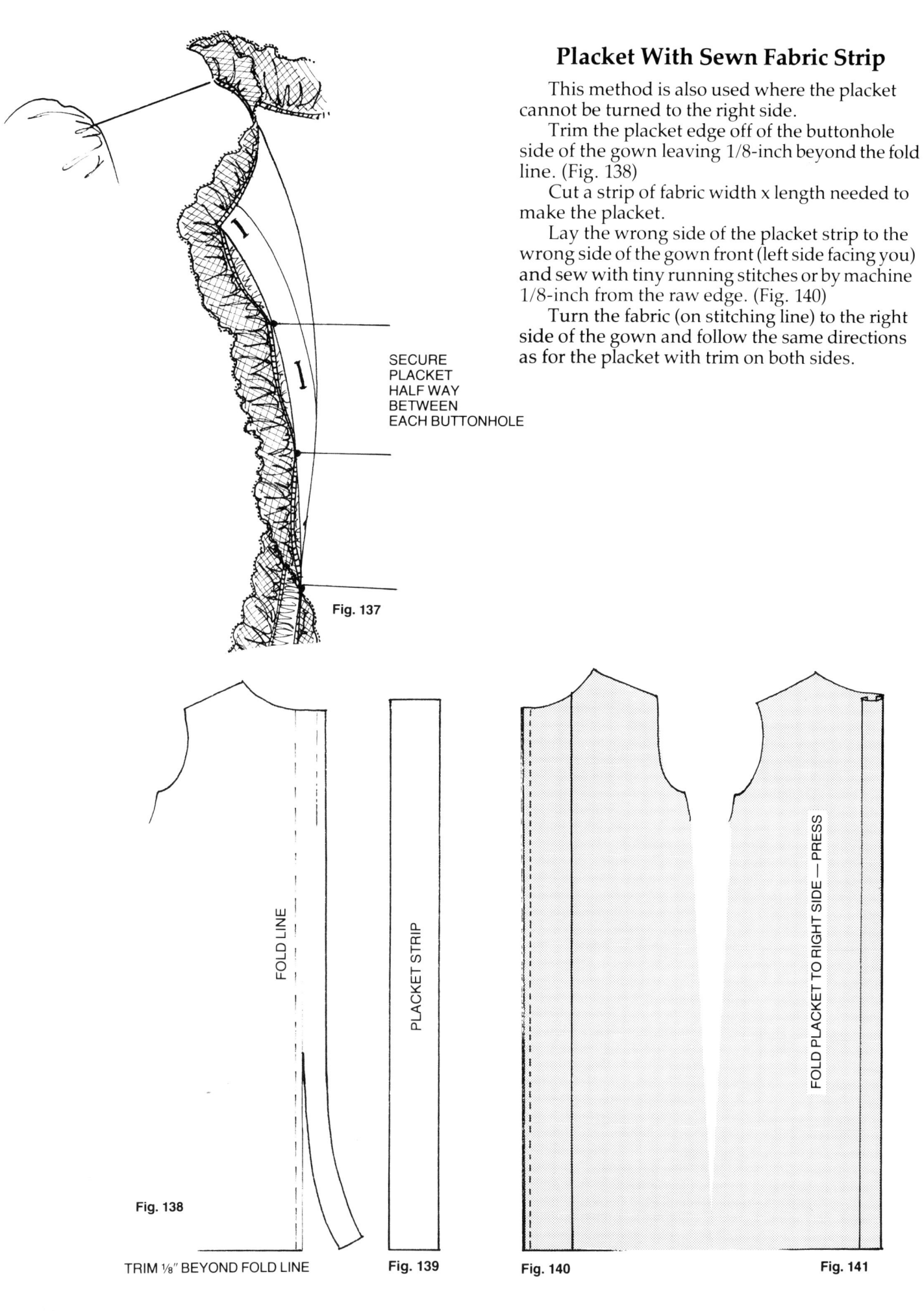

Fig. 139
PLACKET STRIP

Fig. 140

Fig. 141
FOLD PLACKET TO RIGHT SIDE — PRESS

Placket Trimmed with Ruffle

Fold fabric for plackets down either side of gown front 3/4-inch and another 3/4-inch, forming a double thickness. Baste and then blindstitch. (Fig. 142)

Roll and whip the neck edge to 10½-inches from end to end. (Fig. 143A) Turn the bottom edge of the gown up 1½-inches for hem. Turn the raw edge under 1/4-inch and baste, working in the excess fullness. Blindstitch hem. (Fig. 143B) Whip entredeux to the fold edge of the left placket facing you and continue around the neck edge. (Fig. 143C).

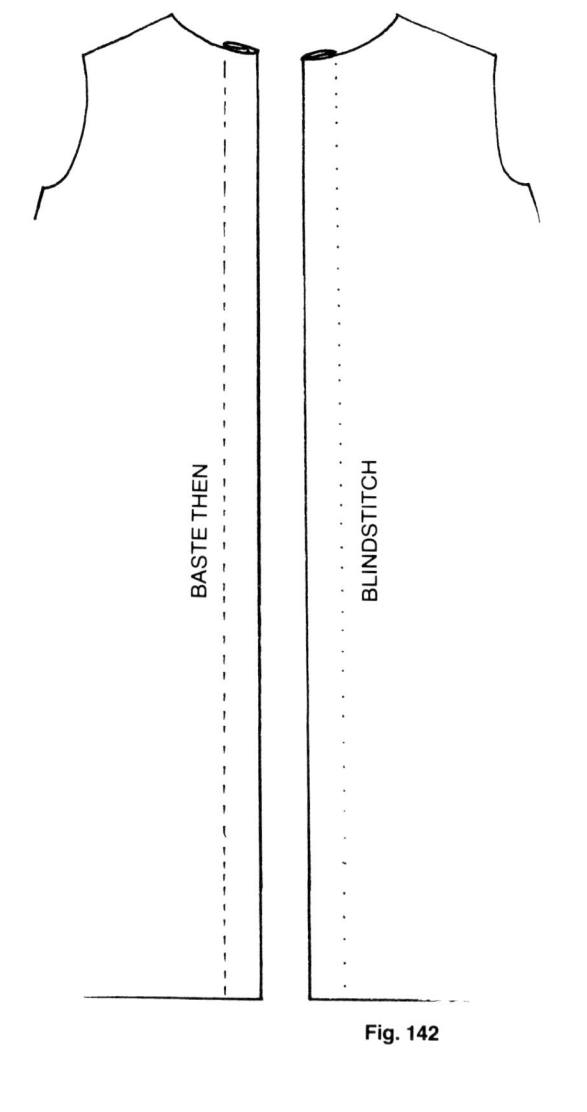

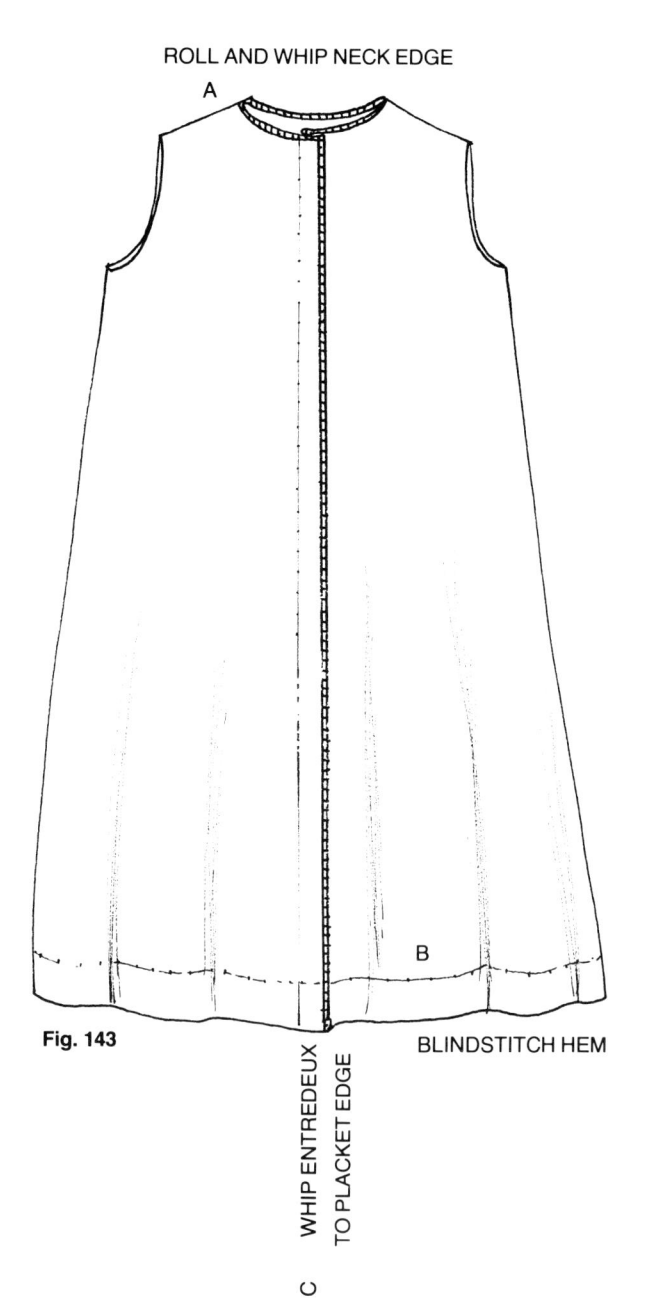

Fig. 142

Fig. 143

96

Make a fabric ruffle 1½-inches wide x one and one-half times the length of the placket. Curve the top of the ruffle (Fig. 144A) and put a tiny hem in the bottom of the ruffle. (Fig. 144B)

Roll and whip the curved side of the ruffle, and whip lace edging to the curved side, (Fig. 144C) leaving enough lace edging extending at the top to be gathered around the neck. (Fig. 144D) Roll and whip and gather the other side of the ruffle to fit the entredeux on the front placket. Whip to the entredeux. (Fig. 145A) Whip lace edging to the rest of the neck. (Fig. 145B) Ruffles are pretty made of a different color fabric. The ruffle may be omitted and lace edging used in place of the ruffle.

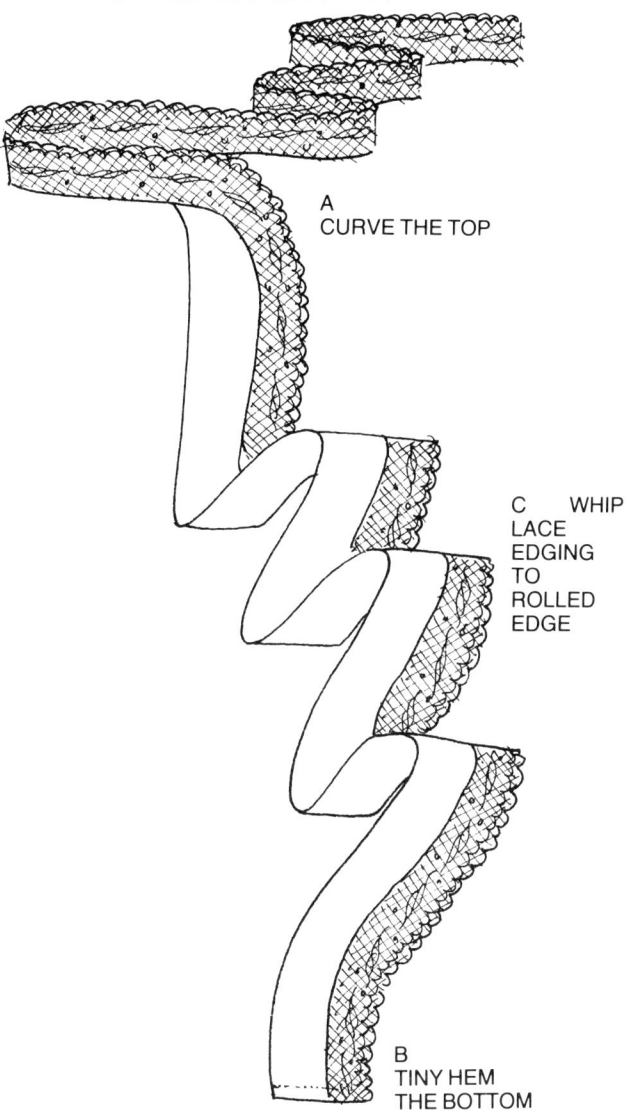

Fig. 144

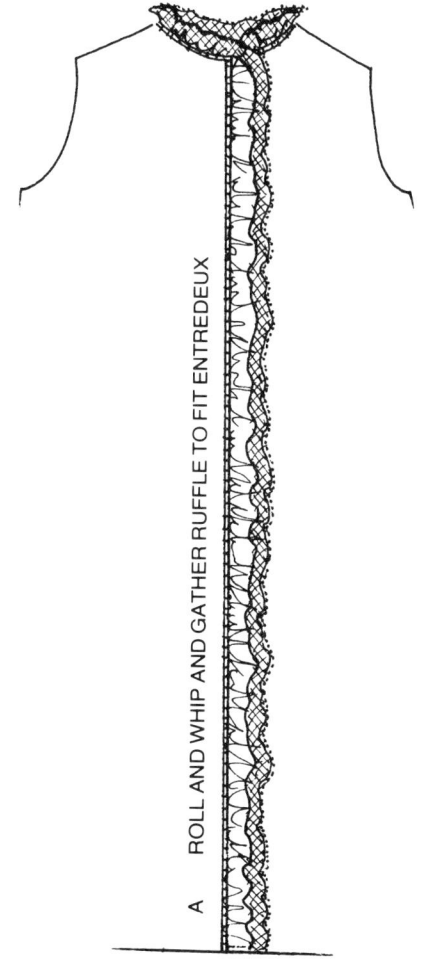

Fig. 145

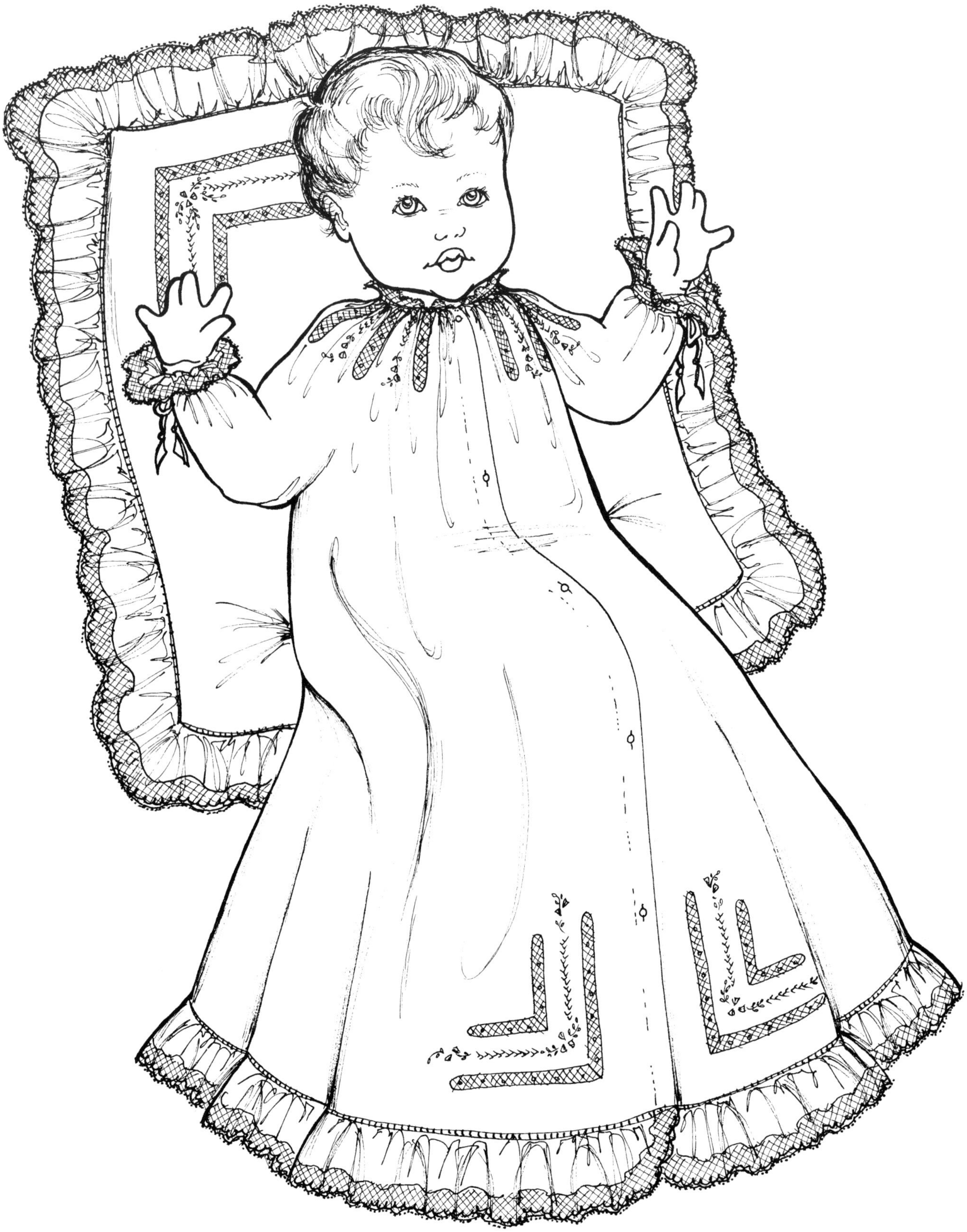

Gowns with Raglan Sleeves

This gown has strips of lace insertion applied in a spoked effect around the neck. The lace is basted to the fabric with tiny running stitches and secured with a buttonhole, satin, or pin stitch. The ends of the lace are folded under, forming a rounded effect at the end. (Fig. 146)

Lace insertion is applied on the skirt in the same manner. Embroider with a featherstitch and rosebuds between the lace. The plain placket is turned under on both sides.

The neck edge is rolled and whipped to 10½ inches from end to end. The bottom edge of the gown is rolled and whipped, and entredeux is whipped to the rolled edge.

A fabric ruffle edged with lace (2½ inches wide x 1½ times the length and shaped at each end) is whipped to the entredeux.

The bottom of the sleeves (5½ inches around) may be finished with beading enhanced with a lace or fabric ruffle.

This gown is made with a ruffle applied to a placket edge. The top of the ruffle is shaped to fit the neck. A tiny hem finishes the bottom of the ruffle. The ruffle should be approximately 1½ inches wide and one and one-half times the length of the placket.

Hem the gown (by turning the bottom edge up 1½ inches, turning raw edge under 1/4 inch, and basting and blindstitching) and roll and whip the neck before whipping the entredeux and ruffle to the front.

Featherstitch the inside of the placket (one stitch on placket, one stitch off placket) and work rosebuds between the buttonholes.

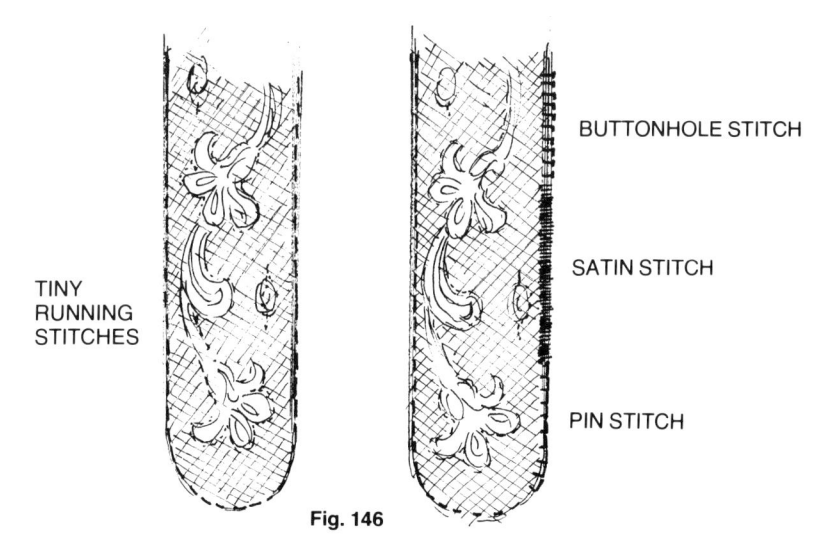

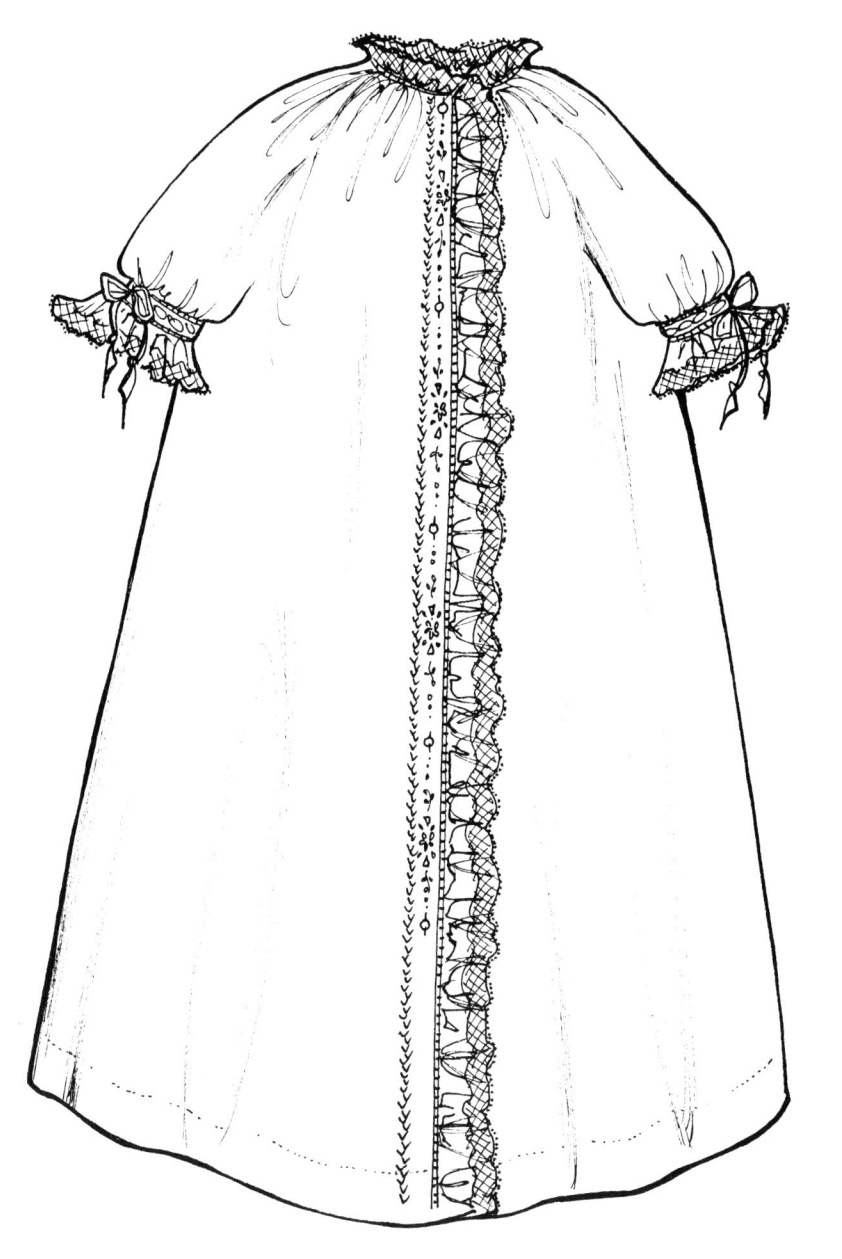

Fig. 146

Gowns with Set-In Sleeves

This dainty gown has fine pin tucks and embroidery on each side of the placket. The back neck edge is gathered.

The gown is hemmed, and both sides of the placket are enhanced with gathered lace edging. Embroidery on the placket is optional.

The sleeves are set into the armhole with entredeux.

EMBROIDERY DESIGNS FOR USE BETWEEN OR

AROUND BUTTONHOLES

Whipped tucks embellished with embroidery and a placket with a sewn placket strip of a different color, edged with entredeux and lace, makes a lovely garment for a boy or girl.

The ruffle on the sleeves should match the placket color.

Choose embroidery floss and ribbon for the sleeves that will enhance the color placket and ruffle you choose.

For the fathers who object to too much lace on their sons (even though a baby is a baby whether born a girl or boy and should be treated as such), this gown is ideal. It features tiny pin tucks on each side of the placket. The back can have a box pleat (Fig. 147), more tucks (Fig. 148), or gathers to make the neck the proper size (Fig. 149).

The petite collar, placket, and binding at the bottom of the sleeves are trimmed with tatting.

FOR USE AROUND BUTTONHOLE

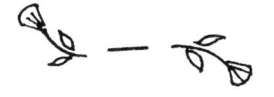

Fig. 147

Fig. 148

Fig. 149

Gowns with Yokes

We offer a pattern for this gown; it is the yoked daygown that I designed from an old baby dress pattern.

I have added insertion and lace edging down the skirt fronts. The yoke and skirt are embroidered with french roses.

The fabric is tucked deeply enough to form the yoke. It is tucked front and back with 1/8 to 1/4-inch tucks. Leave enough fabric plain to form the placket on each side of the front.

Gather fullness in before cutting out.

Make a false placket of handloomed embroidery or eyelet insertion.

This yoked gown can be made from the round yoke dress pattern. Cut the back yoke on the fold and add a placket to the front yoke. Open the skirt front down the center.

Make a false placket of puffing with entredeux and edging.

The yoke may be made of all lace, lace and puffing, or fabric edged at the bottom with insertion. A lace ruffle enhances the yoke and sleeves.

If you do not use a false placket, you must use the placket with a sewn fabric strip.

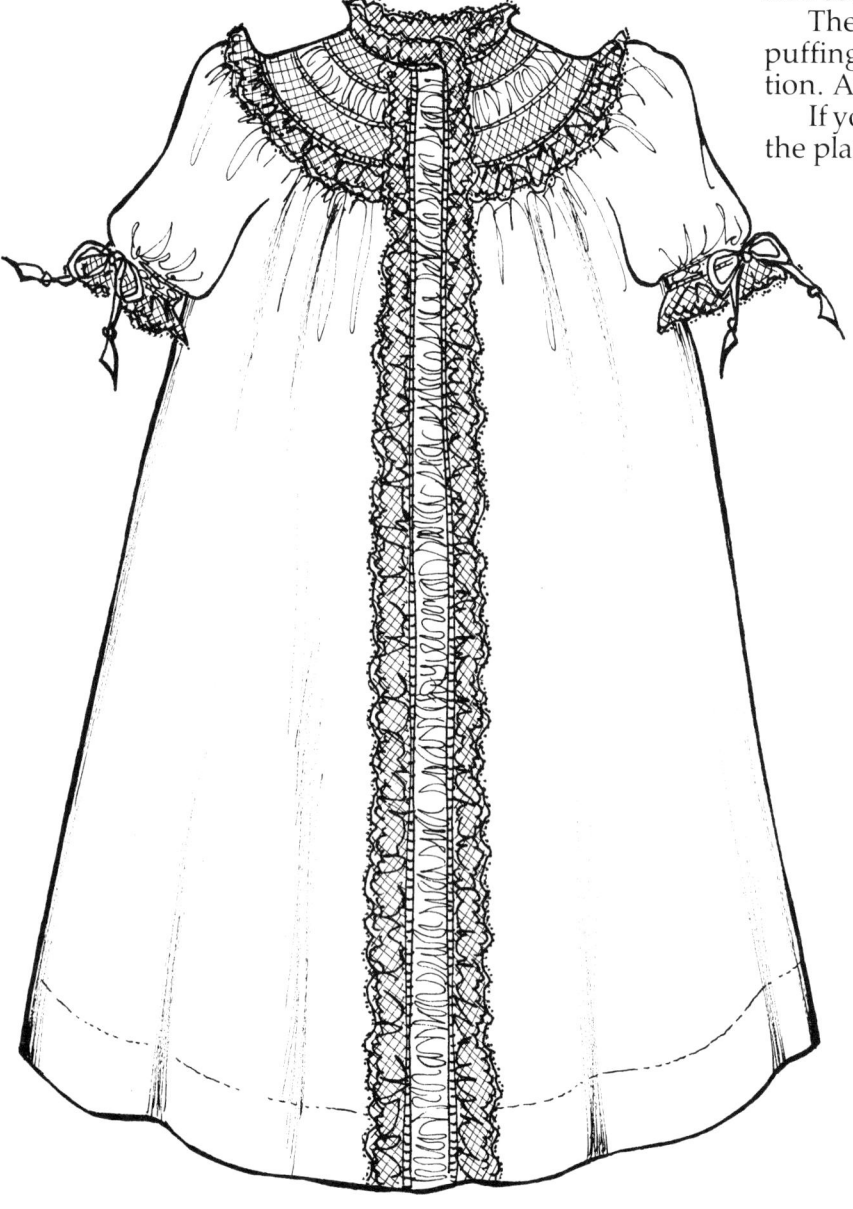

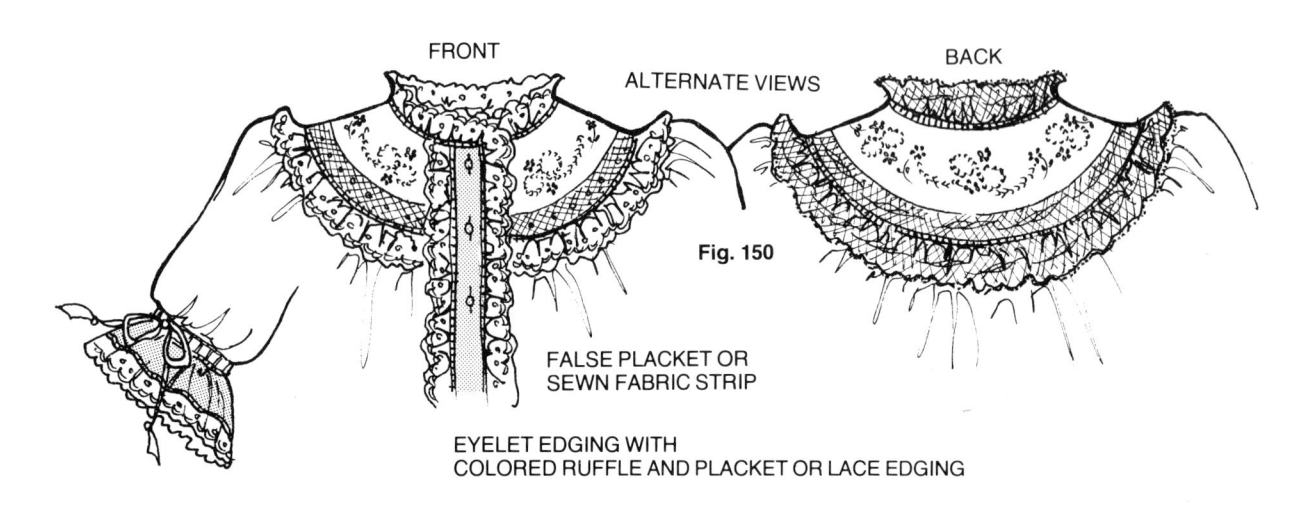

FRONT ALTERNATE VIEWS BACK

Fig. 150

FALSE PLACKET OR
SEWN FABRIC STRIP

EYELET EDGING WITH
COLORED RUFFLE AND PLACKET OR LACE EDGING

A-Line Gown with Back Opening

Make a block of tucks, lace, and eyelet insertion the length you need x the widest bottom measurement. (Fig. 151)

The back has 1/4-inch tucks to form fullness. (Fig. 152)

The bottom is trimmed with eyelet or lace insertion edged with a ruffle. NOTE: The ruffle can be eyelet or fabric trimmed with lace.

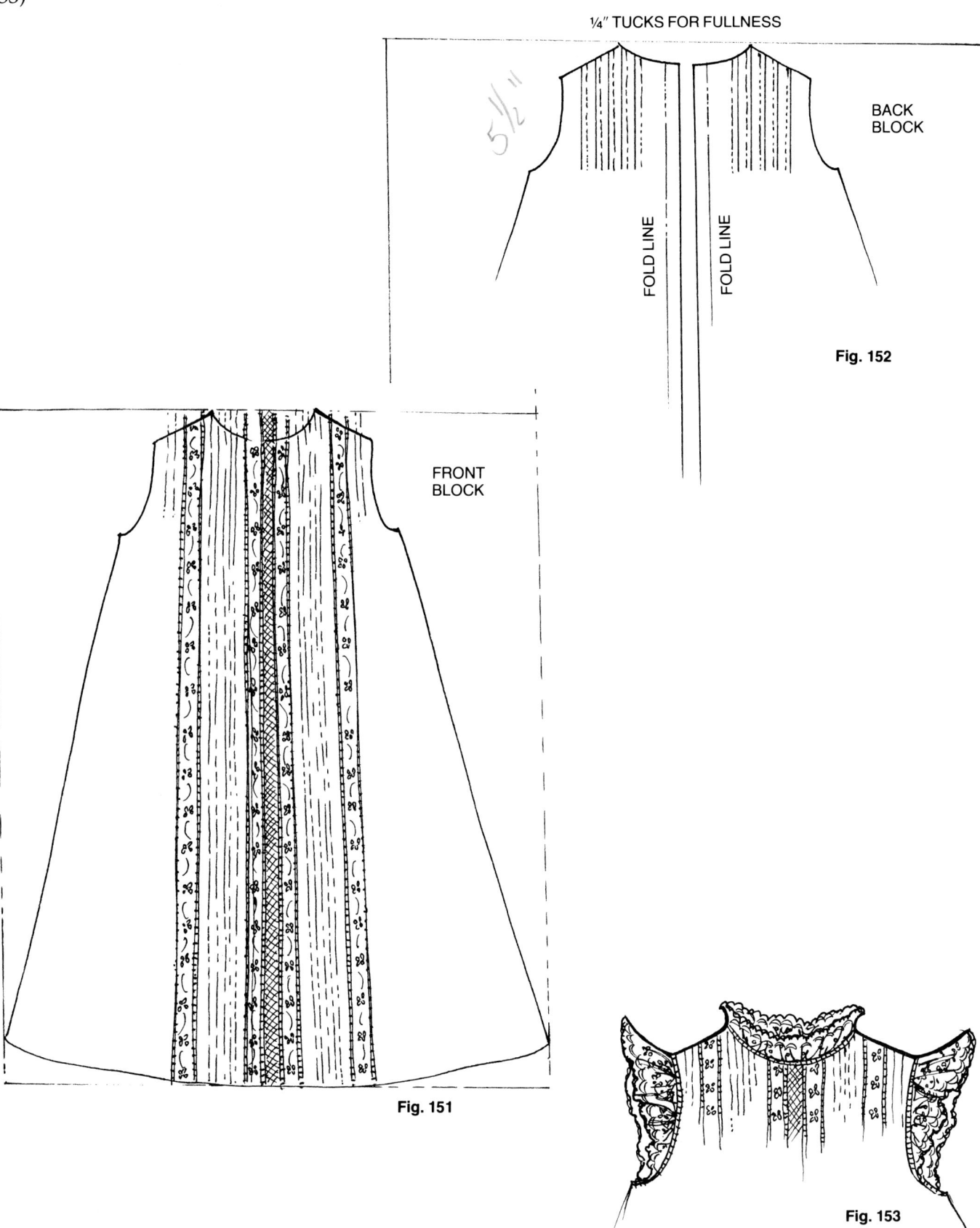

For summer babies, an eyelet ruffle in the armhole may be substituted for the sleeve. (Fig. 153)

¼" TUCKS FOR FULLNESS

5½"

FOLD LINE

FOLD LINE

BACK BLOCK

work out from center

Fig. 152

FRONT BLOCK

Fig. 151

Fig. 153

108

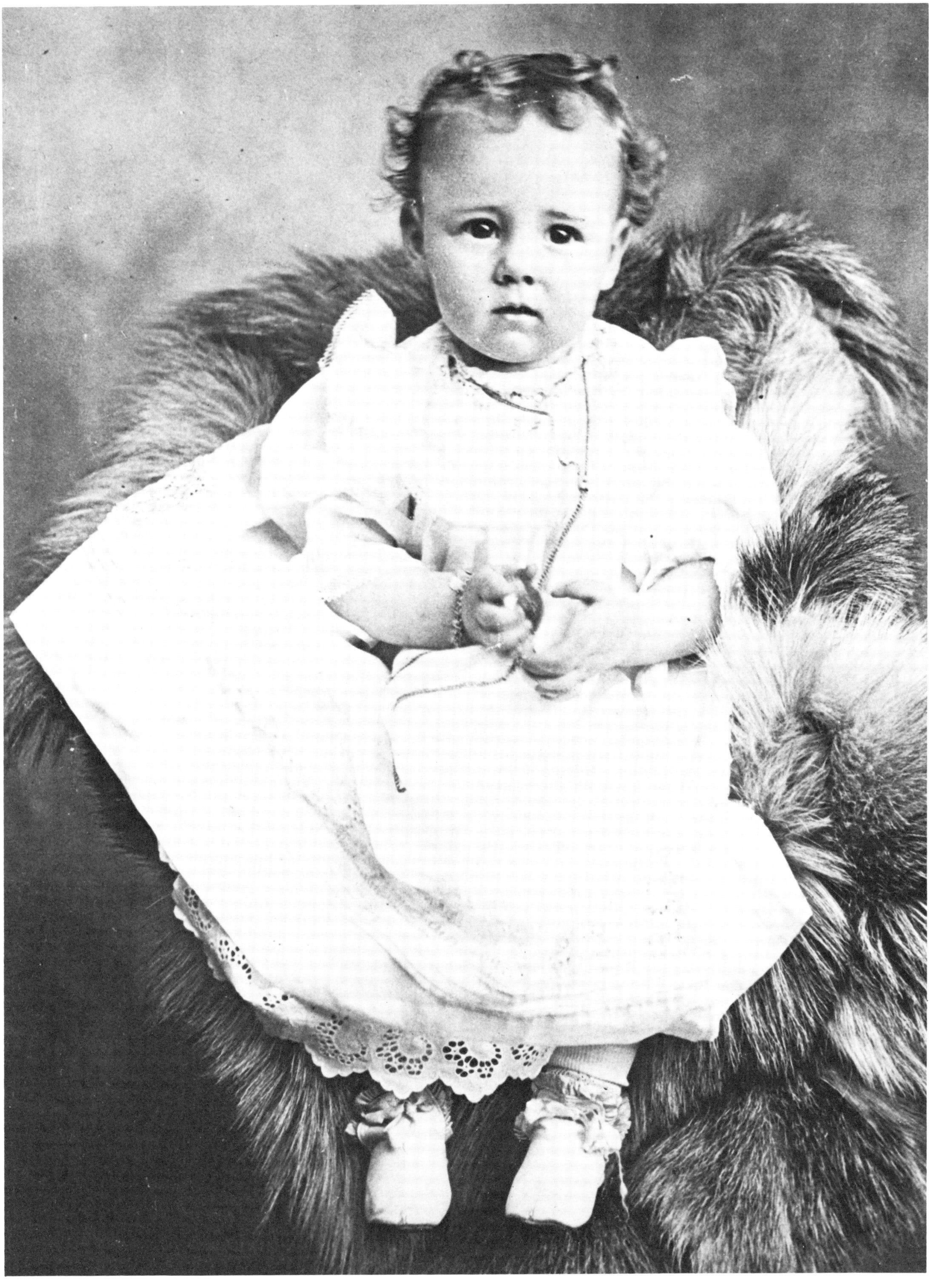

TROUSSEAU TREASURES

Pillow Shams 113
Handkerchief Pillow 117
Pin Cushions 118
Carriage Covers 120
Receiving Blankets 123
Sacques and Kimonos 125
Coats 131
Bibs 133
Diaper Shirts 135
Diaper Covers and Panties 137

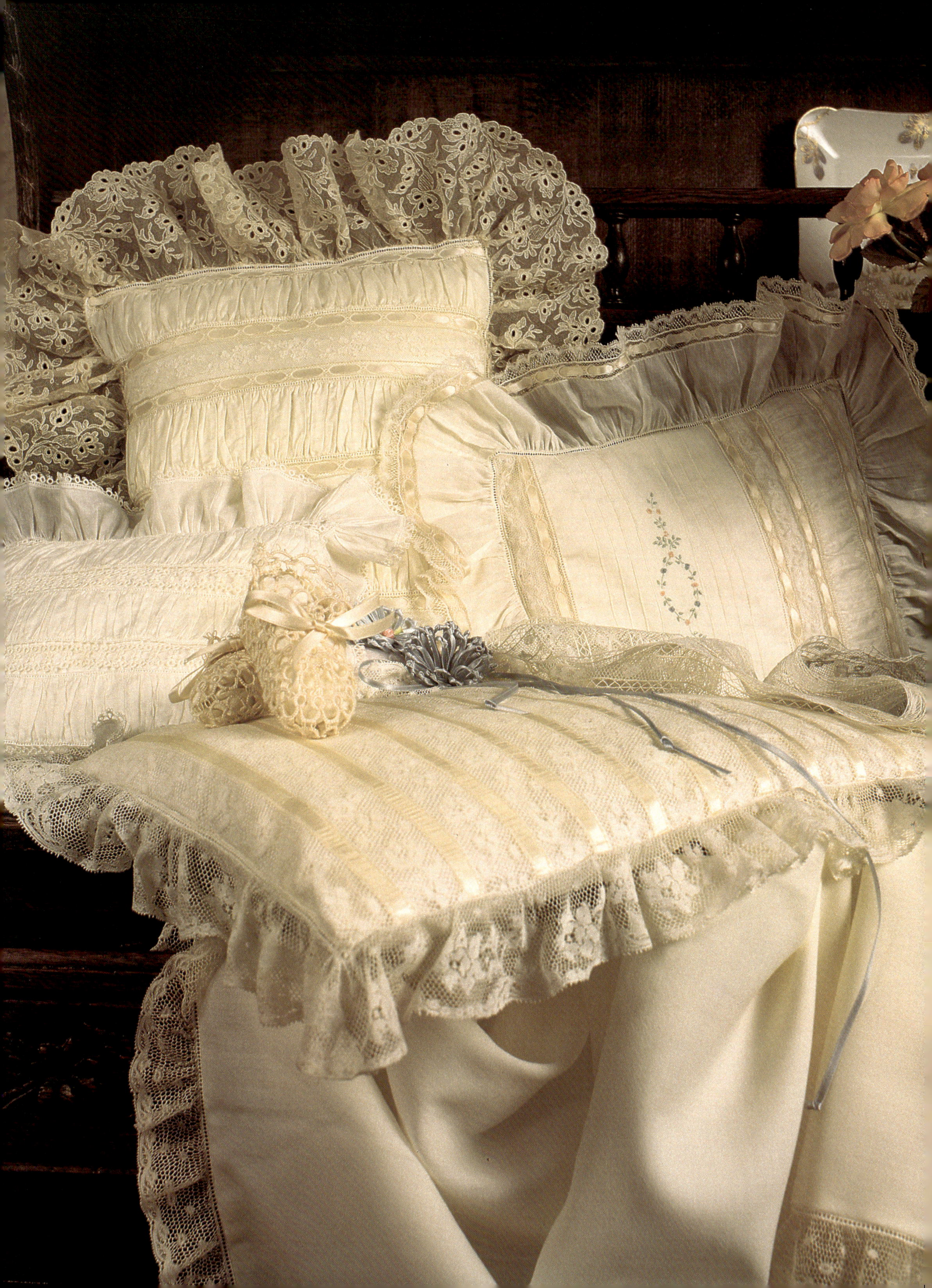

INTRODUCTION

In this chapter, you will find ideas for gifts that are fun to make and give as well as to receive. Some are luxury items, while others are necessities.

Let these suggestions get you started; then use your imagination to create your own designs.

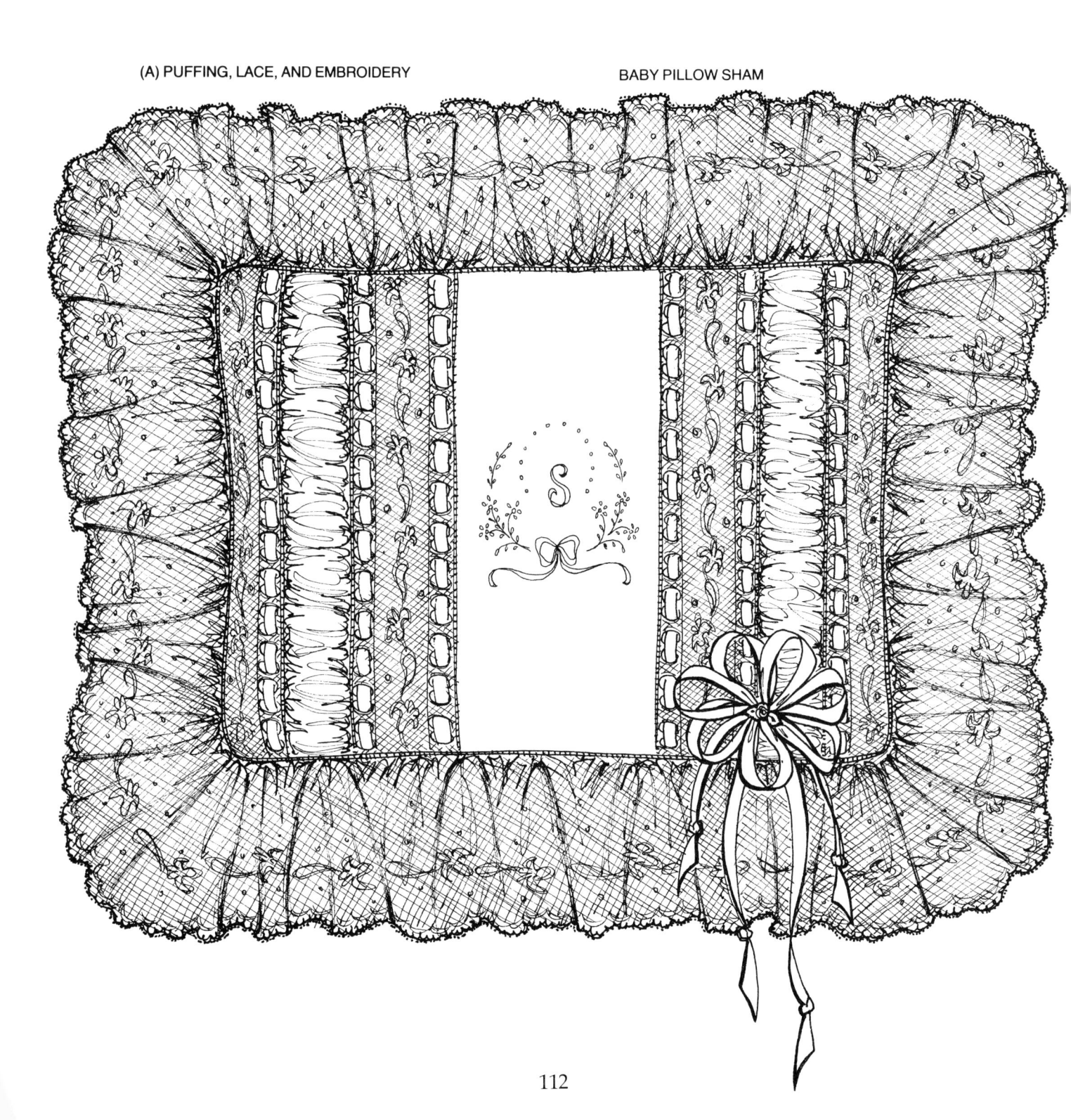

(A) PUFFING, LACE, AND EMBROIDERY **BABY PILLOW SHAM**

Pillow Shams

Standard measurements for baby pillows are 12 x 16 inches (finished). If the outer edge of the pillow top is lace insertion, you can make the pillow top to the exact measurement. If the outer edge of the pillow top is fabric, you should add 1/4-inch seam allowances all around. (Fig. 154)

The pillow back is made of two overlapping fabric pieces. Each must have a 1/4-inch seam allowance on the three outer edges. The fourth, overlapping edge of each piece will have a 1/2-inch

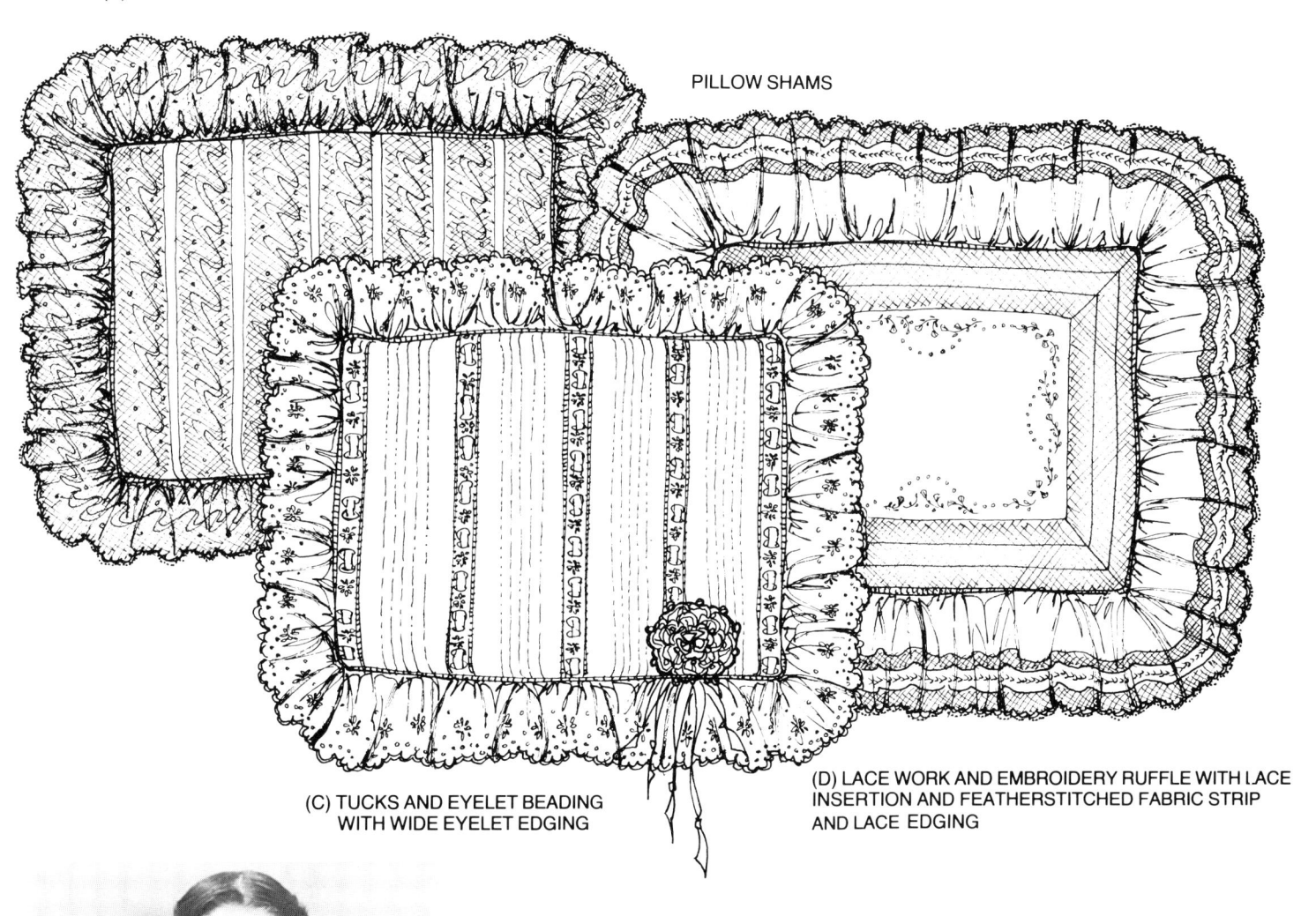

(B) WIDE LACE AND RIBBON

PILLOW SHAMS

(C) TUCKS AND EYELET BEADING WITH WIDE EYELET EDGING

(D) LACE WORK AND EMBROIDERY RUFFLE WITH LACE INSERTION AND FEATHERSTITCHED FABRIC STRIP AND LACE EDGING

ADD ¼" SEAM ALLOWANCE
IF OUTER EDGE IS FABRIC

PILLOW FRONT

IF OUTER EDGE IS LACE YOU CAN MAKE THE PILLOW TOP TO THE EXACT MEASUREMENT

12

16

Fig. 154

FOR PILLOW SHAM FRONT VIEW A, B, OR C ADD ¼" SEAM ALLOWANCE TOP AND BOTTOM.

FOR PILLOW SHAM FRONT D NO SEAM ALLOWANCE IS NECESSARY.

THE LACE FOR PILLOW SHAM D IS JOINED TOGETHER IN ONE LONG STRIP THEN MITERED TO FIT THE PILLOW TOP.

PILLOW BACK

CENTER BACK

FOLD LINE

FOLD LINE

CUT 2 BACKS 10" WIDE FOR BUTTON BACK

CUT 2 BACKS 11-14" WIDE FOR OVERLAPPED BACK

Fig. 155

* ADD ¼" ON 3 OUTER EDGES FOR SEAM ALLOWANCE

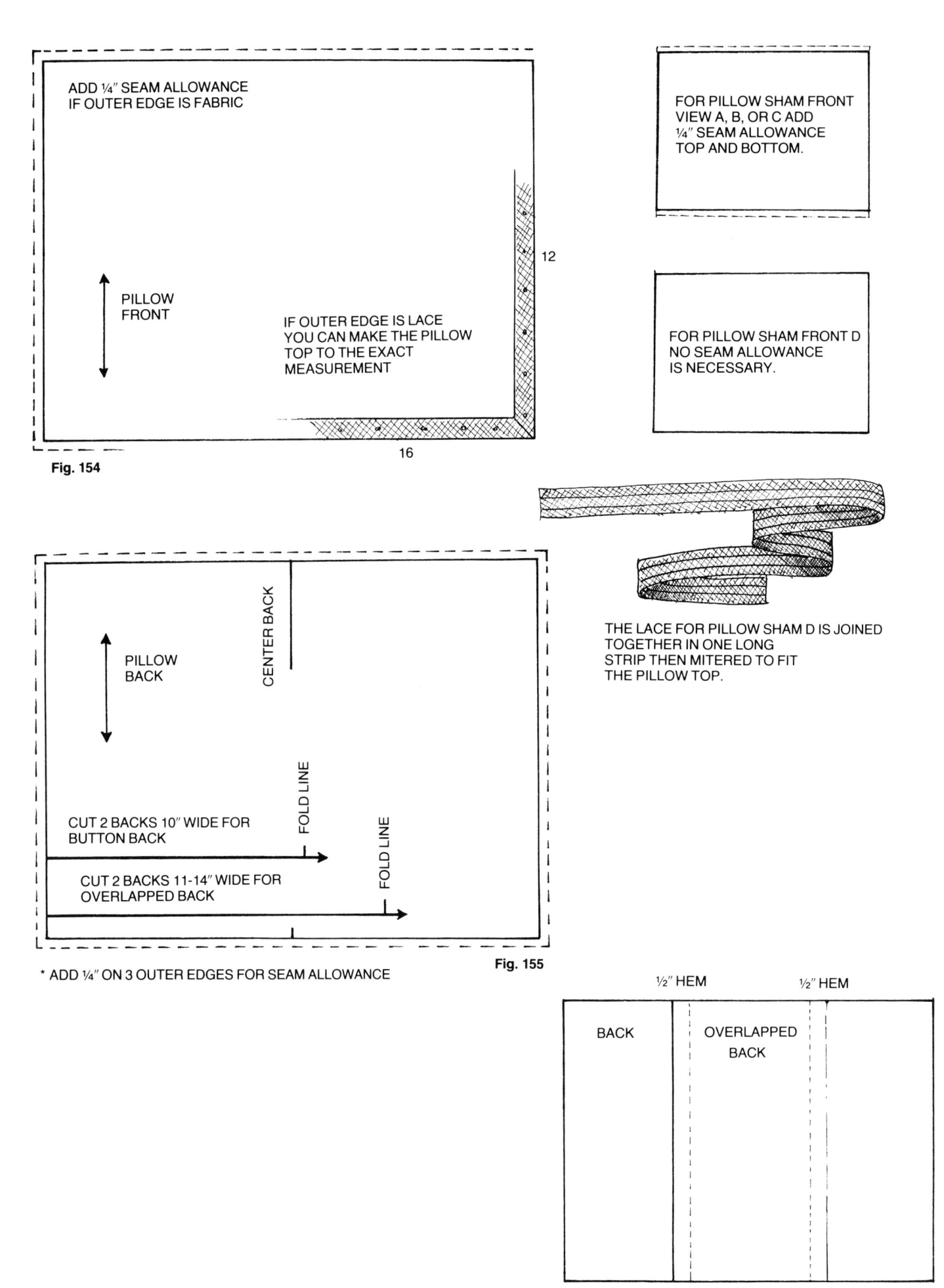

½" HEM   ½" HEM

BACK | OVERLAPPED BACK

Fig. 156

114

hem. (Fig. 156) You can cut the two back pieces with a wide overlap, so that the pillow back will not require buttons, (Fig. 156) or you can make the two pieces overlap the width of the hem only and button to close. (Fig. 157)

Whip entredeux to the entire finished outer edge. Whip a fabric, lace, or eyelet ruffle to the entredeux on the outer edge (gathered 2 x the measurement around the pillow, for fullness). Gather more of the ruffle at the corners, so that it will turn without cupping.

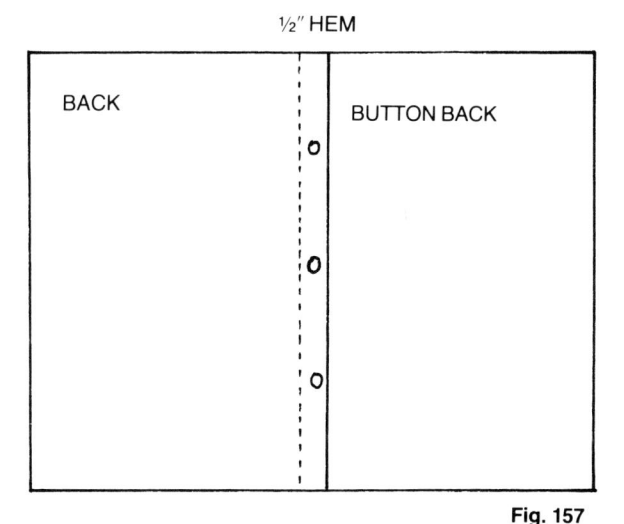

HOW TO MAKE PILLOW SHAMS

FOLD UNDER ¼" FOLD UNDER AGAIN TO FINISH ½" WIDE

½ PILLOW BACK

R & W (a)

PILLOW FRONT

JOIN THE BACKS TO THE PILLOW FRONT (RIGHT SIDES TOGETHER) (a) BY ROLLING AND WHIPPING THE ONE SIDE AND WHIPPING THE ROLLED EDGE TO PILLOW TOPS FINISHED WITH LACE INSERTION OR (b) SEWING ¼" FROM THE EDGE FOR TOPS THAT HAVE A FABRIC EDGE.

¼" SEAM (b)

½ PILLOW BACK

½" HEM

BACK	BUTTON BACK
	o
	o
	o

Fig. 157

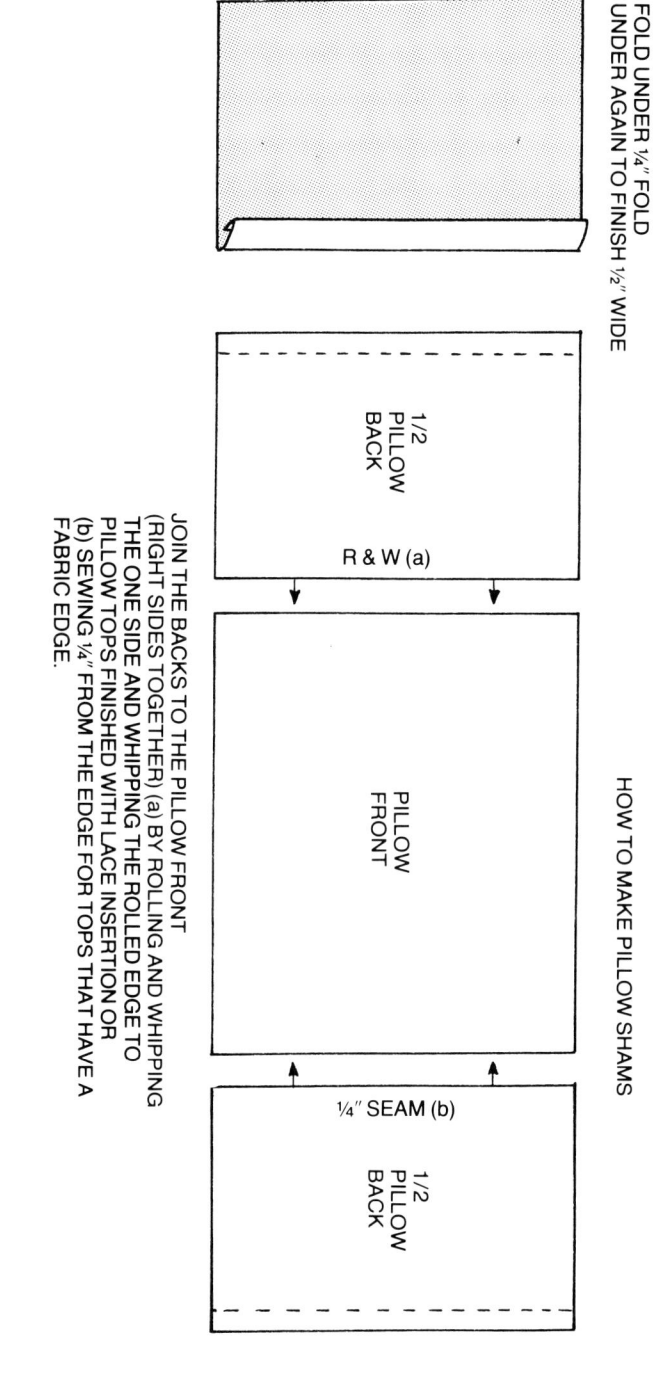

WITH RIGHT SIDES TOGETHER OVERLAP BACKS TO FIT PILLOW TOP. MACHINE STITCH OR TINY BASTE THE LONG SIDES ¼" FROM RAW EDGE
TURN TO RIGHT SIDE AND PRESS.
OR
ROLL AND WHIP THE ¼" SEAM ALLOWANCE AT THE TOP AND BOTTOM OF THE PILLOW BACK (AFTER THE BACK HAS BEEN FOLDED TO MATCH THE FRONT) AND WHIP THE ROLLED EDGE TO THE LACE INSERTION ON THE PILLOW TOP.

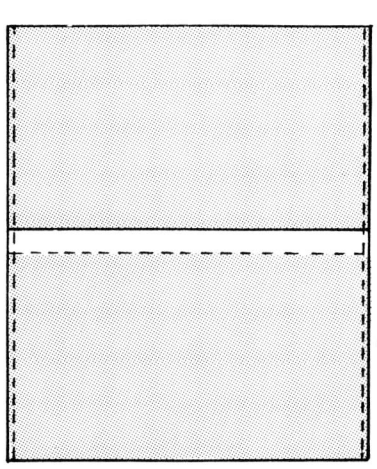

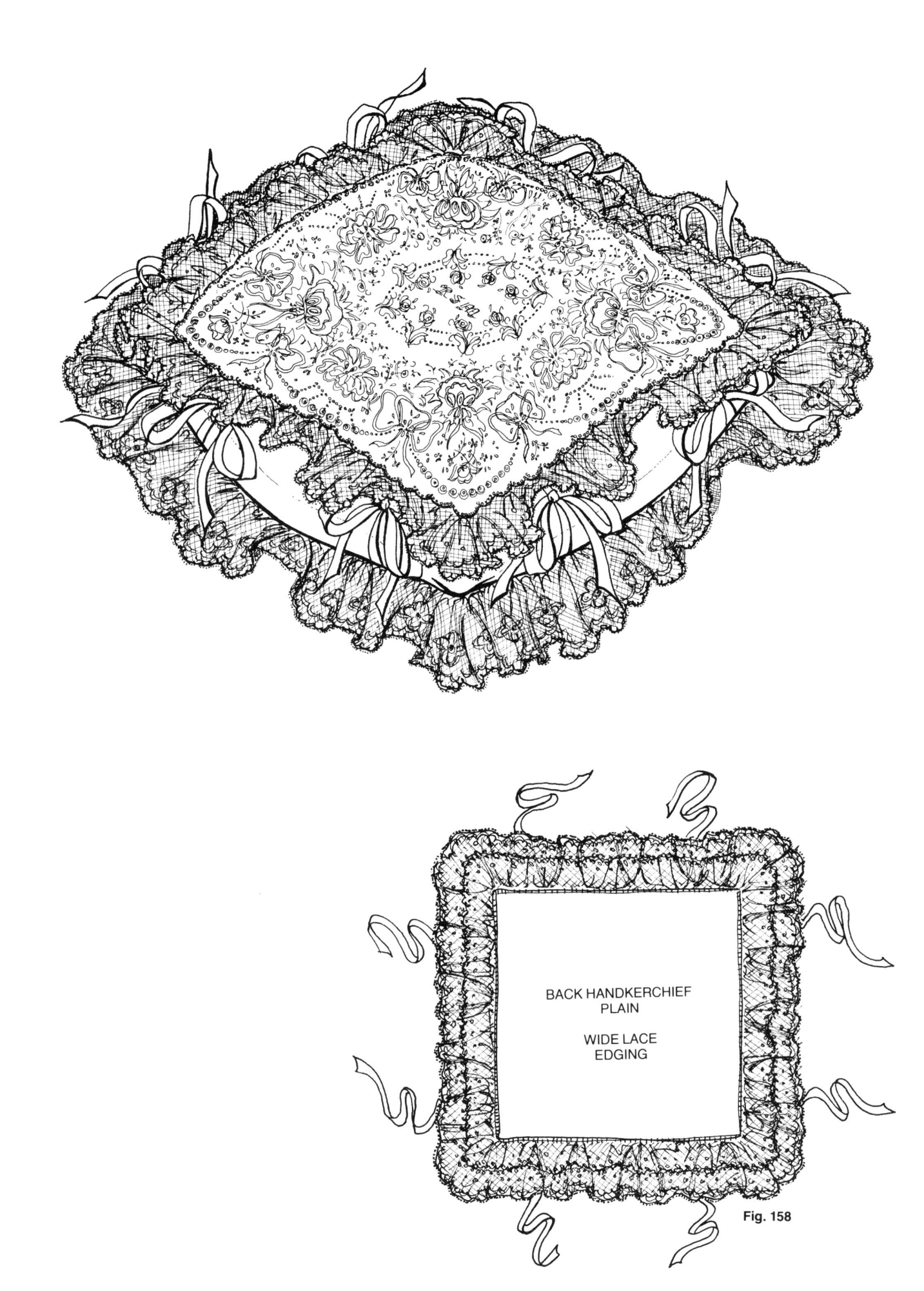

BACK HANDKERCHIEF
PLAIN

WIDE LACE
EDGING

Fig. 158

Handkerchief Pillow

Select two handkerchiefs, one fancy (for pillow top) and one plain (for pillow back), or two fancy. They must be the same size.

Whip wide gathered lace edging around the back handkerchief. (Fig. 158) Whip narrow or approximately 5/8-inch-wide edging around the front one. (Fig. 159)

Make two 1/4-inch satin ribbon ties on all four sides of the handkerchiefs. Make a pillow to fit inside the handkerchiefs and tie ribbons to hold the pillow in place. (Fig. 160)

MAKE PILLOW THE SIZE OF THE HANDKERCHIEF

Fig. 160

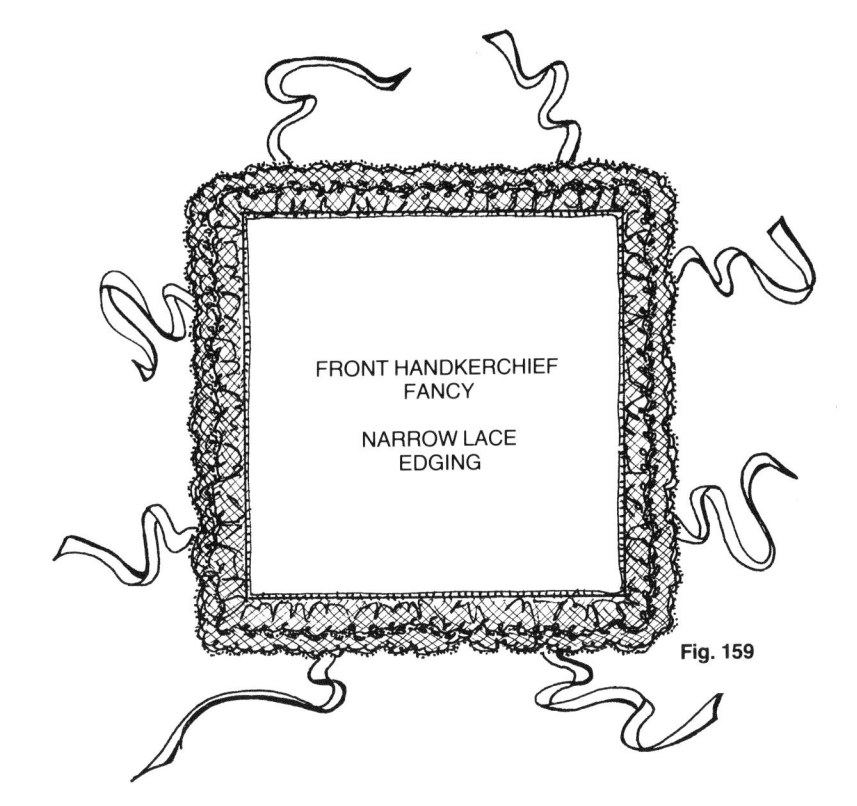

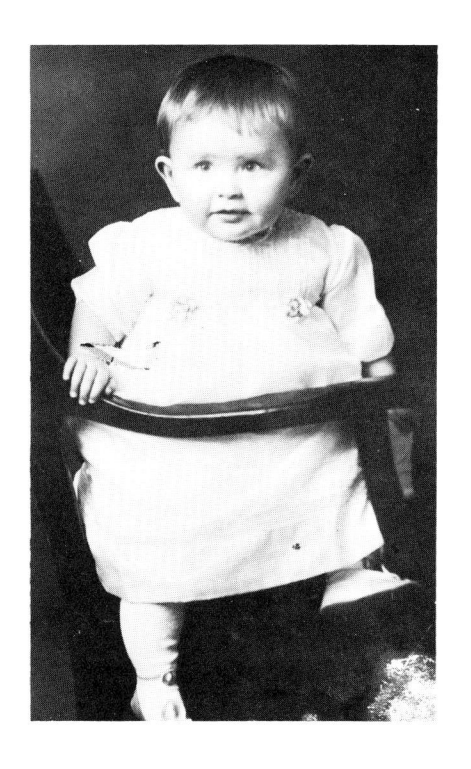

FRONT HANDKERCHIEF
FANCY

NARROW LACE EDGING

Fig. 159

Pin Cushions

Pin cushions are made from tiny squares or circles embellished in many different ways. The top of the pin cushion is underlined with satin or velvet, and the back is made of the same fabric as the underlay.

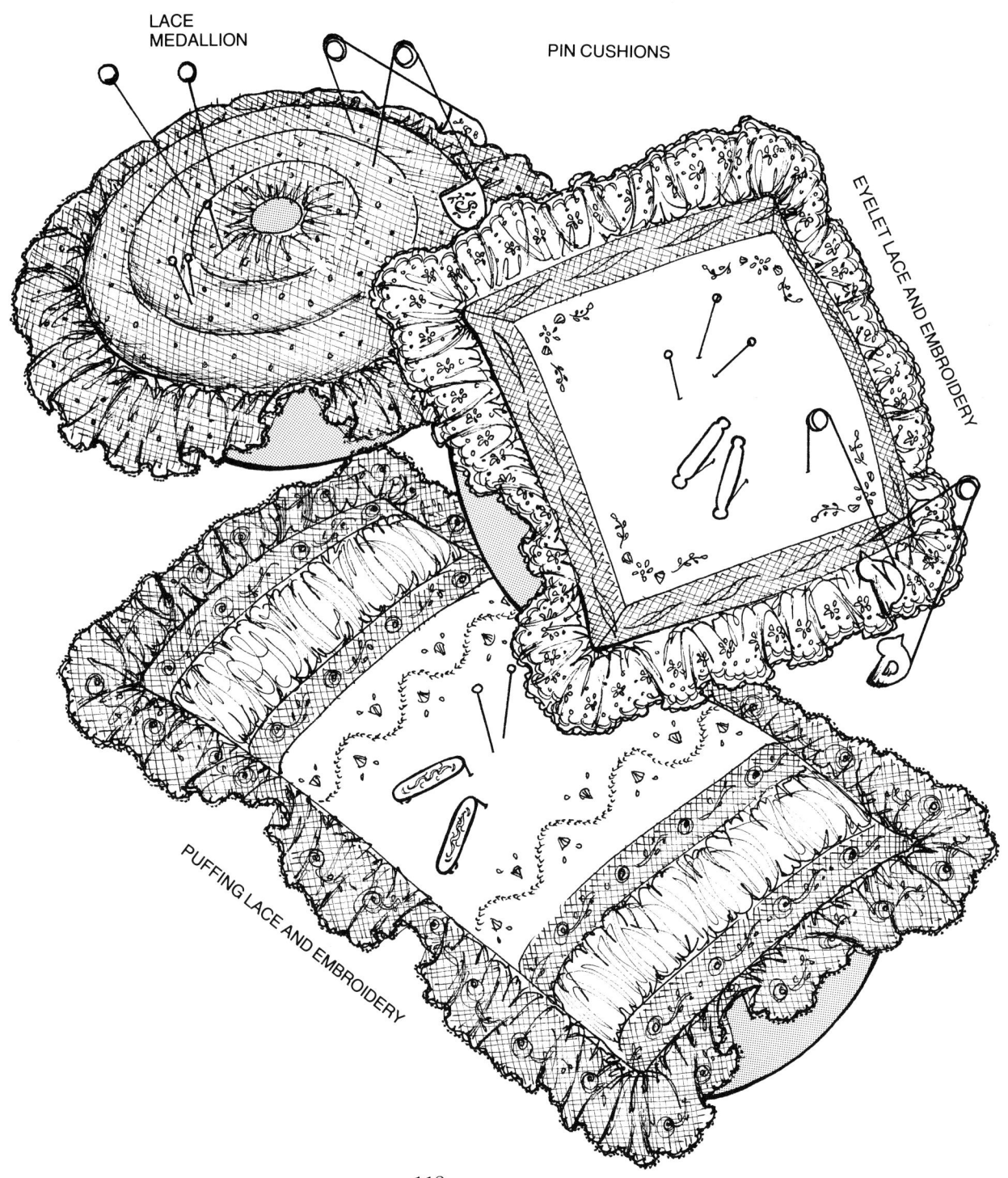

Put the right sides of lined front and back together and sew around all four sides, leaving a small opening in one side to turn through. Turn, press, and fill pin cushion with dacron fiberfill. (Fig. 161) Whip the opening to close.

Whip a fabric, lace, or eyelet ruffle around the outer edge.

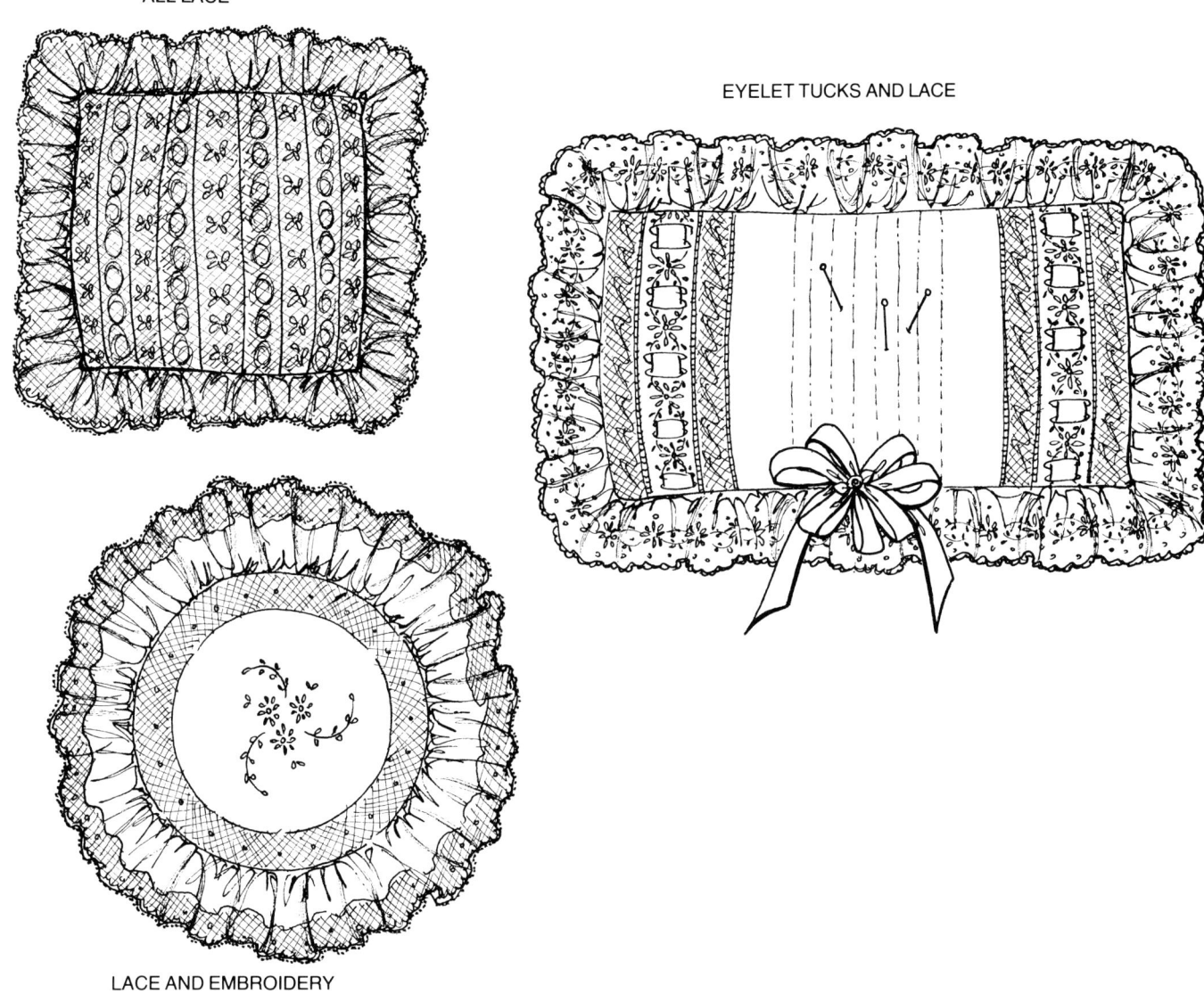

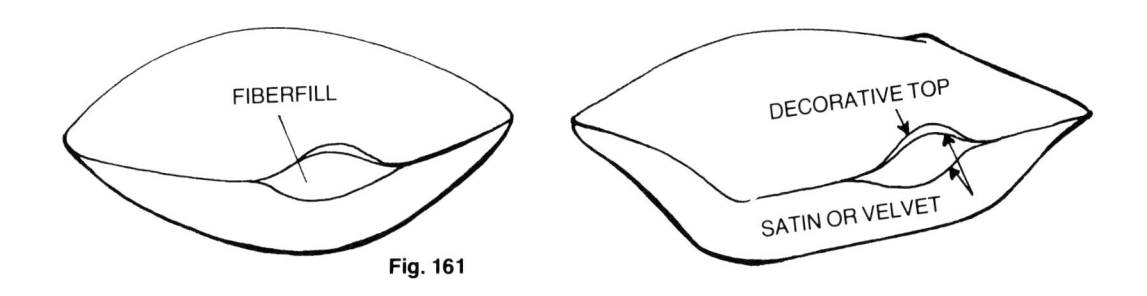

ALL LACE

EYELET TUCKS AND LACE

LACE AND EMBROIDERY

FIBERFILL

DECORATIVE TOP

SATIN OR VELVET

Fig. 161

Carriage Covers

Carriage covers can be made any size you wish and from many fabrics. They can, if you desire, have matching pillow shams. Among the fabrics you might choose are batiste, broadcloth, linen, silk, and challis. Here are a few ideas for construction. (See Figures 162-164)

CARRIAGE COVER

Fig. 162

CARRIAGE COVERS PUFFING AND LACE

Fig. 163

OPTIONAL YOU MAY ADD EDGING AROUND THE SIDES AND BOTTOM

BAND & RUFFLE WRONG SIDE FACING YOU

JOIN BAND HERE

RIGHT SIDE FACING YOU

ALTERNATE ENDING FOR BAND AND RUFFLE

BAND AND RUFFLE FOLDS TO THE RIGHT SIDE

FINISHED CARRIAGE COVER

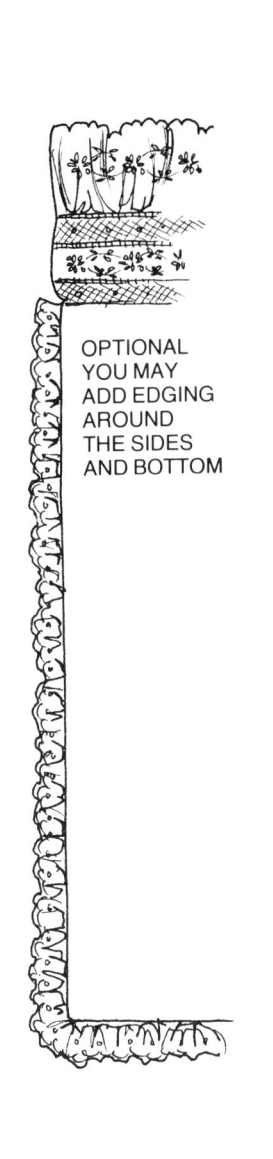

Fig. 164

LINE WITH COLOR TO MATCH RIBBON

TIE BOWS AT BOTTOM EDGE

121

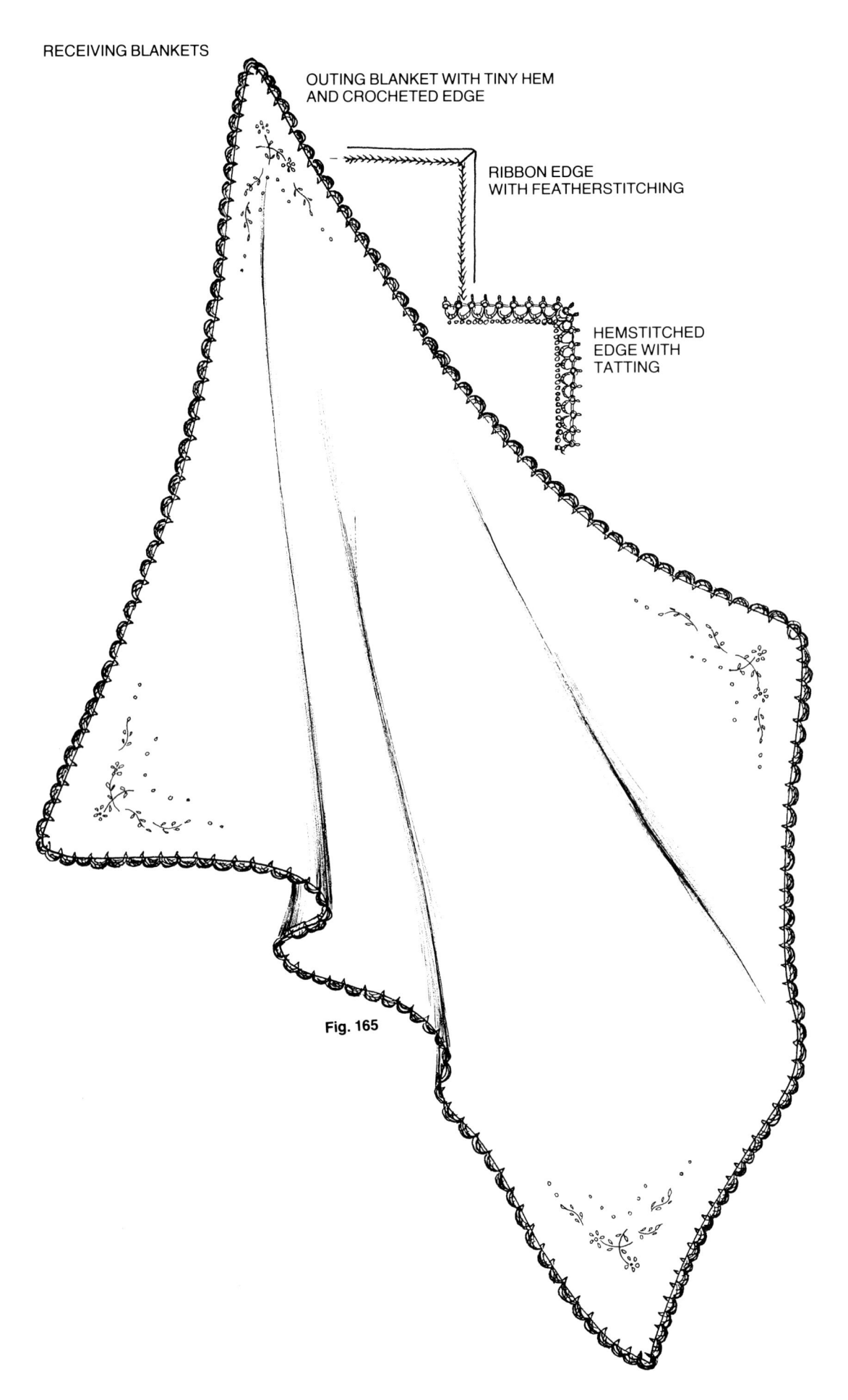

RECEIVING BLANKETS

OUTING BLANKET WITH TINY HEM AND CROCHETED EDGE

RIBBON EDGE WITH FEATHERSTITCHING

HEMSTITCHED EDGE WITH TATTING

Fig. 165

Receiving Blankets

Receiving blankets are usually made of cotton flannel or plisse. The outing flannel ones can be lined with a soft permanent-press batiste. NOTE: Be sure to wash flannel and lining before sewing. I think the plisse is nicer unlined.

When using a single thickness, blankets may be machine hemstitched or tiny hemmed before trimming. If they are made double, sew, right sides together, all around the edge, leaving a 1-inch opening for turning. Or baste the two layers together and hemstitch.

The outing blankets may have a crocheted, tatted, or ribbon edge. NOTE: Make sure that the ribbon is washable. (Fig. 165) The plisse blankets are lovely with a wide lace or eyelet ruffle. (Fig. 166)

Challis blankets may be made of a single layer, or lined with china silk. Embroider the four corners and whip wide lace edging around the outer edge. Rounding the corners gives a pleasing effect. (Fig. 167)

SINGLE LAYER PLISSE BLANKET WITH EYELET BEADING AND WIDE EYELET RUFFLE

Fig. 166

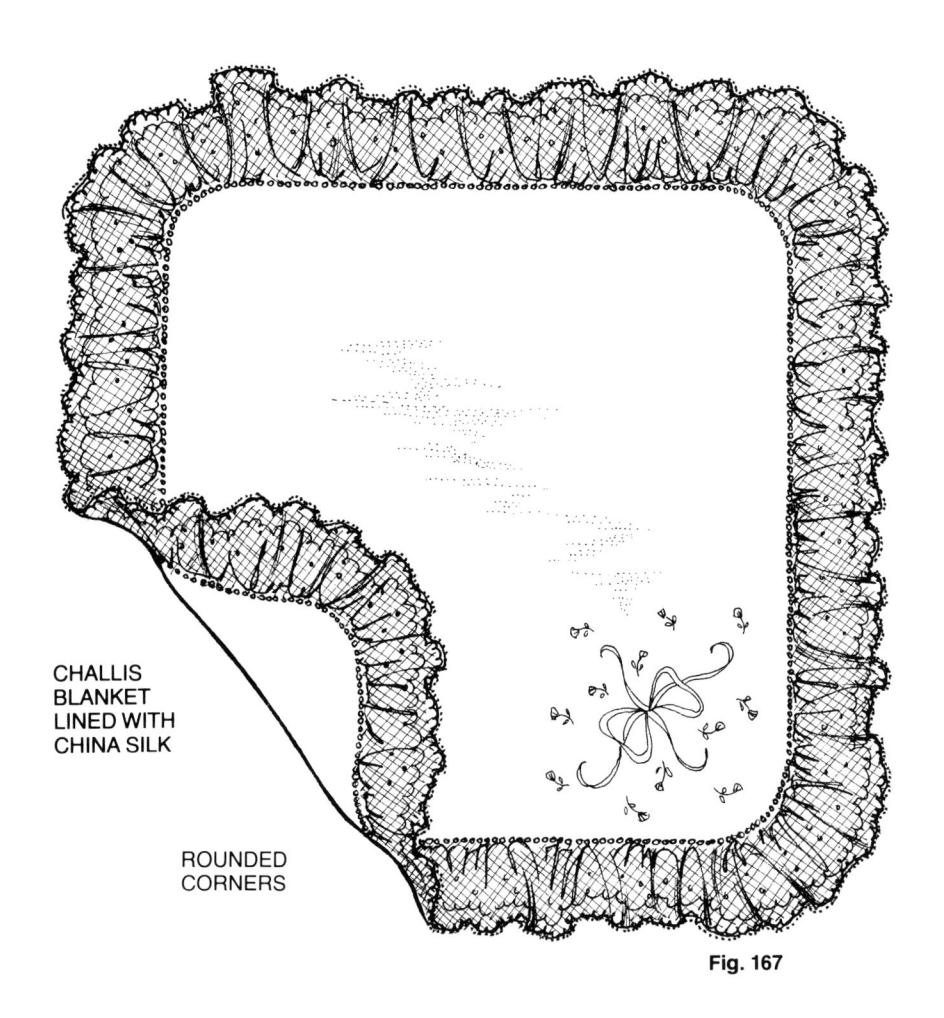

CHALLIS
BLANKET
LINED WITH
CHINA SILK

ROUNDED
CORNERS

Fig. 167

124

Sacques and Kimonos

Sacques and kimonos are ideal wraps for a small infant. The sacque is a shorter version of the kimono. They may be made in one piece to tie with ribbon under the arm and at the neck, or they may have underarm and side seams. Some are made with set-in sleeves. You may use batiste, flannel, silk challis, or plisse, and line them with batiste or china silk.

The first version is trimmed all the way around (including the neck) with lace, tatting, or a crocheted edging. You can use embroidery thread

KIMONO LINED WITH HEMSTITCHED SCALLOPED EDGES AND RECEIVING BLANKET TO MATCH

SACQUE

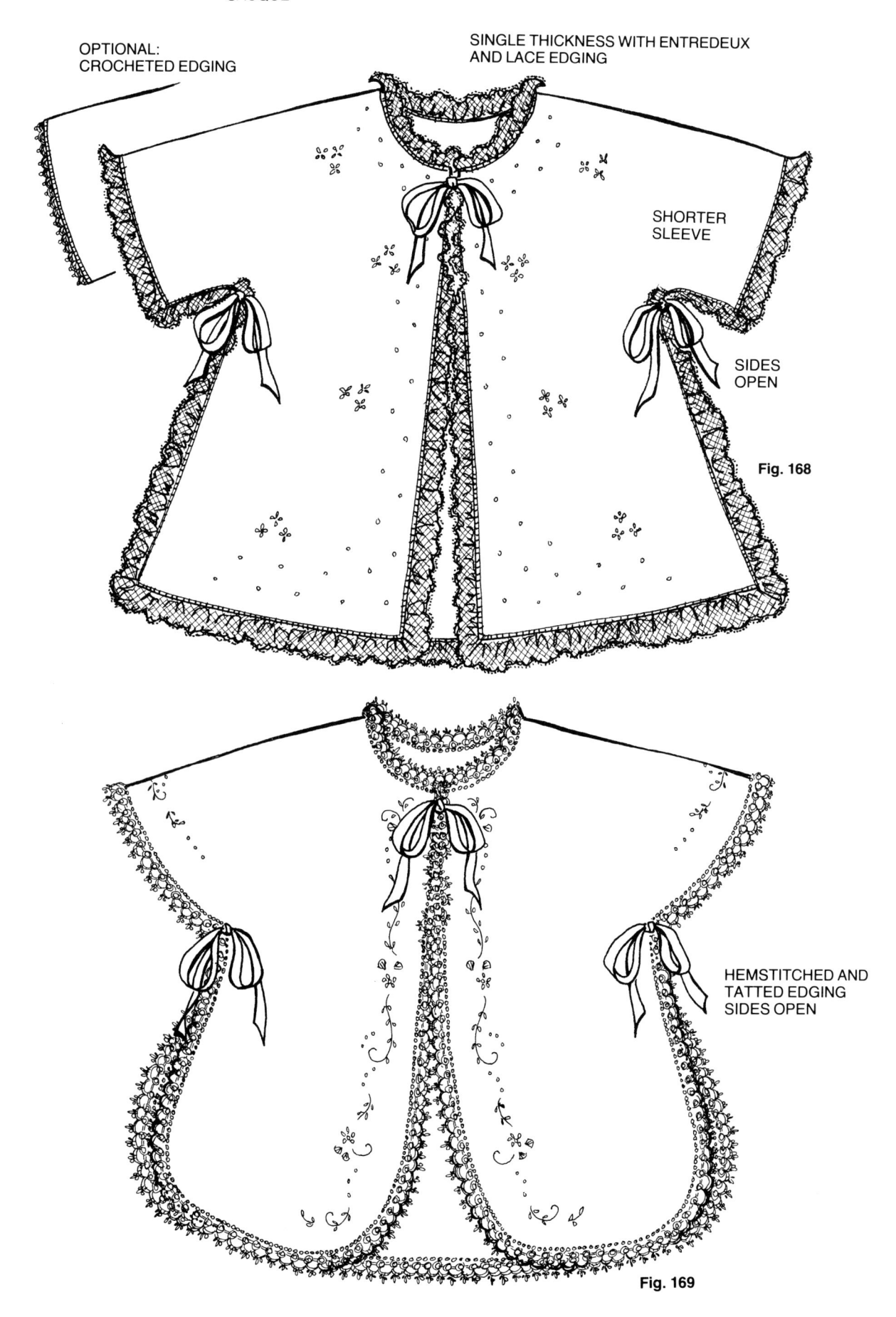

OPTIONAL: CROCHETED EDGING

SINGLE THICKNESS WITH ENTREDEUX AND LACE EDGING

SHORTER SLEEVE

SIDES OPEN

Fig. 168

HEMSTITCHED AND TATTED EDGING SIDES OPEN

Fig. 169

126

for the crochet to create a very delicate edging. Embroider before lining. Sew ribbon for ties. (See Figures 168-170)

The second version is better when lined, but the underarm and sides may be french seamed. They can be hemstitched around the neck, extending down each side front and on around the bottom. If you do not hemstitch this garment, sew the lining and the kimono separately before putting them together and sewing the outer edge. Be sure to leave an opening to turn.

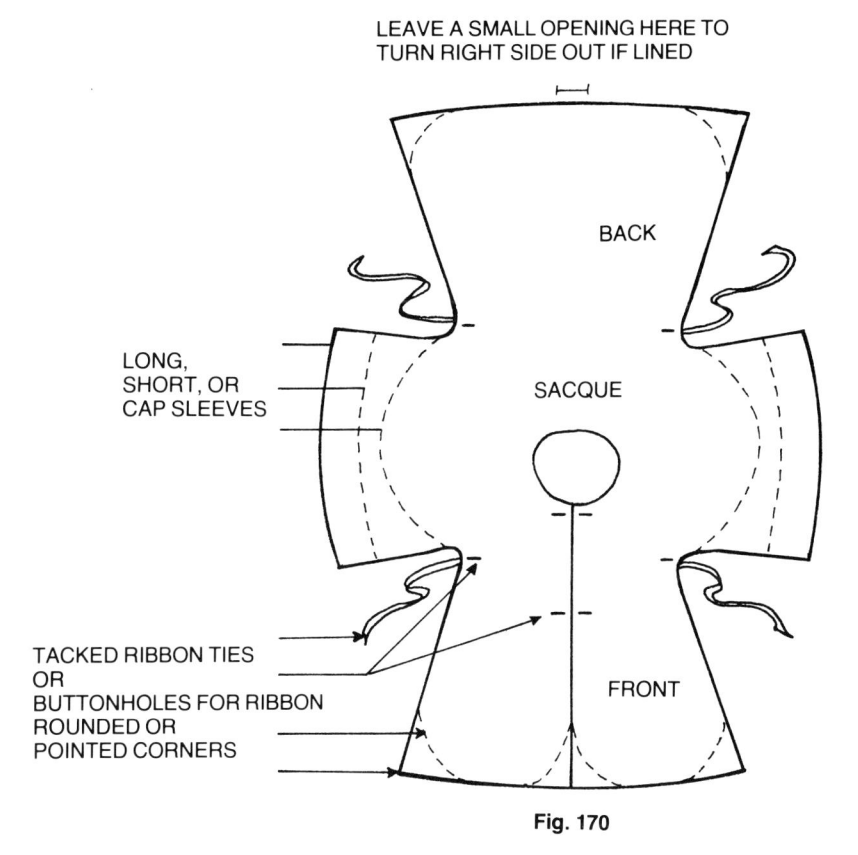

Fig. 170

KIMONO

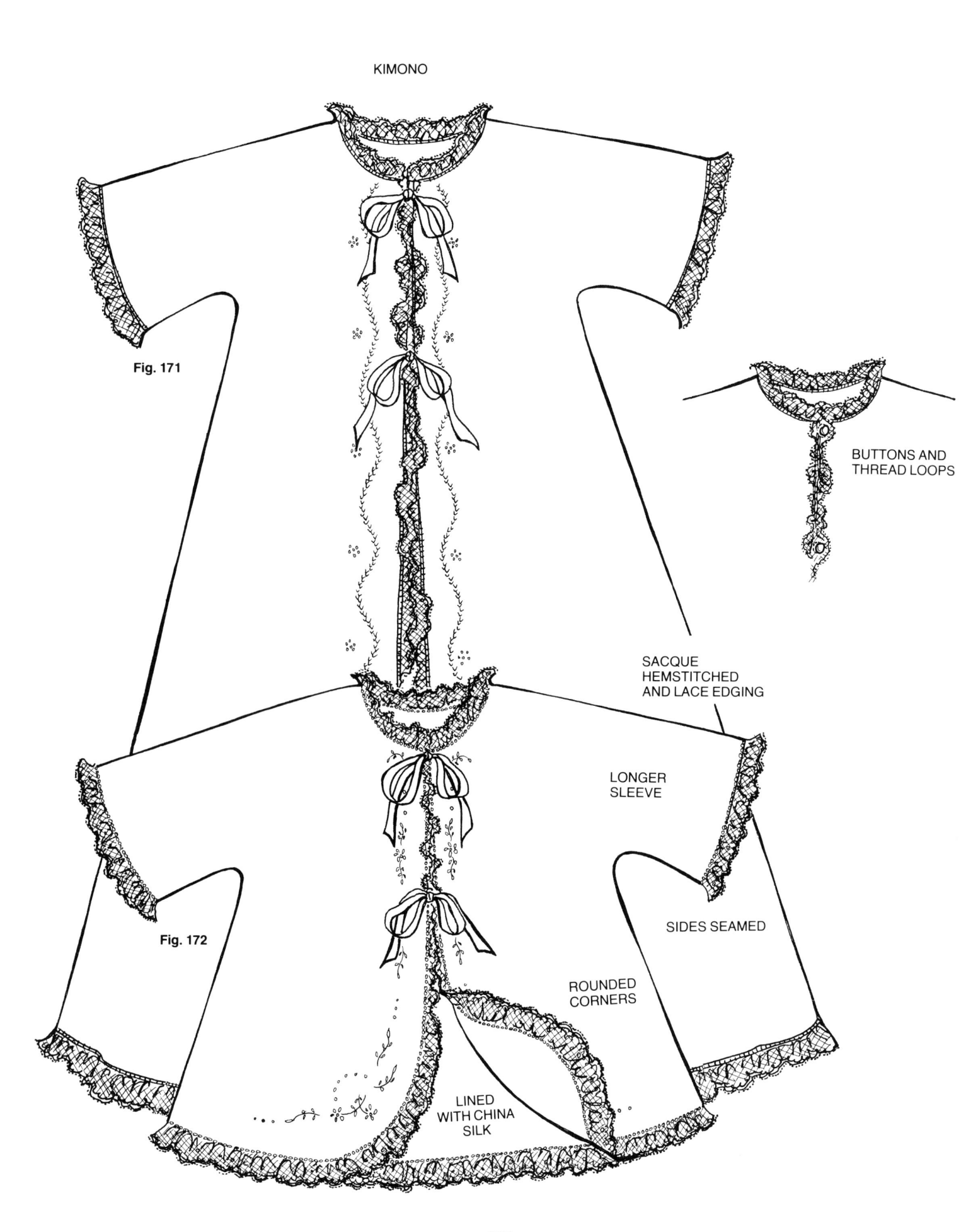

Fig. 171

Fig. 172

BUTTONS AND THREAD LOOPS

SACQUE HEMSTITCHED AND LACE EDGING

LONGER SLEEVE

SIDES SEAMED

ROUNDED CORNERS

LINED WITH CHINA SILK

FOLD　　　　　　　　　　FRONT

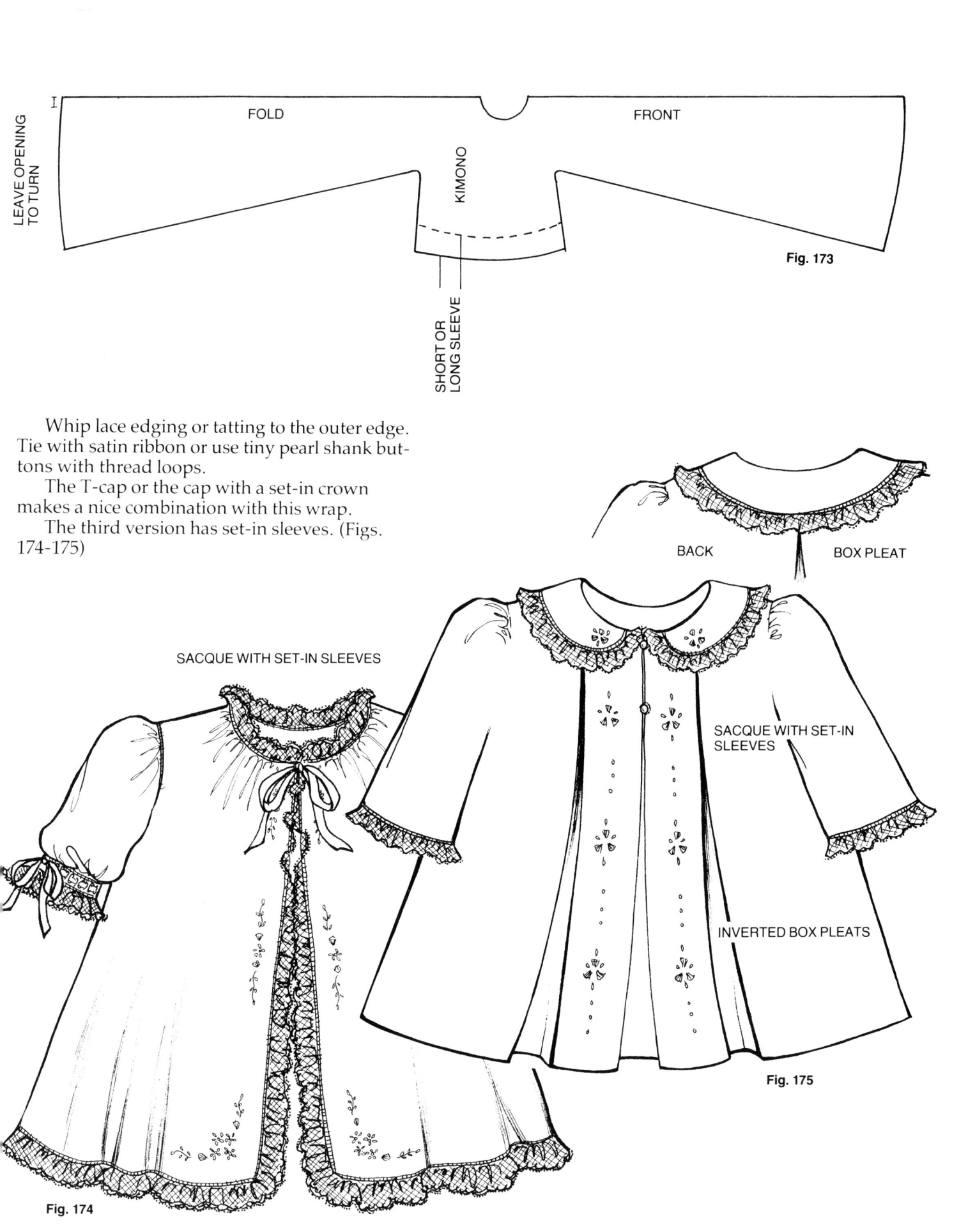

LEAVE OPENING TO TURN

KIMONO

SHORT OR LONG SLEEVE

Fig. 173

Whip lace edging or tatting to the outer edge. Tie with satin ribbon or use tiny pearl shank buttons with thread loops.

The T-cap or the cap with a set-in crown makes a nice combination with this wrap.

The third version has set-in sleeves. (Figs. 174-175)

BACK　　　BOX PLEAT

SACQUE WITH SET-IN SLEEVES

SACQUE WITH SET-IN SLEEVES

INVERTED BOX PLEATS

Fig. 174

Fig. 175

COAT FRONT SECURED WITH SHANK PEARL BUTTON
AND THREAD LOOPS

ALL BATISTE

COAT MADE USING SQUARE YOKE PATTERN

Fig. 176

Coats

Long baby coats are always fashionable. You can make one to go with your christening dress out of batiste or silk or make a warmer version from challis. Line them with batiste or china silk. (Figs. 176-178)

HEMSTITCHED SCALLOPED CAPE AND COLLAR ON A ROUND YOKE PATTERN

¼" TUCKS FORM THE YOKE FRONT AND BACK

SILK LINED WITH CHINA SILK

OVERLAPPING PLACKETS

MAY BE MADE FROM CHALLIS OR PICQUE

Fig. 177

Fig. 178

Fig. 179

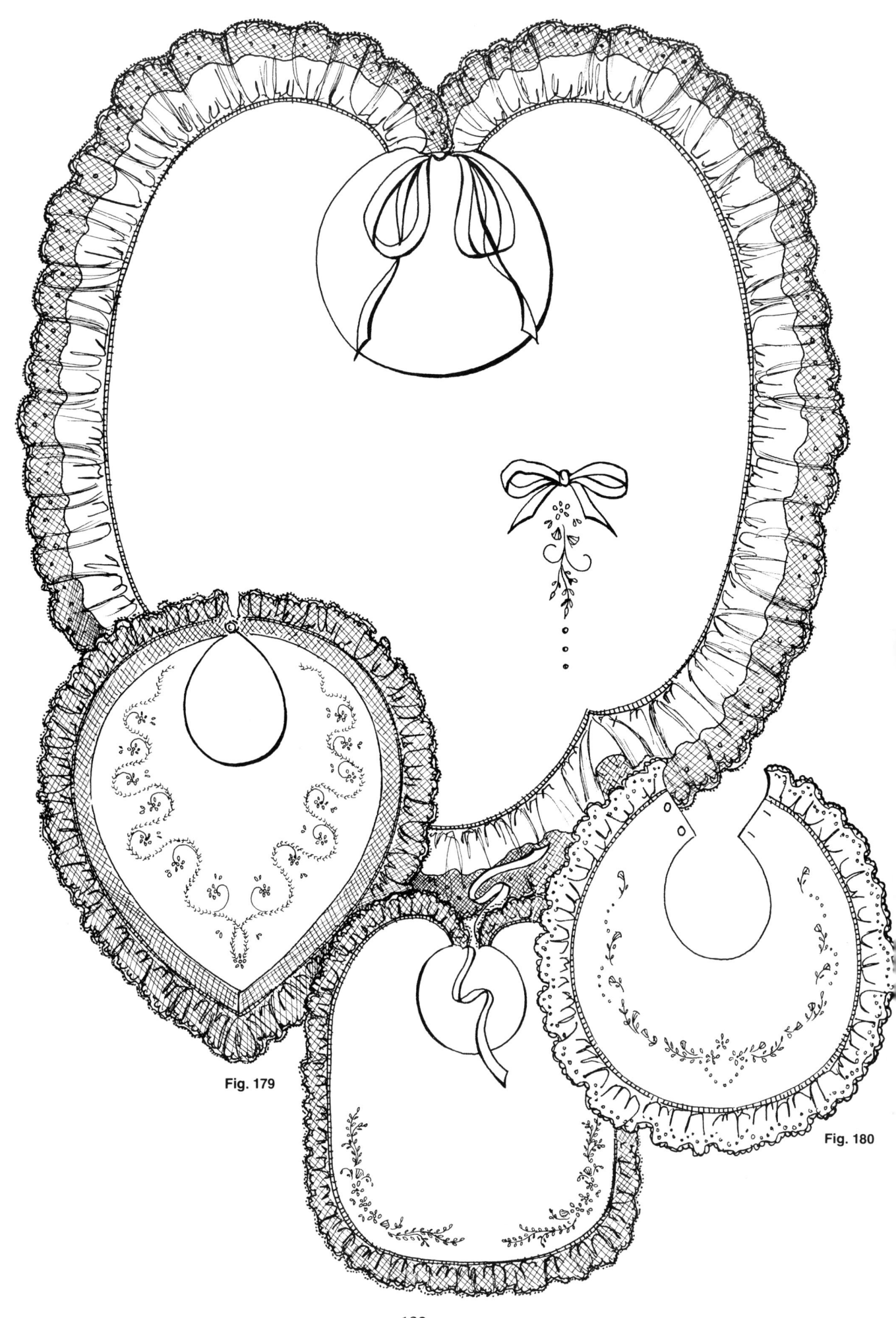

Fig. 180

132

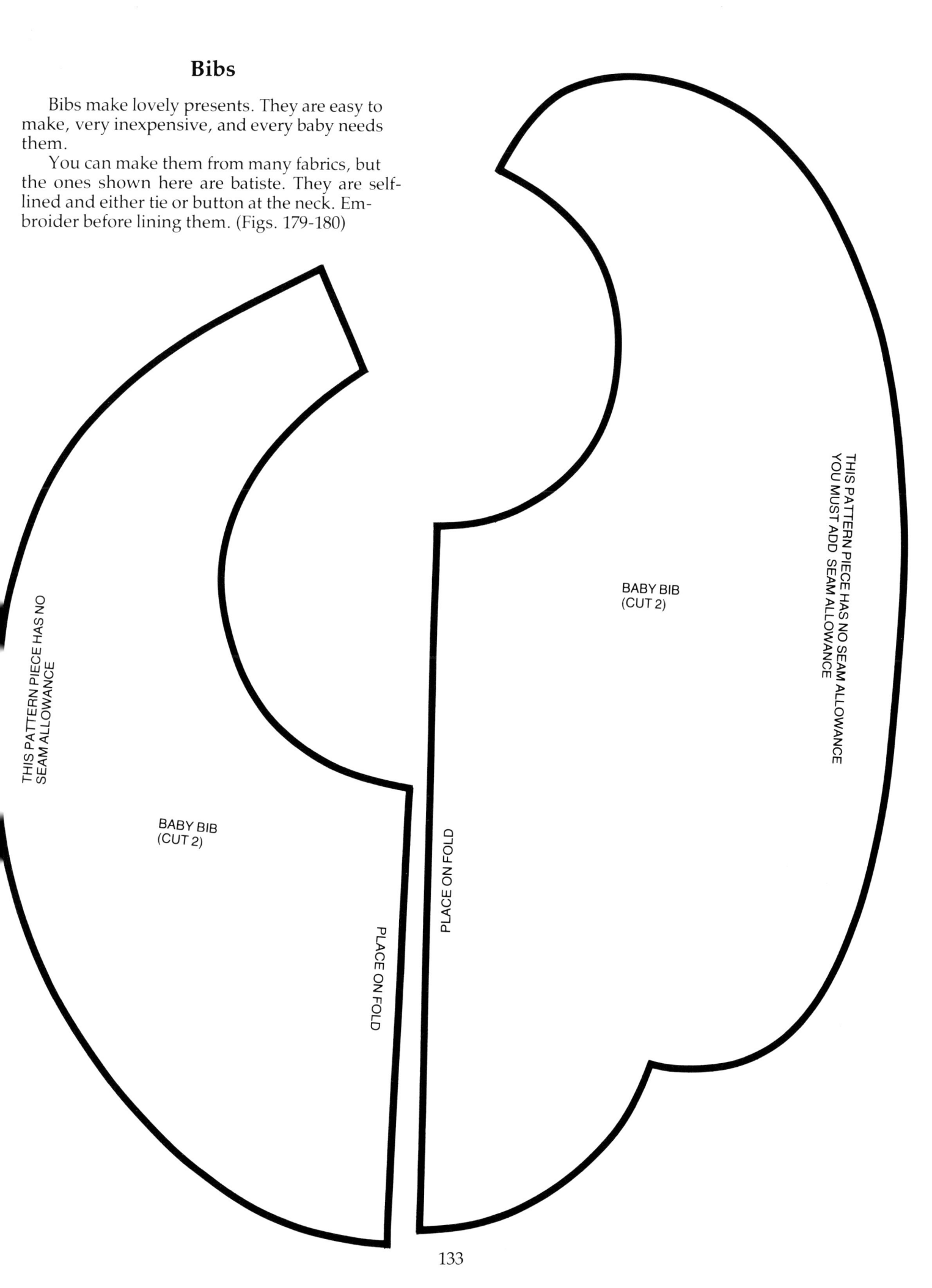

Bibs

Bibs make lovely presents. They are easy to make, very inexpensive, and every baby needs them.

You can make them from many fabrics, but the ones shown here are batiste. They are self-lined and either tie or button at the neck. Embroider before lining them. (Figs. 179-180)

THIS PATTERN PIECE HAS NO SEAM ALLOWANCE

BABY BIB
(CUT 2)

PLACE ON FOLD

BABY BIB
(CUT 2)

PLACE ON FOLD

THIS PATTERN PIECE HAS NO SEAM ALLOWANCE YOU MUST ADD SEAM ALLOWANCE

133

DIAPER SHIRTS (FROM DAYGOWN PATTERN)

SET-IN SLEEVES
OR OMIT THE SLEEVES

OPTIONAL:
BACK GATHERS

OPTIONAL:
BACK BOX PLEAT

Fig. 181

Diaper Shirts

Diaper shirt patterns may be made from several of the daygown patterns by cutting the skirt the desired length and usually excluding the sleeves. They may be trimmed in the same way as the gowns, or use the examples shown here to suggest your own designs. Finish the back neck with a box pleat or gathers. Trim the neck just as for a nightshirt for boys or trim with ruffles and lace for girls. Collars with puffed or cupped sleeves create another variation. Diaper shirts made from these patterns are ample in size for larger babies. (Figs. 181-182)

As many of you know, I learned to sew making diaper shirts. I made one every day for thirty-six days. Figs. 183-184 show the style I made from batiste and plisse. The only seams are the shoulder seams. The back is cut on the fold, creating a bias front.

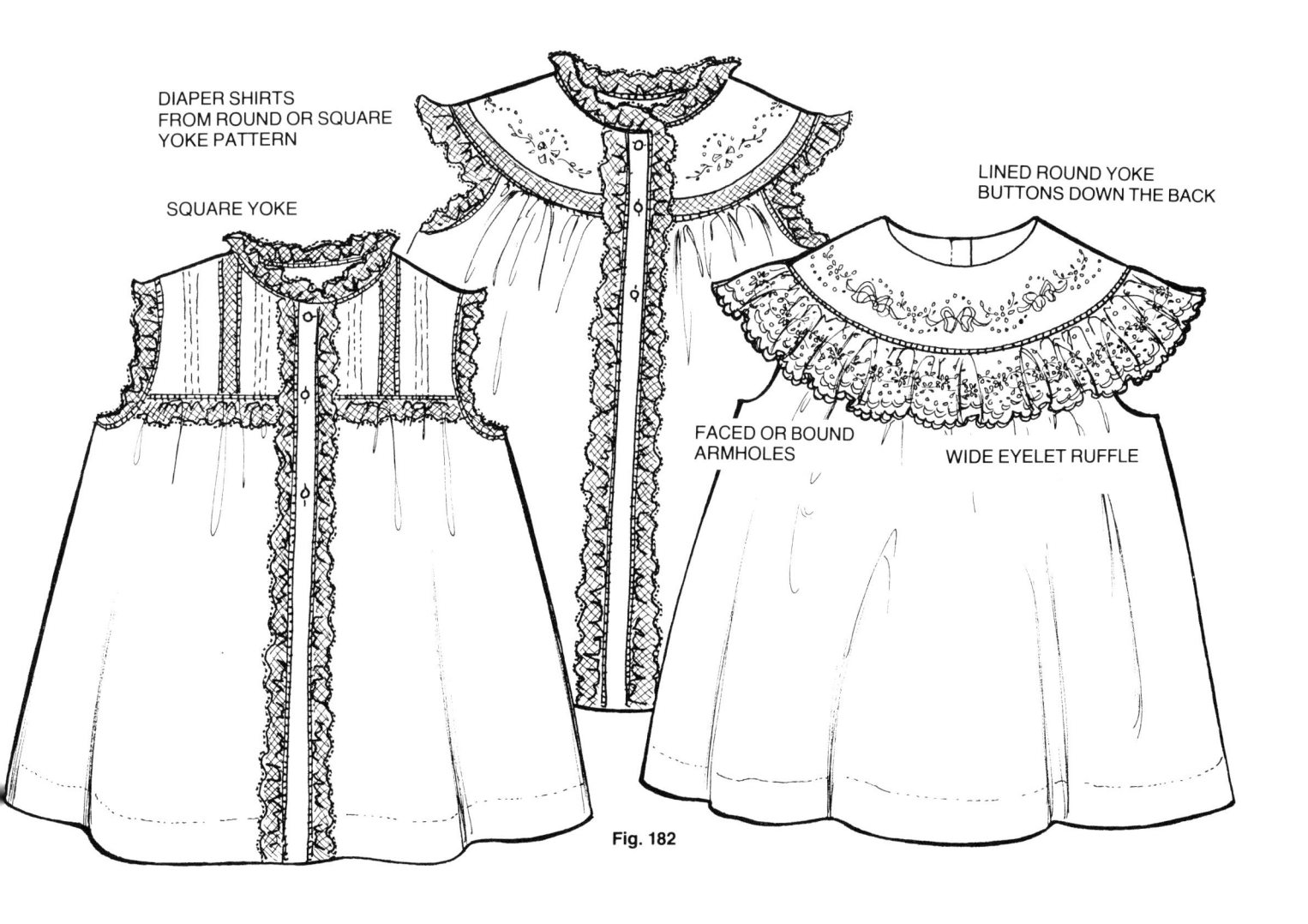

Fig. 182

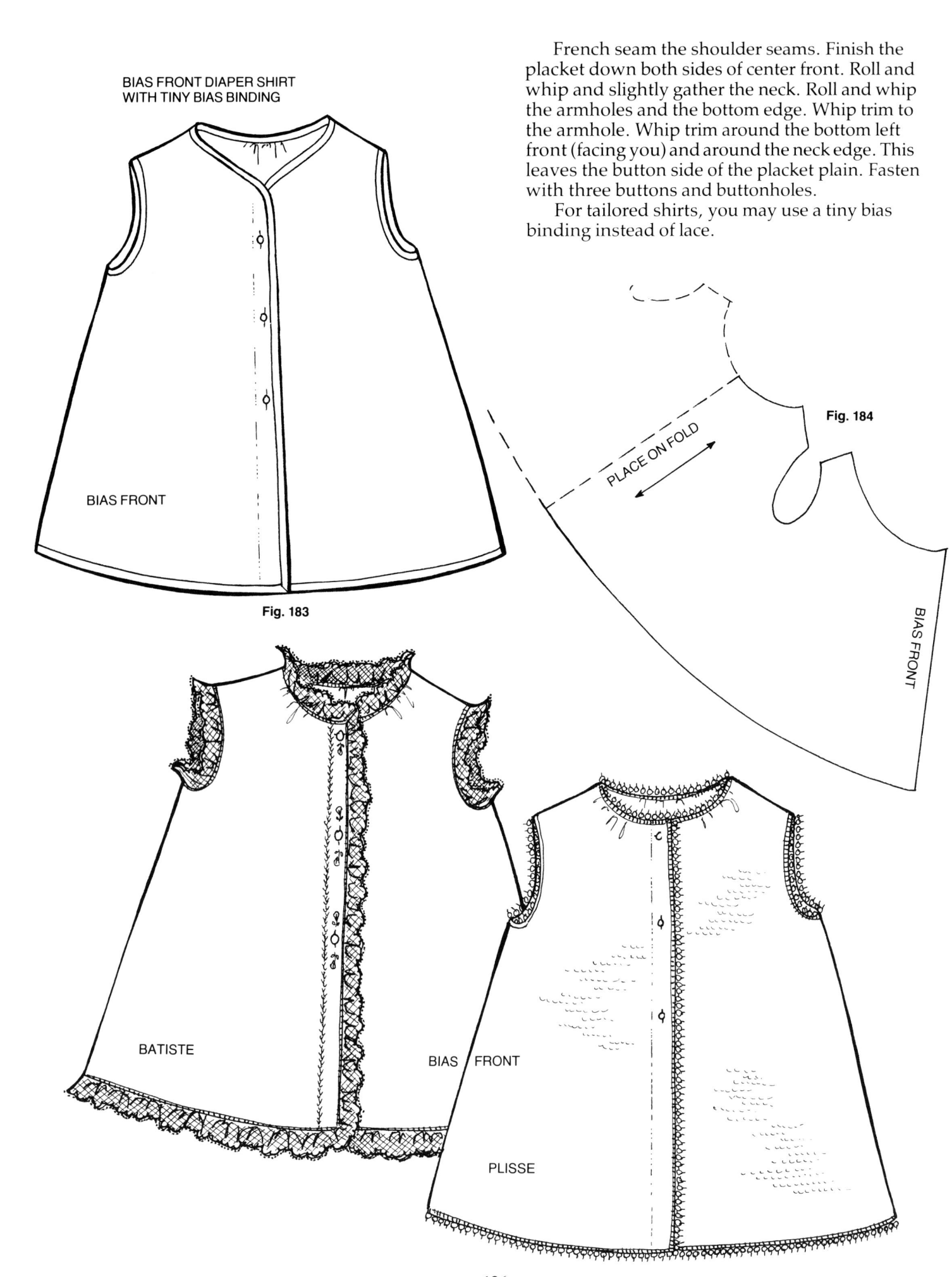

BIAS FRONT DIAPER SHIRT WITH TINY BIAS BINDING

French seam the shoulder seams. Finish the placket down both sides of center front. Roll and whip and slightly gather the neck. Roll and whip the armholes and the bottom edge. Whip trim to the armhole. Whip trim around the bottom left front (facing you) and around the neck edge. This leaves the button side of the placket plain. Fasten with three buttons and buttonholes.

For tailored shirts, you may use a tiny bias binding instead of lace.

Fig. 183

Fig. 184

Diaper Covers and Panties

Today, most babies wear paper diapers. You might wish to make a diaper cover for the little boys and prissy panties for the girls. There are commercial patterns available for diaper covers, and I have a pattern for the panties. The panties are large enough to cover the diapers and will still fit when the child grows older and is trained. (Fig. 185)

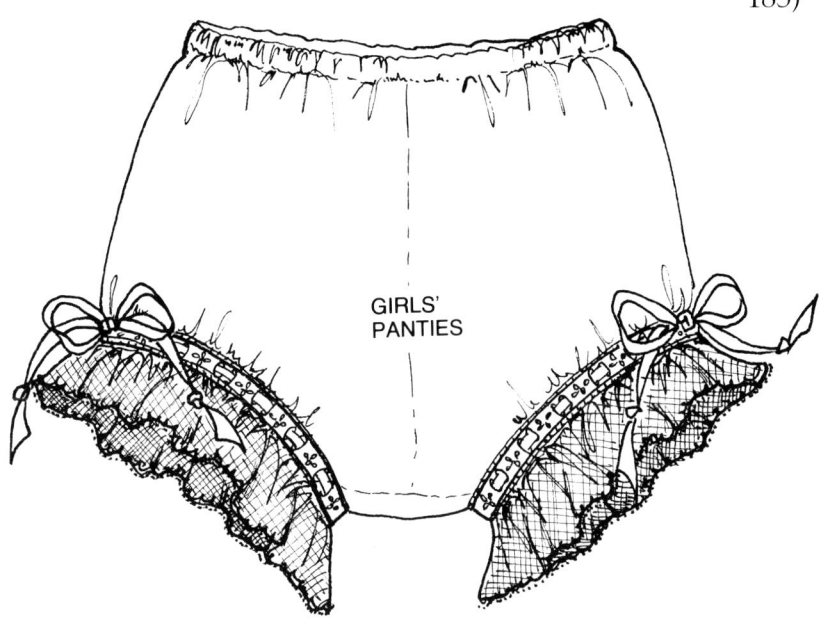

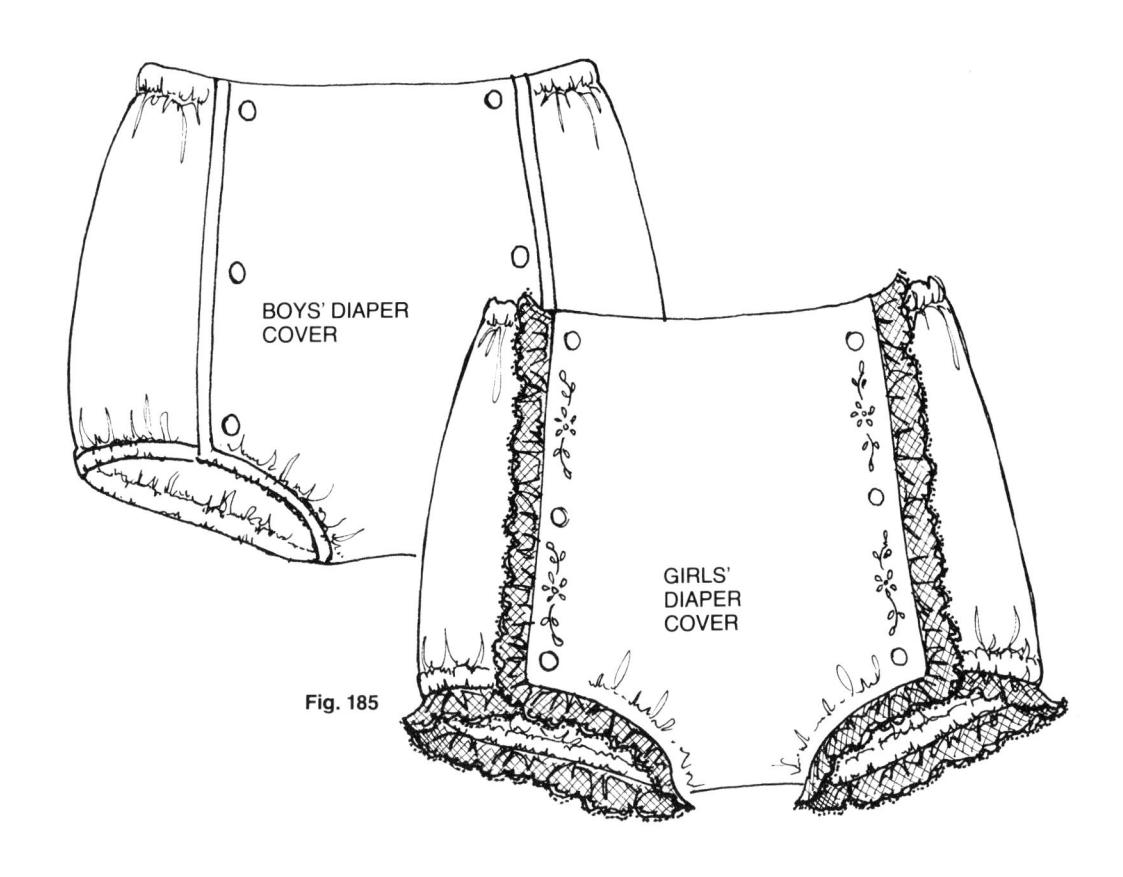

Fig. 185

CARRIAGE COVER
CORNER DESIGN

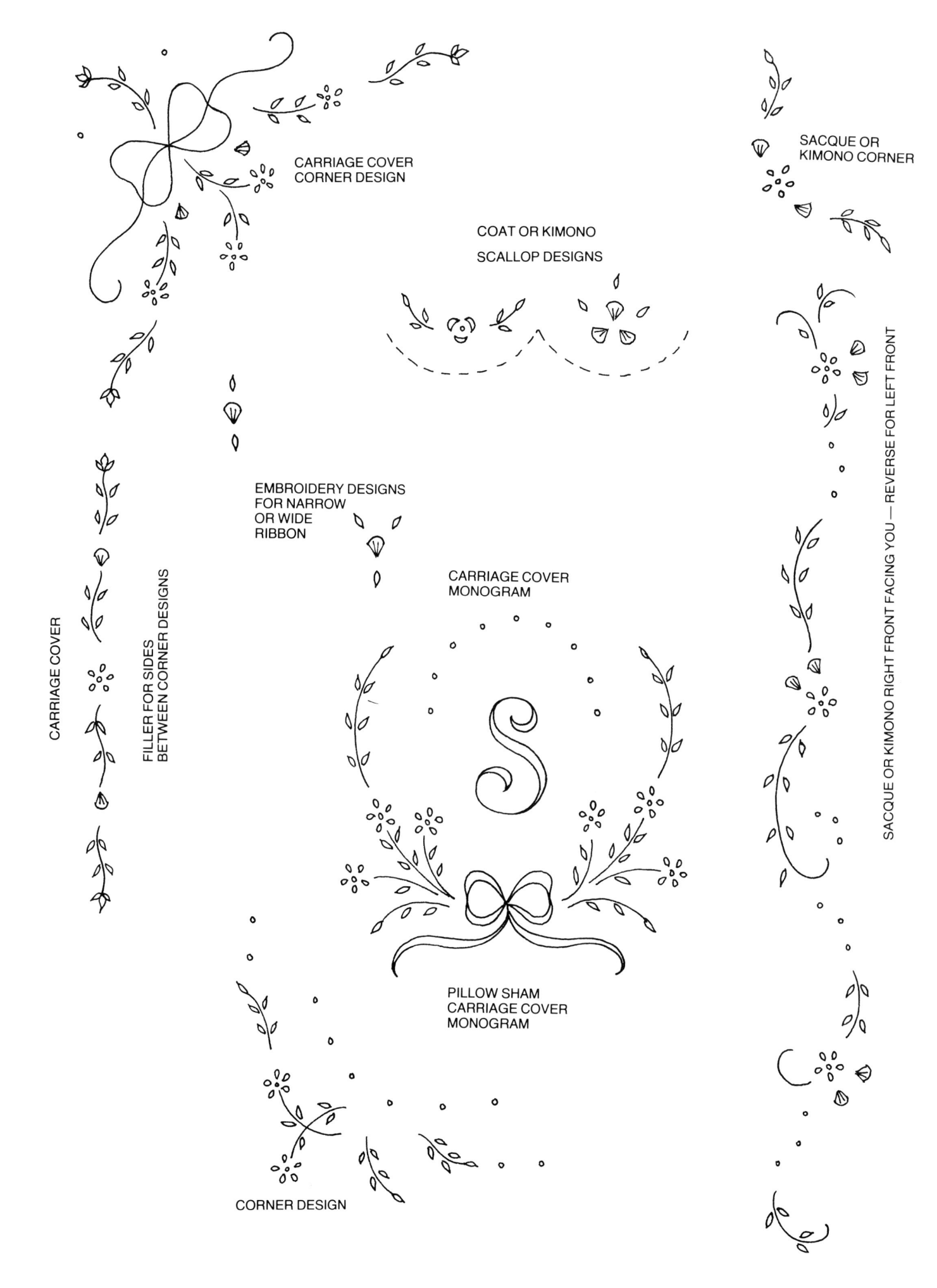

SACQUE OR
KIMONO CORNER

COAT OR KIMONO
SCALLOP DESIGNS

EMBROIDERY DESIGNS
FOR NARROW
OR WIDE
RIBBON

CARRIAGE COVER
MONOGRAM

CARRIAGE COVER

FILLER FOR SIDES
BETWEEN CORNER DESIGNS

SACQUE OR KIMONO RIGHT FRONT FACING YOU — REVERSE FOR LEFT FRONT

PILLOW SHAM
CARRIAGE COVER
MONOGRAM

CORNER DESIGN

SACQUES & KIMONOS

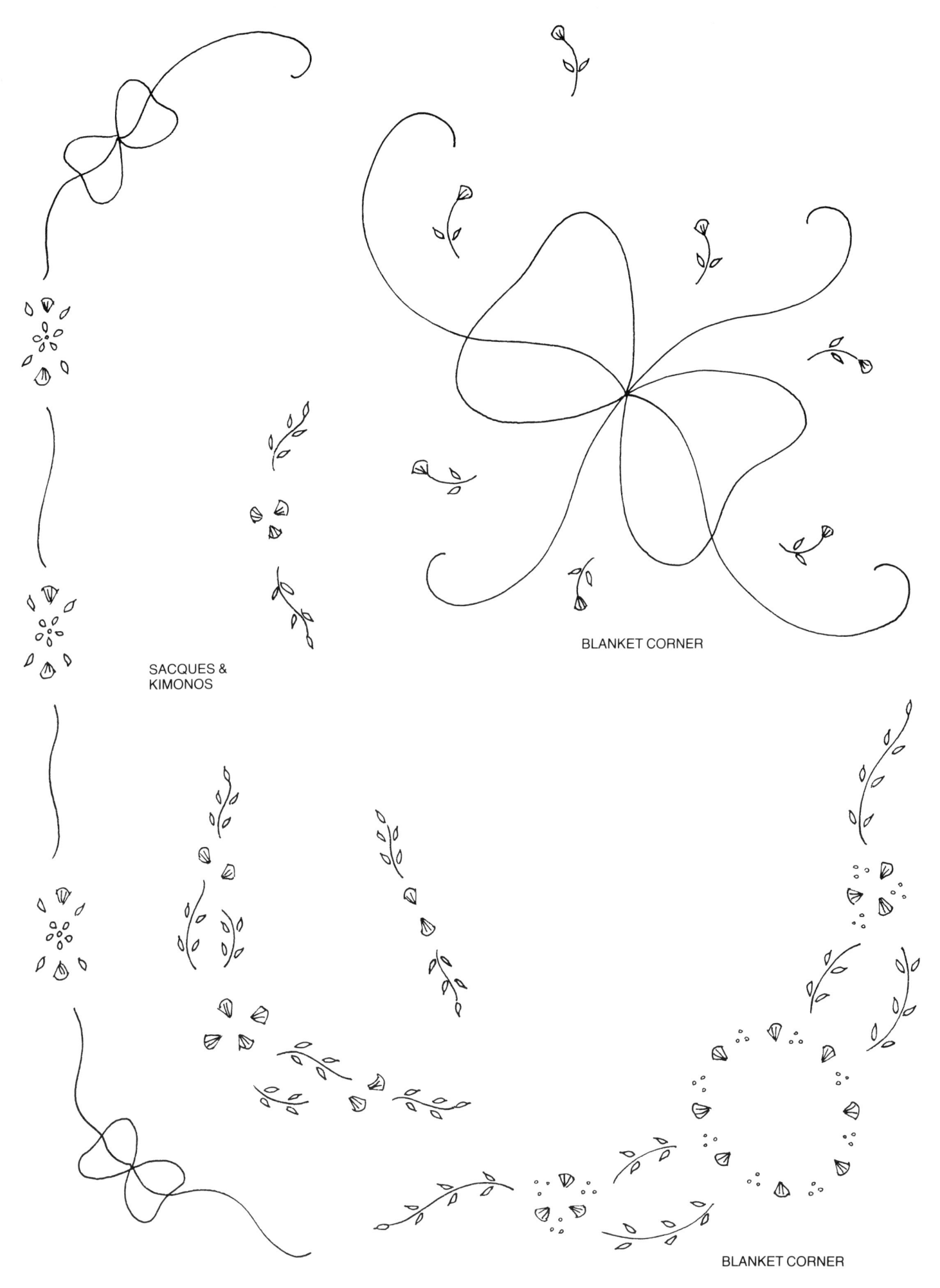

BLANKET CORNER

BLANKET CORNER

BABETTE & BABY DRESSES

Yoke and Panel Dress 143
Square Yoke Dresses 143
Shaped Square Yoke Dresses 147
Round Yoke Dresses 152

Right: Melissa Robinson Marshall
Daughter of Captain & Mrs. Samuel Allen Marsh

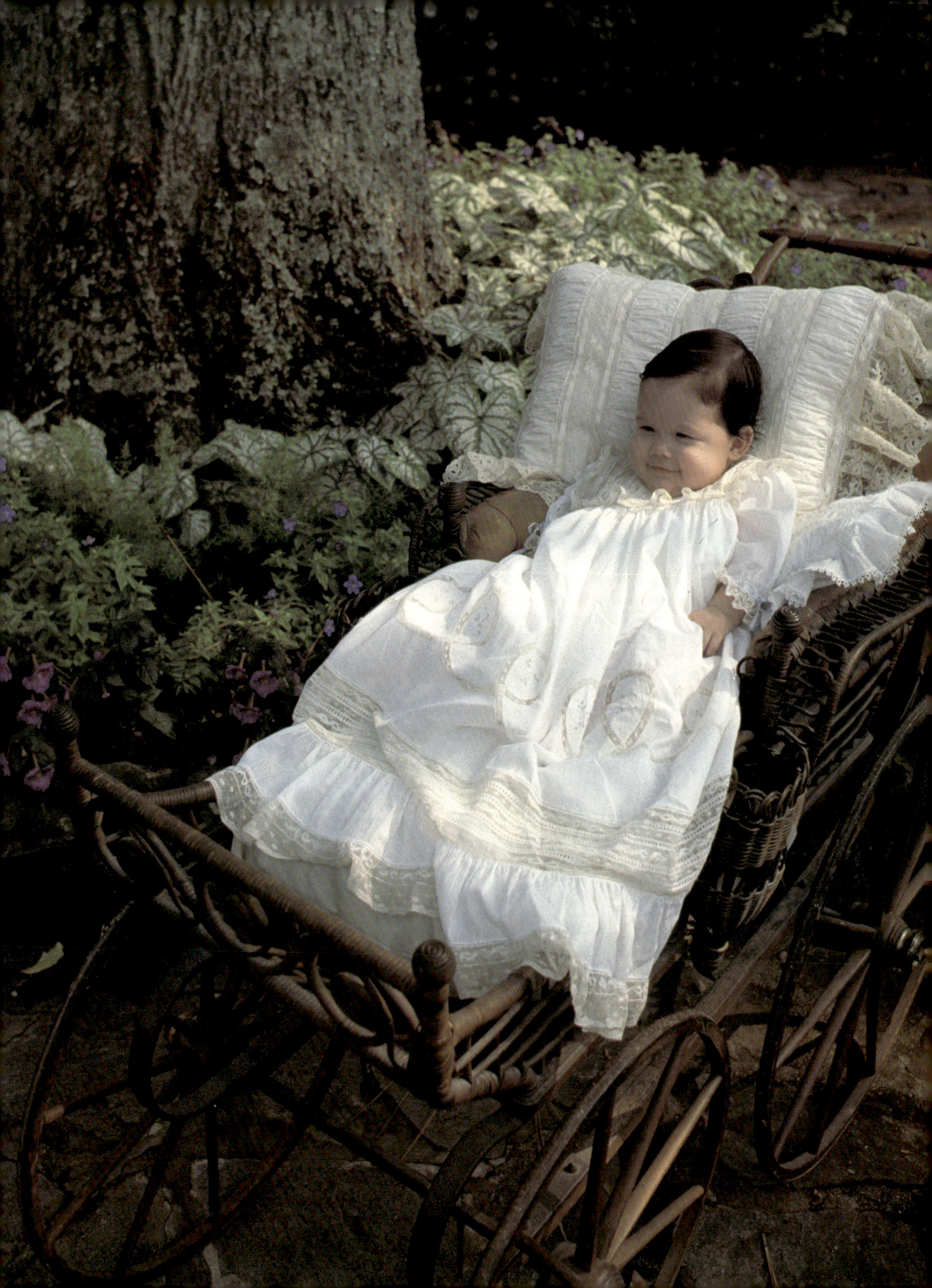

INTRODUCTION

Baby and Babette dresses are made in the same way except for the skirt length and the sleeve. Baby dresses range in length from 22 to 27 inches and usually have a long baby sleeve. Babette dresses range from 14 to 16 inches and have puffed sleeves.

Baby or Babette dresses can be made with any of the yoke designs in Chapter 1. Do not make the Babette dress so elaborate that the dress overpowers the child. You can have more design on the baby dress skirts because you have more length to work with.

The skirt should be sixty-six inches in width (finished); ruffles for the baby dresses can vary, but for Babettes, they should be 1¾ to 2 inches wide. A hemmed skirt can be used in place of a ruffle.

Slips or skirt liners should be made to compliment the dress. (Refer to the slips section in Chapter 1.) I designed a basic yoke and slip pattern that is available. It has a square yoke, but the skirt embellishments can be applied to any shape yoke.

YOKE AND PANEL DRESS

PANEL DRESS WITH LACE BOWS AND FEATHERSTITCHING

Fig. 186

BACK YOKE

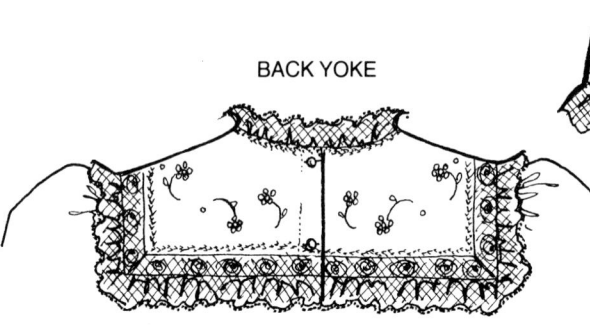

Fig. 187

BOTTOM LACE BOW AND EMBROIDERY DESIGN

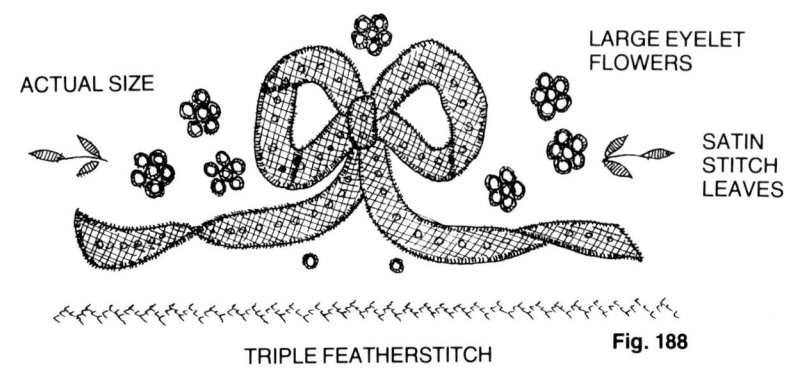

ACTUAL SIZE

LARGE EYELET FLOWERS

SATIN STITCH LEAVES

TRIPLE FEATHERSTITCH

Fig. 188

142

Yoke and Panel Dress

The lace bows are accented with delicate embroidery. The tiny bows encircle the skirt. Tiny featherstitching adds the final touch.

The skirt and sleeves are edged with lace insertion and edging that has been slightly gathered. (Fig. 186-188)

Square Yoke Dresses

Lace, eyelet, and French embroidery form the motif on the yoke. Tucks and eyelet insertion encircle the skirt. The eyelet ruffle is edged with lace. Handloomed embroidery may be used in place of the eyelet. Matching embroidered edging or a fabric ruffle trimmed with lace may be substituted for the eyelet ruffle. (Fig. 189)

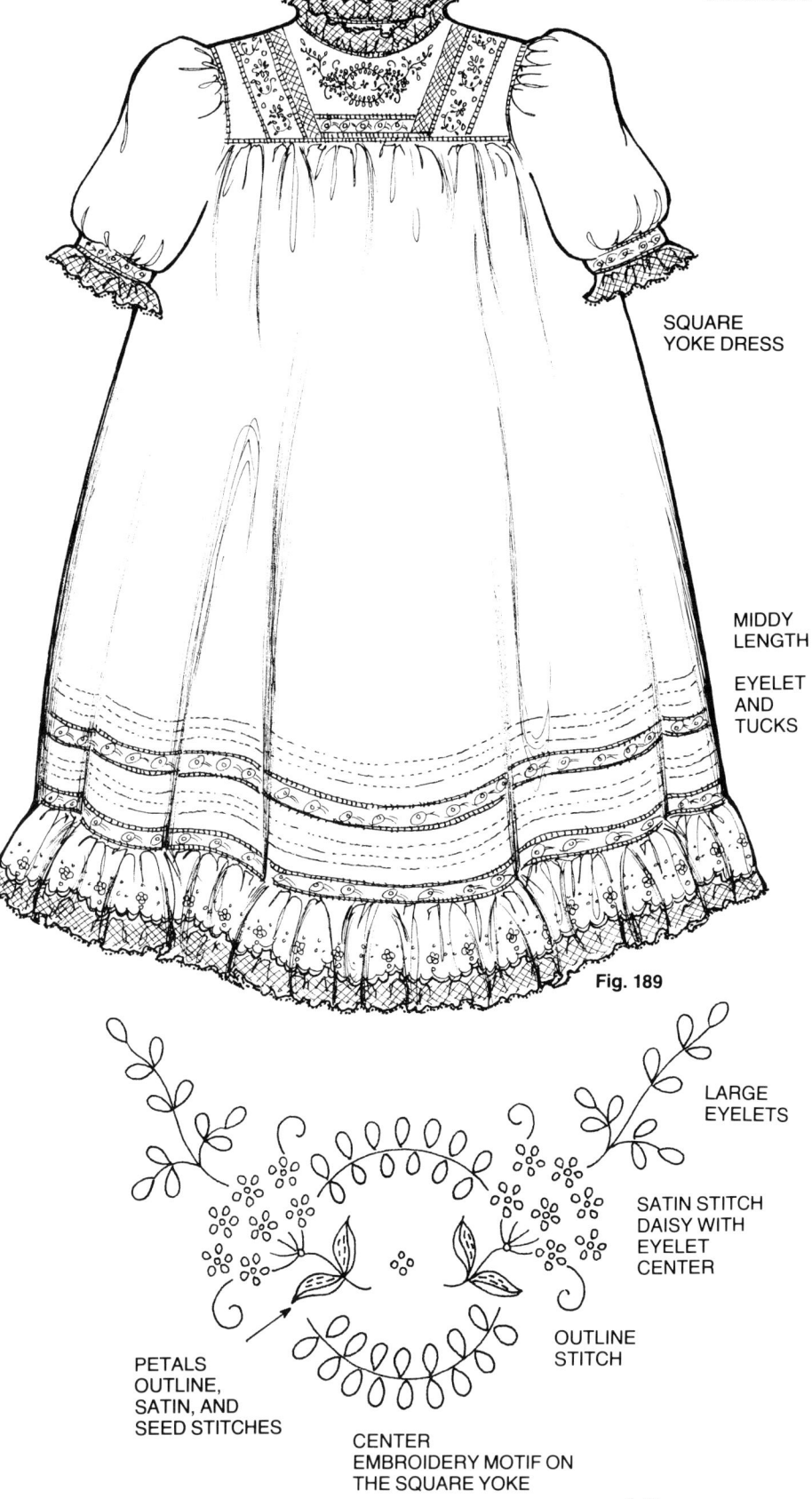

SQUARE YOKE DRESS

MIDDY LENGTH

EYELET AND TUCKS

Fig. 189

LARGE EYELETS

SATIN STITCH DAISY WITH EYELET CENTER

OUTLINE STITCH

PETALS OUTLINE, SATIN, AND SEED STITCHES

CENTER EMBROIDERY MOTIF ON THE SQUARE YOKE

Horizontal Variations

This square yoke features a horizontal band of lace and beading across the bottom edge. Sprays of embroidery are worked on the fabric part of the yoke. A matching lace band and ruffle encircle the skirt. The same dress may be made with many variations, including puffing, tucks, and feather-stitching. (Figs. 190-191)

Fig. 190

SHORT SQUARE YOKE DRESS
WITH LACE AND BEADING AND
SPRAYS OF EMBROIDERY

LEFT SHOULDER
DESIGN

RIGHT SHOULDER
DESIGN FACING YOU

CENTER
DESIGN

BACK YOKE DESIGN
(REVERSE FOR OTHER BACK YOKE)

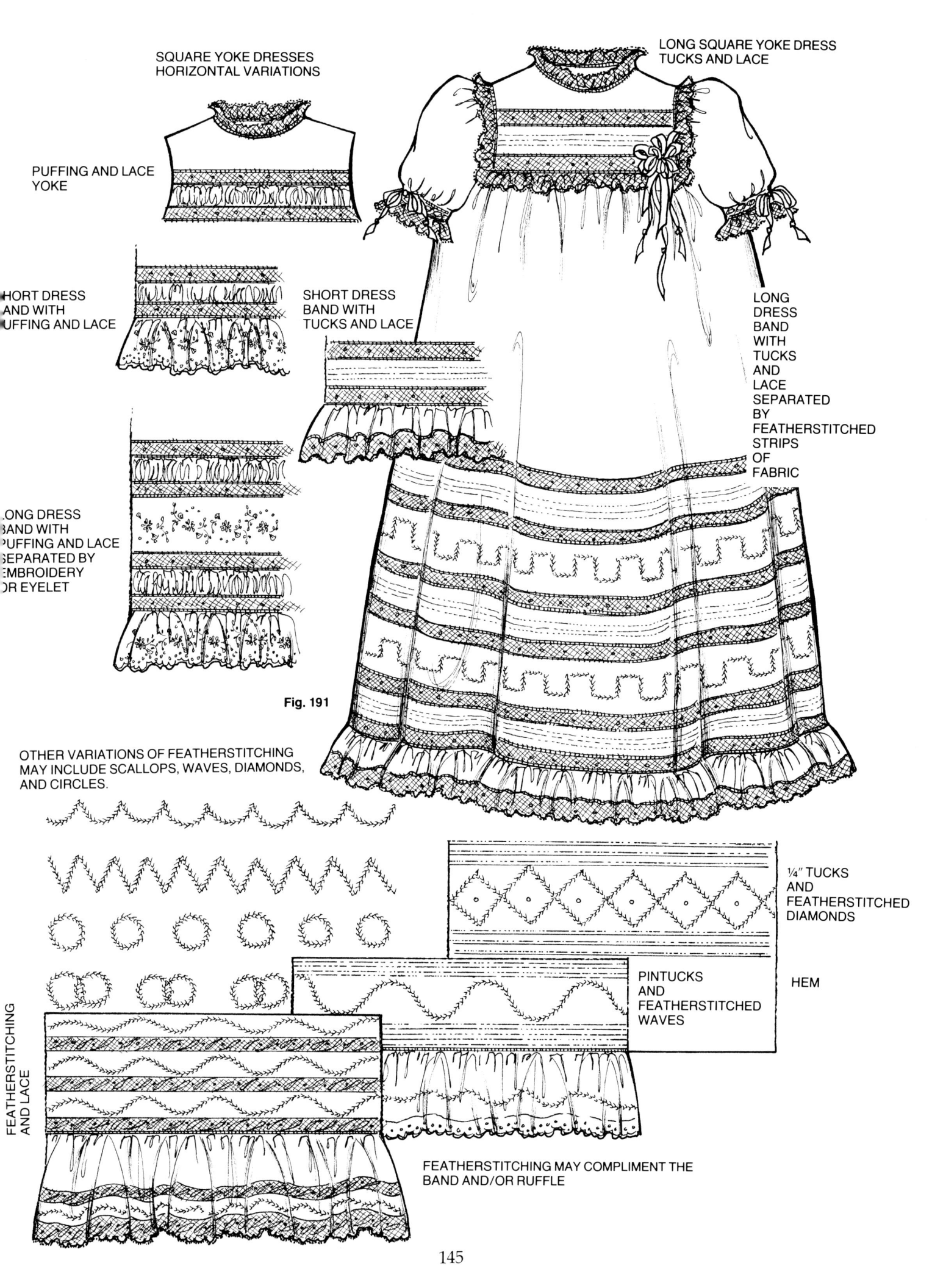

SQUARE YOKE DRESSES
HORIZONTAL VARIATIONS

LONG SQUARE YOKE DRESS
TUCKS AND LACE

PUFFING AND LACE
YOKE

SHORT DRESS
BAND WITH
PUFFING AND LACE

SHORT DRESS
BAND WITH
TUCKS AND LACE

LONG
DRESS
BAND
WITH
TUCKS
AND
LACE
SEPARATED
BY
FEATHERSTITCHED
STRIPS
OF
FABRIC

LONG DRESS
BAND WITH
PUFFING AND LACE
SEPARATED BY
EMBROIDERY
OR EYELET

Fig. 191

OTHER VARIATIONS OF FEATHERSTITCHING
MAY INCLUDE SCALLOPS, WAVES, DIAMONDS,
AND CIRCLES.

¼" TUCKS
AND
FEATHERSTITCHED
DIAMONDS

PINTUCKS
AND
FEATHERSTITCHED
WAVES

HEM

FEATHERSTITCHING
AND LACE

FEATHERSTITCHING MAY COMPLIMENT THE
BAND AND/OR RUFFLE

145

Vertical Variations

The square yoke can be made with many vertical variations, as well. Here you will see different ways to embellish the vertical square yoke with matching skirt designs. The plain part of the skirt can be long or short. Add puffed or baby sleeves. Edge the yoke with a lace ruffle. (Fig. 192)

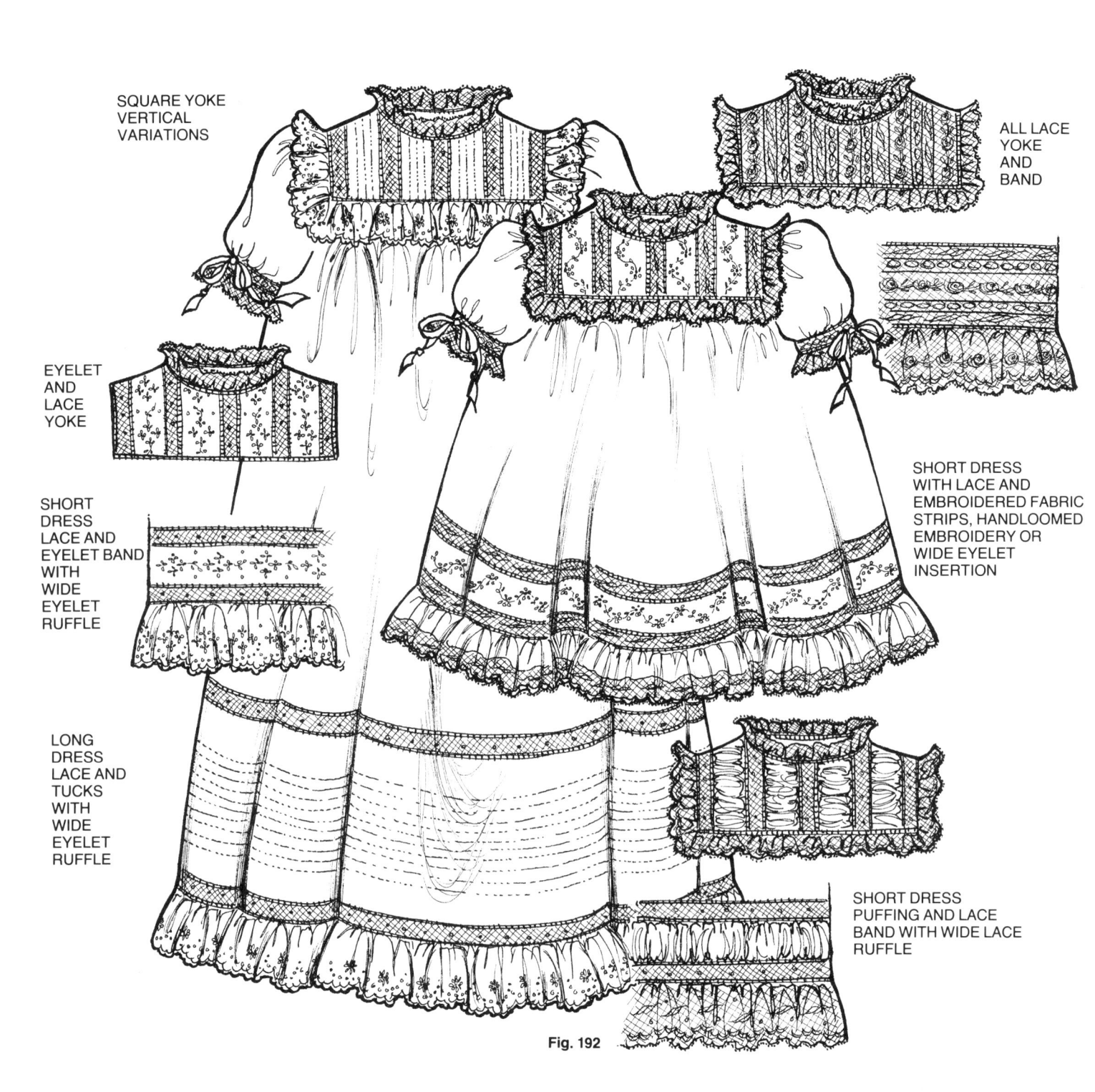

Fig. 192

Shaped Square Yoke Dresses

This shaped yoke has three scallops across the front outlined with lace insertion. The back yoke is straight across the bottom edge. The yoke is outlined with a lace ruffle.

The front skirt is shaped to fit the scallop and the back skirt is straight across the top. The bottom of the skirt is scalloped and embroidered with bows or flowers. The scallops are formed with lace insertion. The bottom edge is enhanced with a fabric or lace ruffle. (Fig. 193A, B, C).

SHAPED YOKE

BACK YOKE
STRAIGHT ACROSS BOTTOM EDGE

Fig. 193

33½" INCLUDING SEAMS →

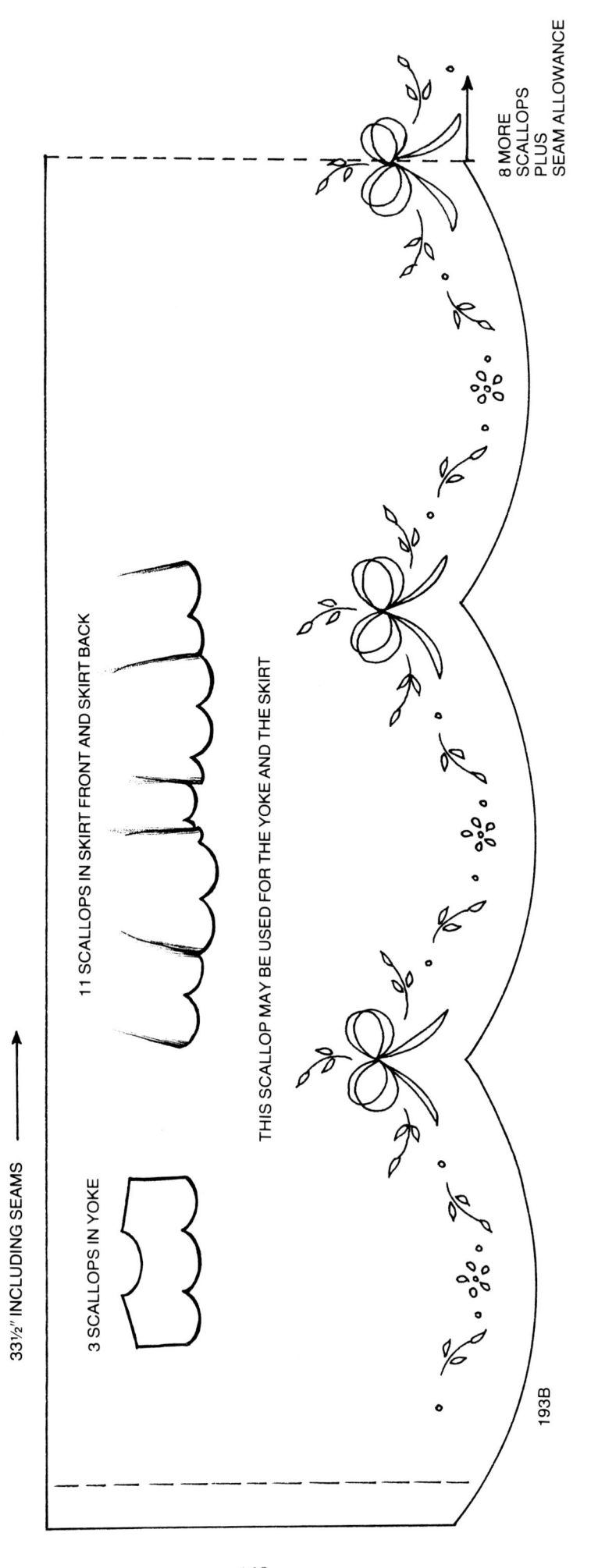

11 SCALLOPS IN SKIRT FRONT AND SKIRT BACK

3 SCALLOPS IN YOKE

THIS SCALLOP MAY BE USED FOR THE YOKE AND THE SKIRT

8 MORE SCALLOPS PLUS SEAM ALLOWANCE

193B

148

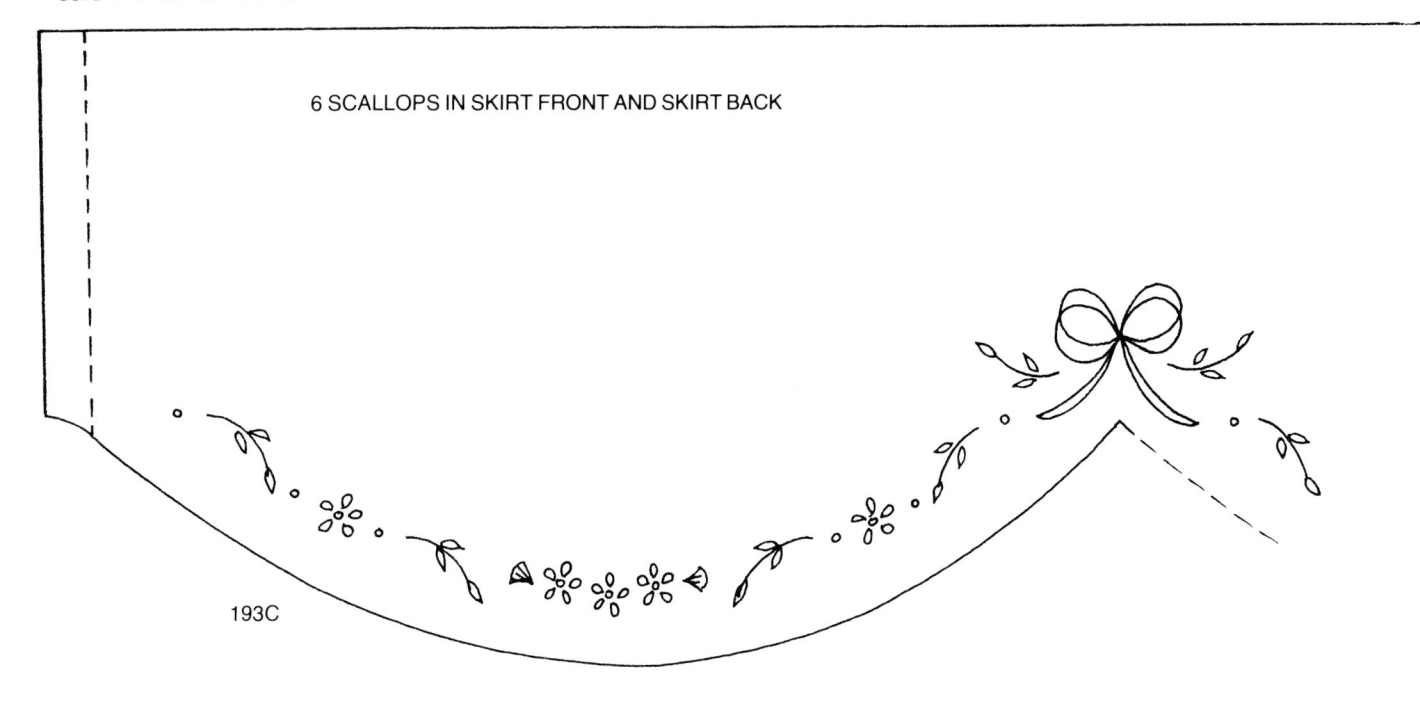

33½" INCLUDING SEAMS

6 SCALLOPS IN SKIRT FRONT AND SKIRT BACK

193C

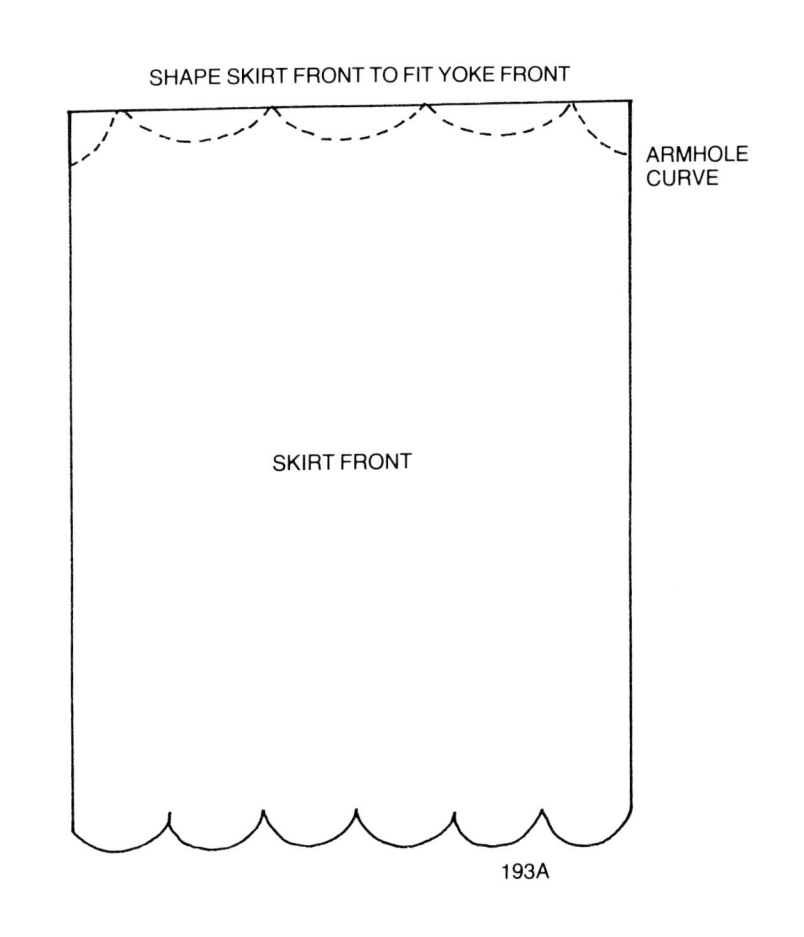

SHAPE SKIRT FRONT TO FIT YOKE FRONT

ARMHOLE CURVE

SKIRT FRONT

193A

This pointed yoke is outlined with lace insertion that is mitered at all points. The center is embroidered. The yoke is square across the back. Matching sprays of embroidery are worked on the skirt, which can be edged with a fabric or lace ruffle. (Fig. 194)

The inside of the yoke could be tucked fabric edged with insertion and the bottom could be made in points edged with lace insertion and edging.

SHAPED SQUARE YOKE DRESSES

YOKE SQUARE ACROSS THE BACK

EMBROIDERED YOKE OUTLINED WITH LACE INSERTION EDGED WITH LACE RUFFLE

TUCKED YOKE

ALTERNATE LONG SKIRT VIEW

POINTS OUTLINED WITH LACE INSERTION EDGED WITH LACE RUFFLE

Fig. 194

This yoke is made like a square yoke, but has been rounded at the bottom edge (front and back). The back yoke placket is double lace insertion. You can use any of the vertical yoke and skirt variations.

The shoulder edge is enhanced with a fabric eyelet or lace ruffle like the all-lace christening dress in Chapter 1.

The outline of the yoke is edged with a lace ruffle.

Other skirt options include a scalloped edge with lace insertion or a scalloped hem. (Fig. 195)

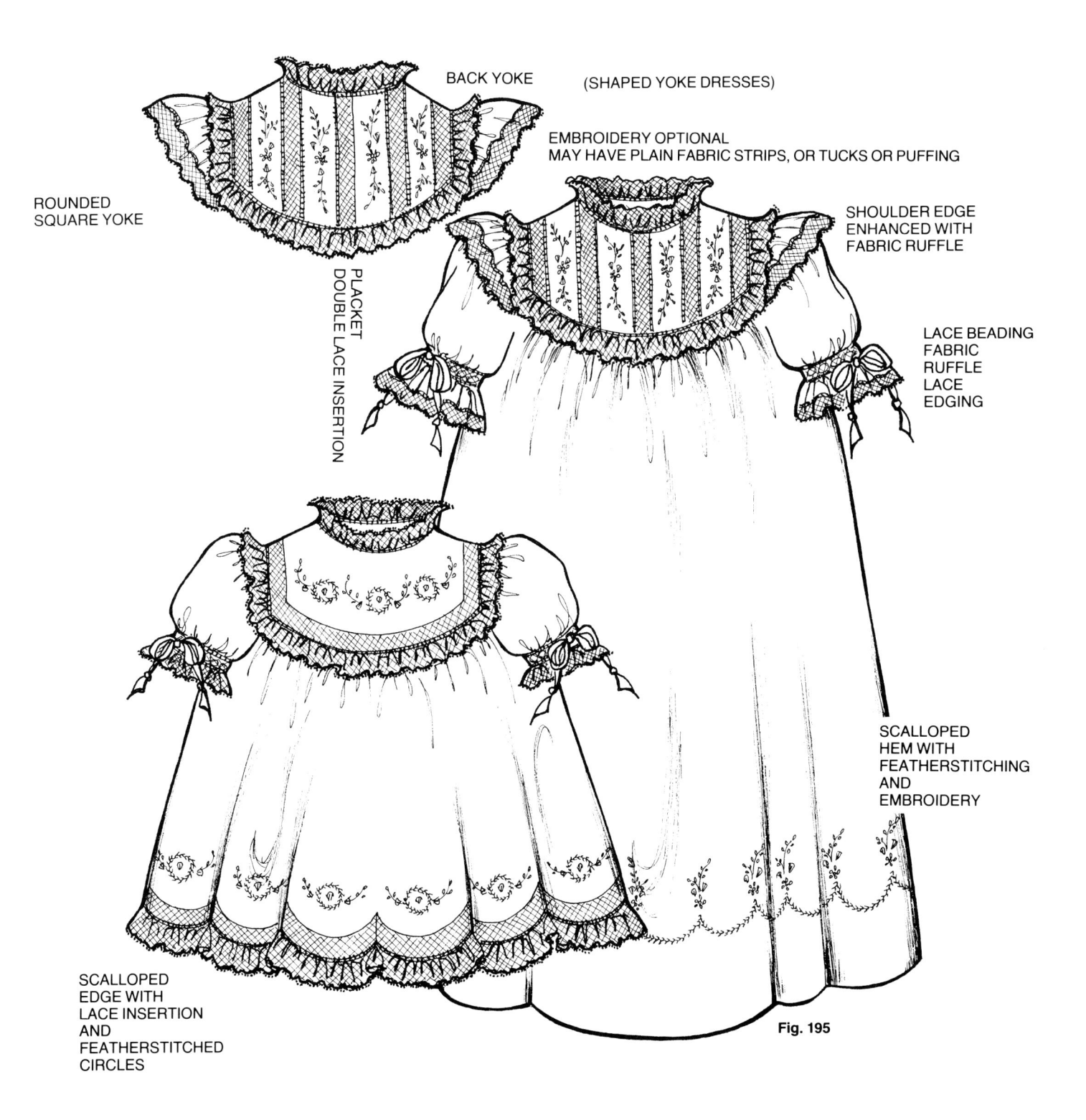

Fig. 195

Round Yokes

Round yokes can be made from a vertical block of trim (refer to Chapter 1), trim going around the yoke, lace applied to form a spoked effect, or simply from fabric enhanced with embroidery or tucks. Use any of the skirt designs from the square yoke dresses. (Fig. 196)

ROUND YOKES

PUFFING AND LACE YOKE WITH LACE RUFFLE

ALL LACE YOKE

EMBROIDERY AND LACE YOKE

SPOKED LACE YOKE AND EMBROIDERY

TUCKS AND LACE YOKE

FINISHED BACK

ENTREDEUX THEN EYELET RUFFLE

ALL LACE YOKE MADE IN 3 PIECES

FINISHED BACK

DOUBLE LACE PLACKET

ENTREDEUX THEN FABRIC RUFFLE WITH LACE EDGING

Fig. 196

152

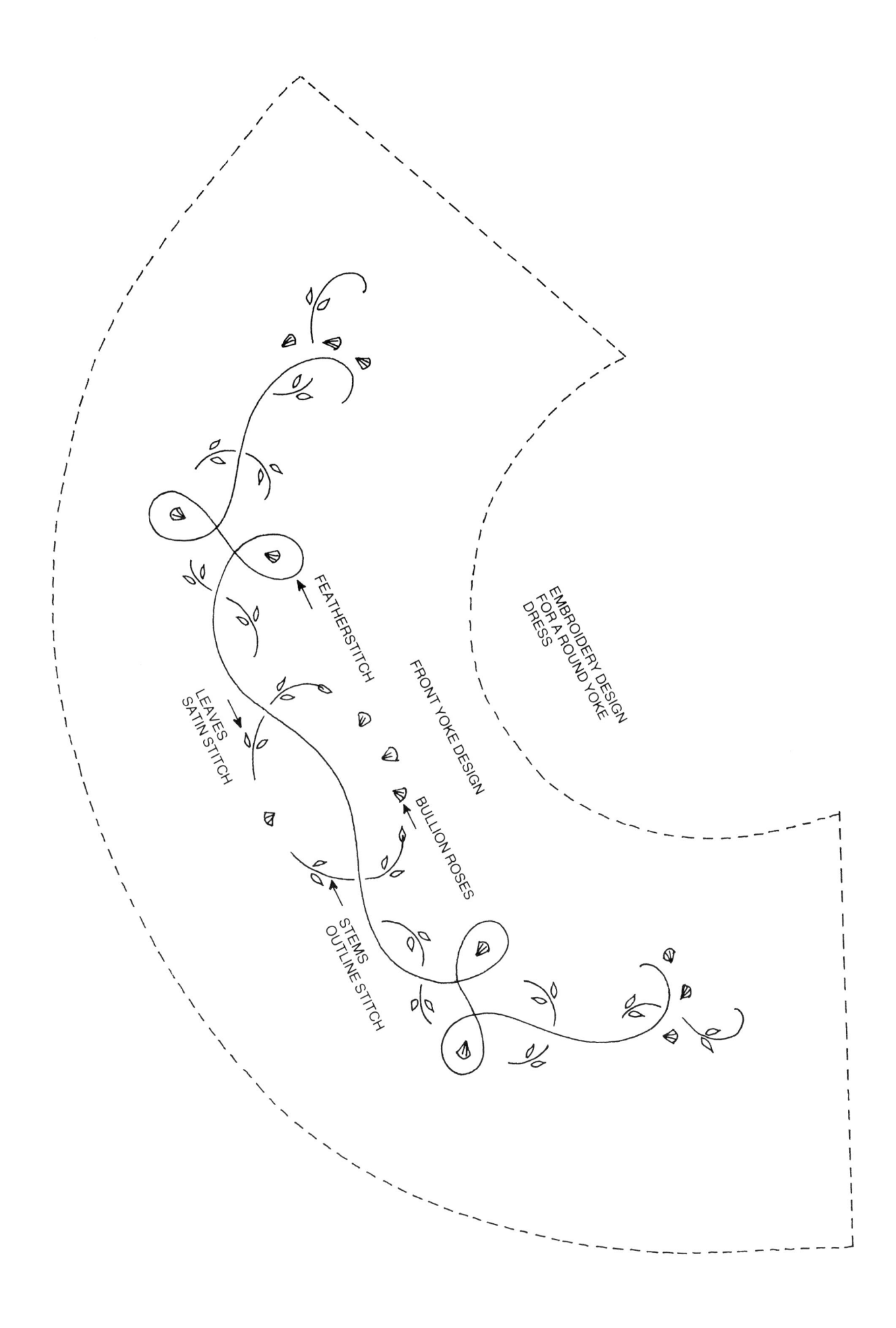

BACK YOKE

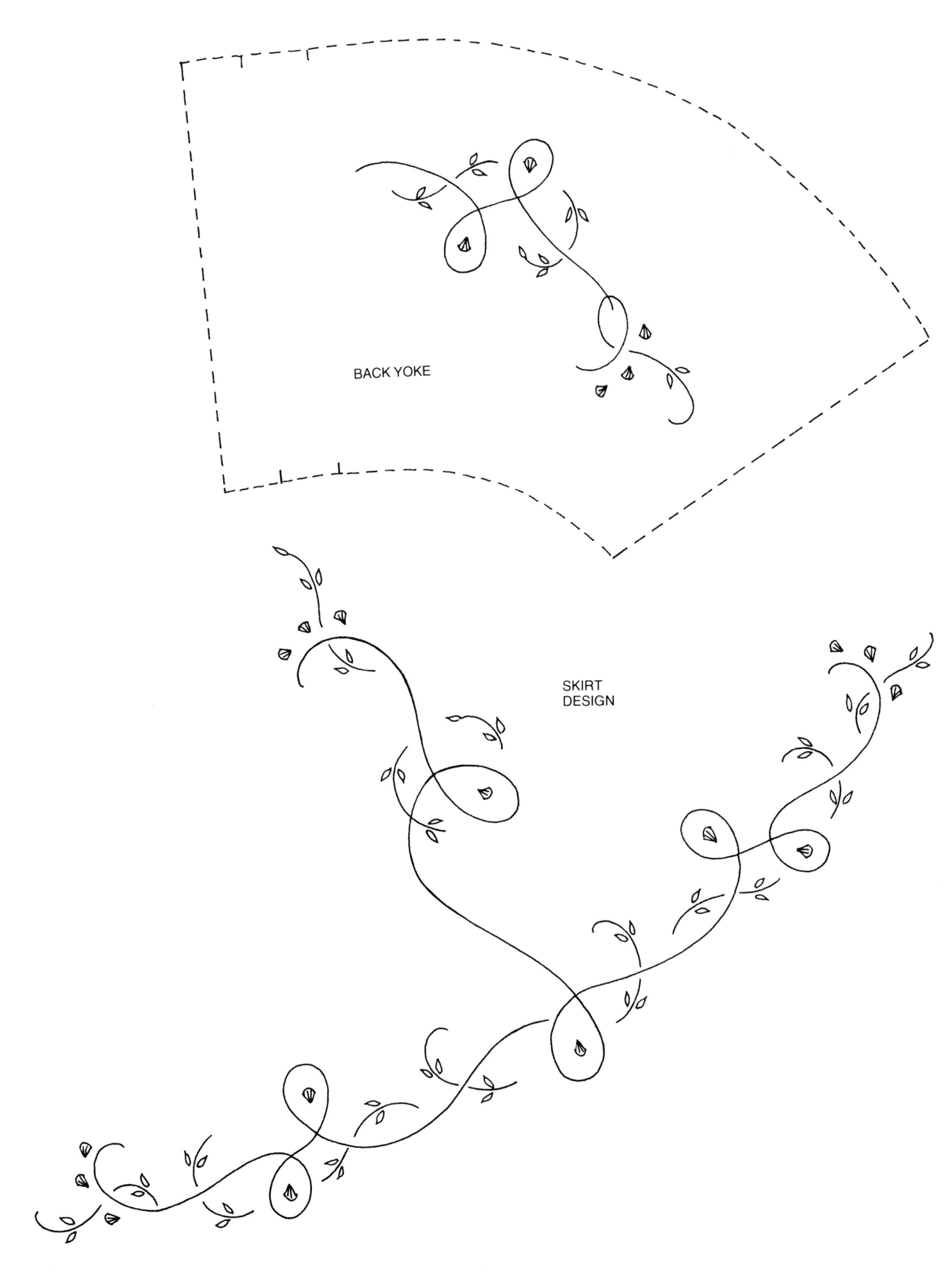

SKIRT
DESIGN

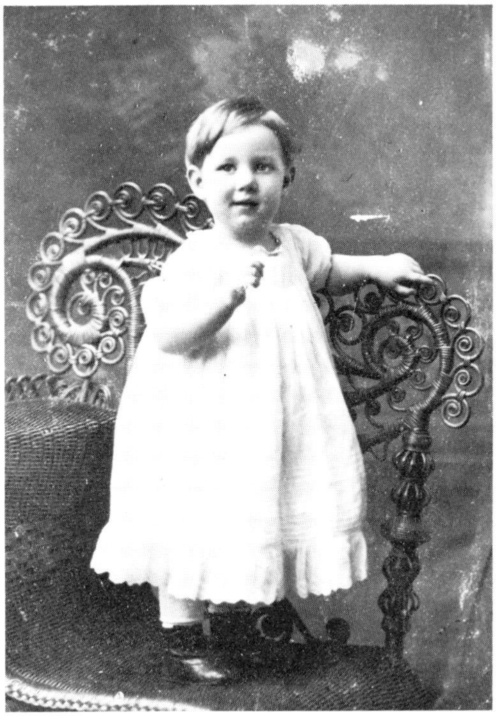
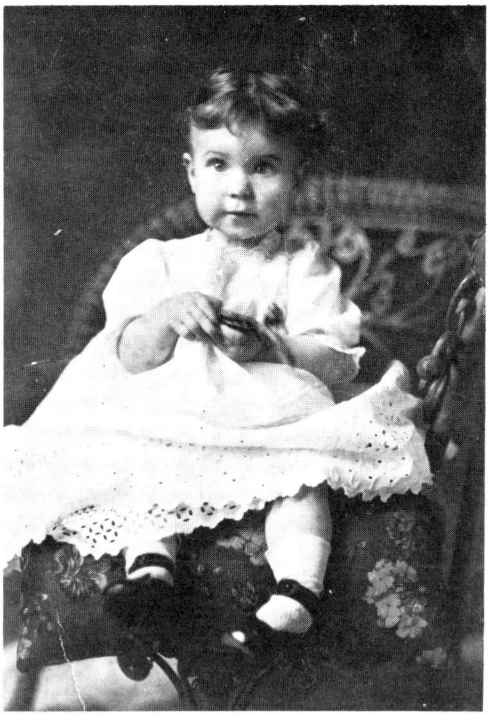
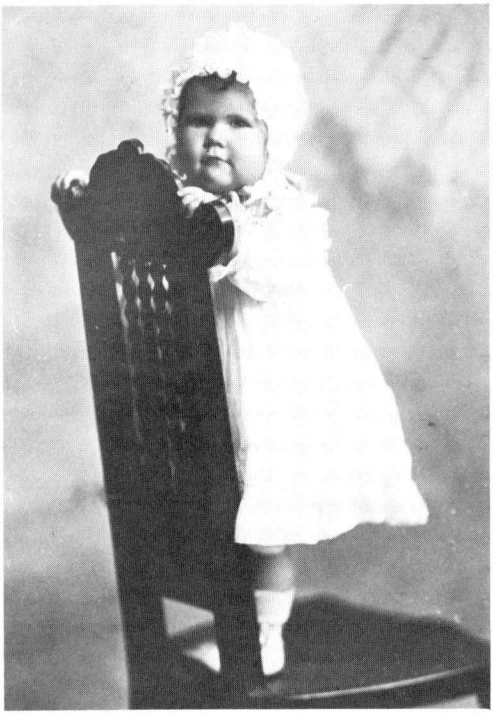
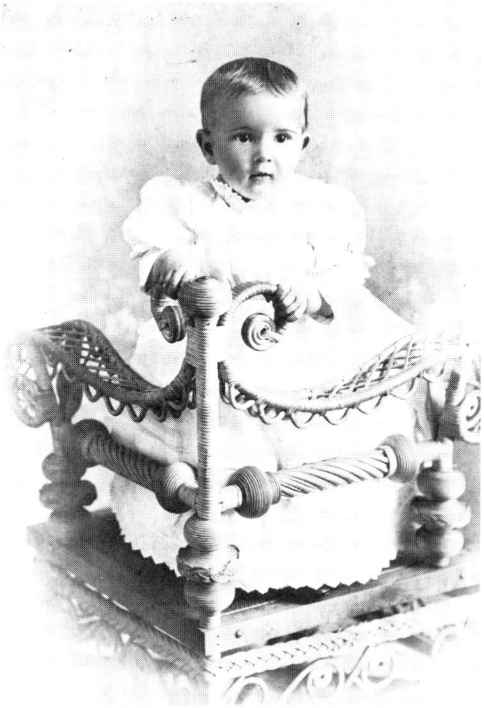

BOY DRESSES

A-Line Dresses 158
Pleated Dresses 162
Side Opening Dress 174

Right: Benton Douglass Stone

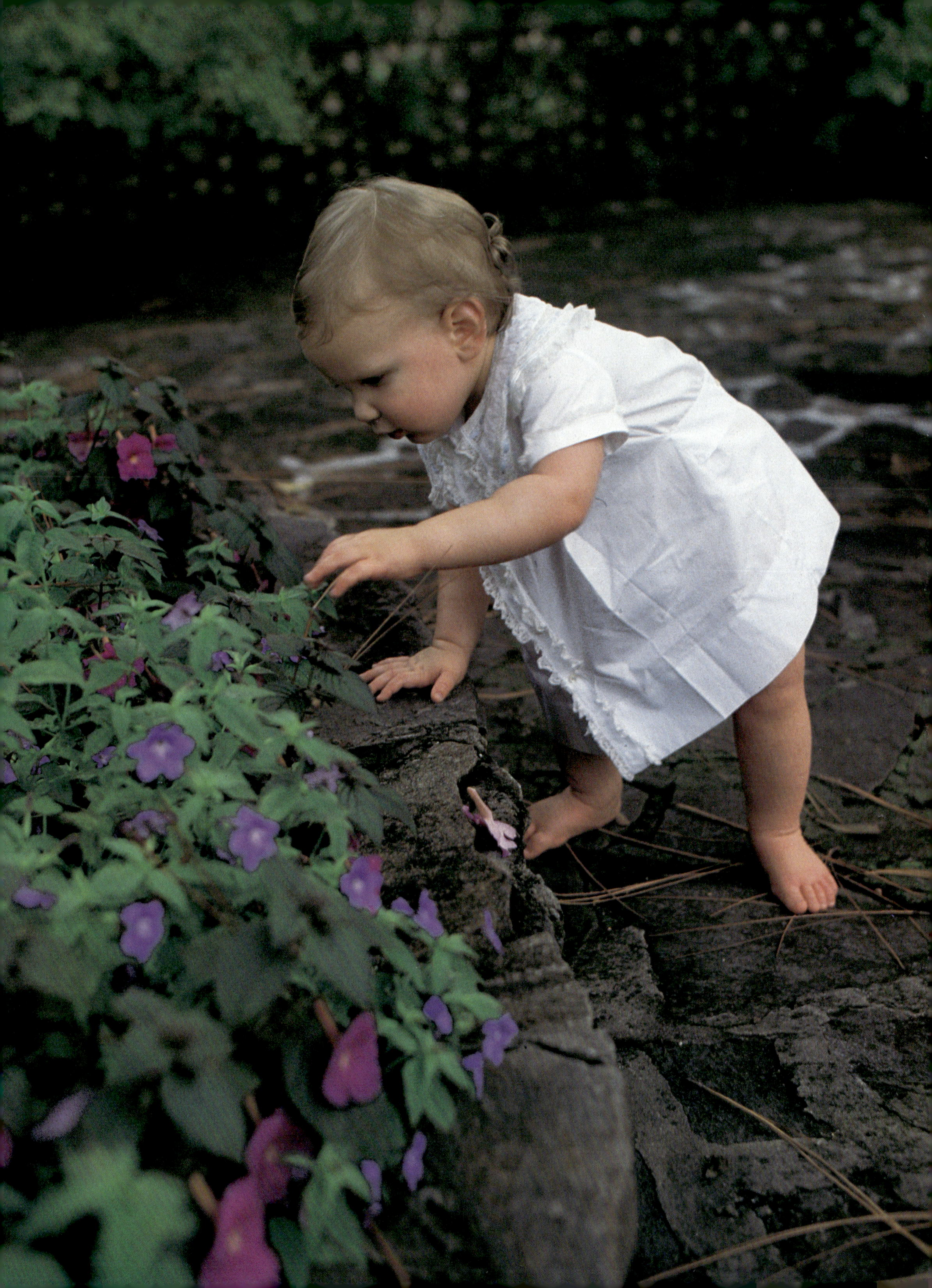

INTRODUCTION

There are several boy dress patterns available on the market today. You can adapt any of the styles shown here to basic patterns. Boy dresses or aprons, as they are sometimes called, are the most practical garments you can have for your little son. Rompers are adorable, but are outgrown lengthwise all too soon. It is my conviction that no "bottom" should be covered that has to be changed. . . . In times past, the male heirs of royalty were put in dresses for fear that they might be kidnapped, and so the tradition began.

I have never known a little boy dressed in lace who was "sissy" — quite the opposite — my grandsons have caught every frog and bug, climbed every tree, and played in every mud puddle in the vicinity, and I can truly say they are **all boy** in spite of the lace.

Broadcloth, gingham, and pima plaids are ideal fabrics to use for boy dresses. Collars and cuffs may be made of batiste or handkerchief linen that is trimmed with eyelet or lace. Pearl buttons in a variety of styles and sizes are very appropriate.

For more information on making fancy plackets, see the chapter on Daygowns.

These dress designs will work beautifully for little girls if you use puff sleeves and use a sash instead of a belt.

A-Line Dresses

Tiny tucks the depth of a yoke (front and back) with a monogram are the accents for this A-line dress. The collar and long sleeves (bound at the bottom edge) are trimmed with tatting. This dress opens down the back and is belted across the back. NOTE: Short sleeves with a cuff can be used instead of the long one. (Fig. 197A)

The second dress, too, opens in the back. (Fig. 197B) The collar and cuffs are scalloped with a lace or tatted edging.

The front panel is made separately and is lined with a light fabric. Put the two fabrics together and stitch along each scalloped edge. Turn. Press and sew trim to the finished edge. Lay the scalloped piece on the front of the dress and secure at neck. The buttons and the hem will hold it in place, or you might blind stitch it down each side.

The belt is secured in the front under the scalloped edge, and buttons in the back.

A-LINE

BELT ATTACHED AT SIDE

LONG BOUND SLEEVES

TUCKS AND MONOGRAM DRESS TRIMMED WITH TATTING

BELT ATTACHED UNDER SCALLOPED PANEL

SCALLOPED COLLAR CUFFS AND FRONT PANEL

A

PANEL SECURED AT NECK BUTTONS AND HEM

Fig. 197

B

This apron or dress is made of white or pastel broadcloth. The bib front is made of batiste, featuring vertical tucks outlined with lace insertion. The space between the insertions is embroidered in the same color as the dress. The bib as well as the collar and cuffs (also made of batiste) are edged with entredeux and lace ruffles. The dress is belted in the back. (Fig. 198)

A-LINE DRESSES

EMBROIDERED SAME COLOR AS DRESS

PASTEL BROADCLOTH

BELTED BACK

BATISTE BIB COLLAR AND CUFF

Fig. 198

BIB PATTERN
FOR FIGURE 198

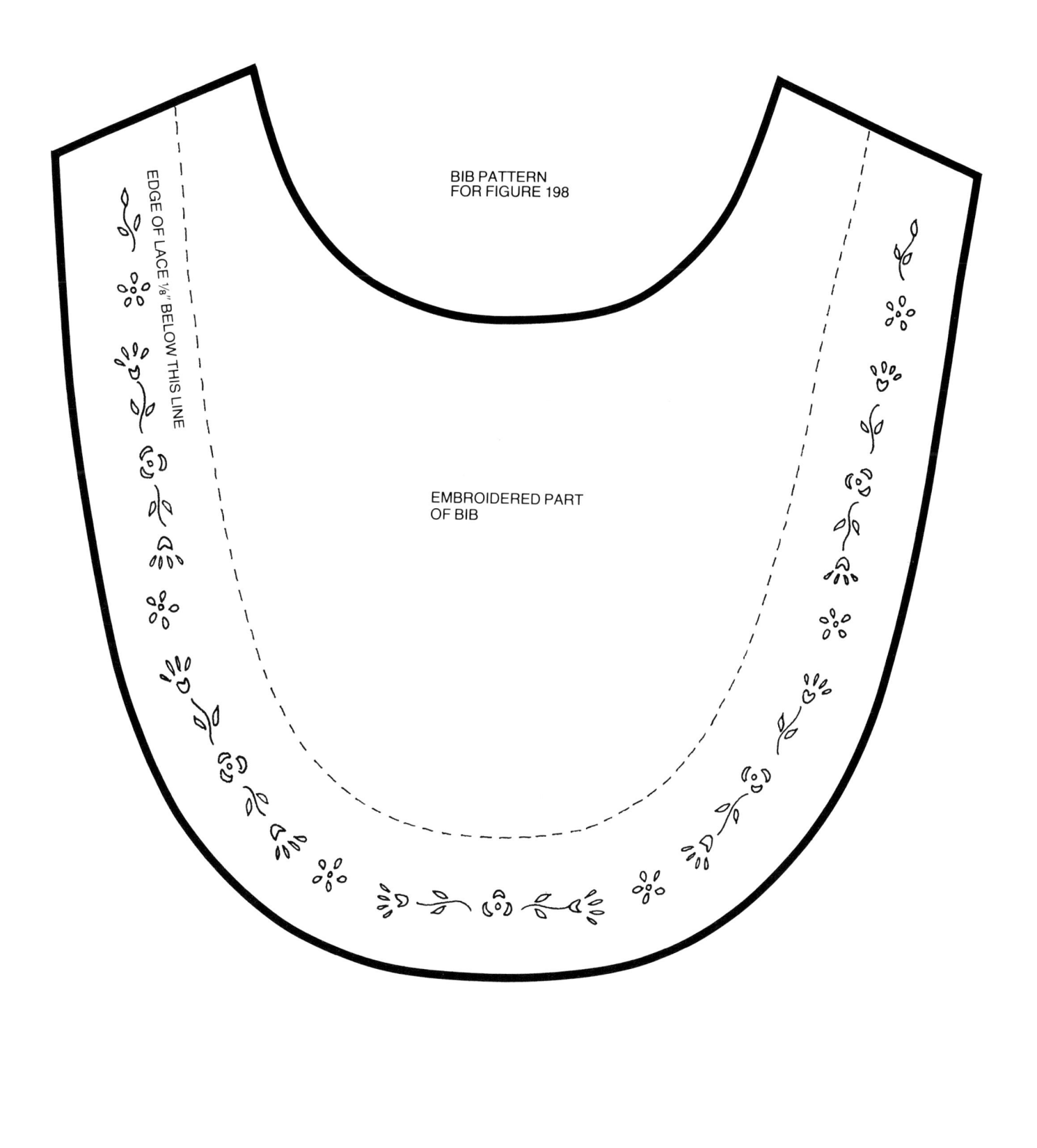

EDGE OF LACE ⅛" BELOW THIS LINE

EMBROIDERED PART OF BIB

161

BIB PATTERN
FOR FIGURE 198

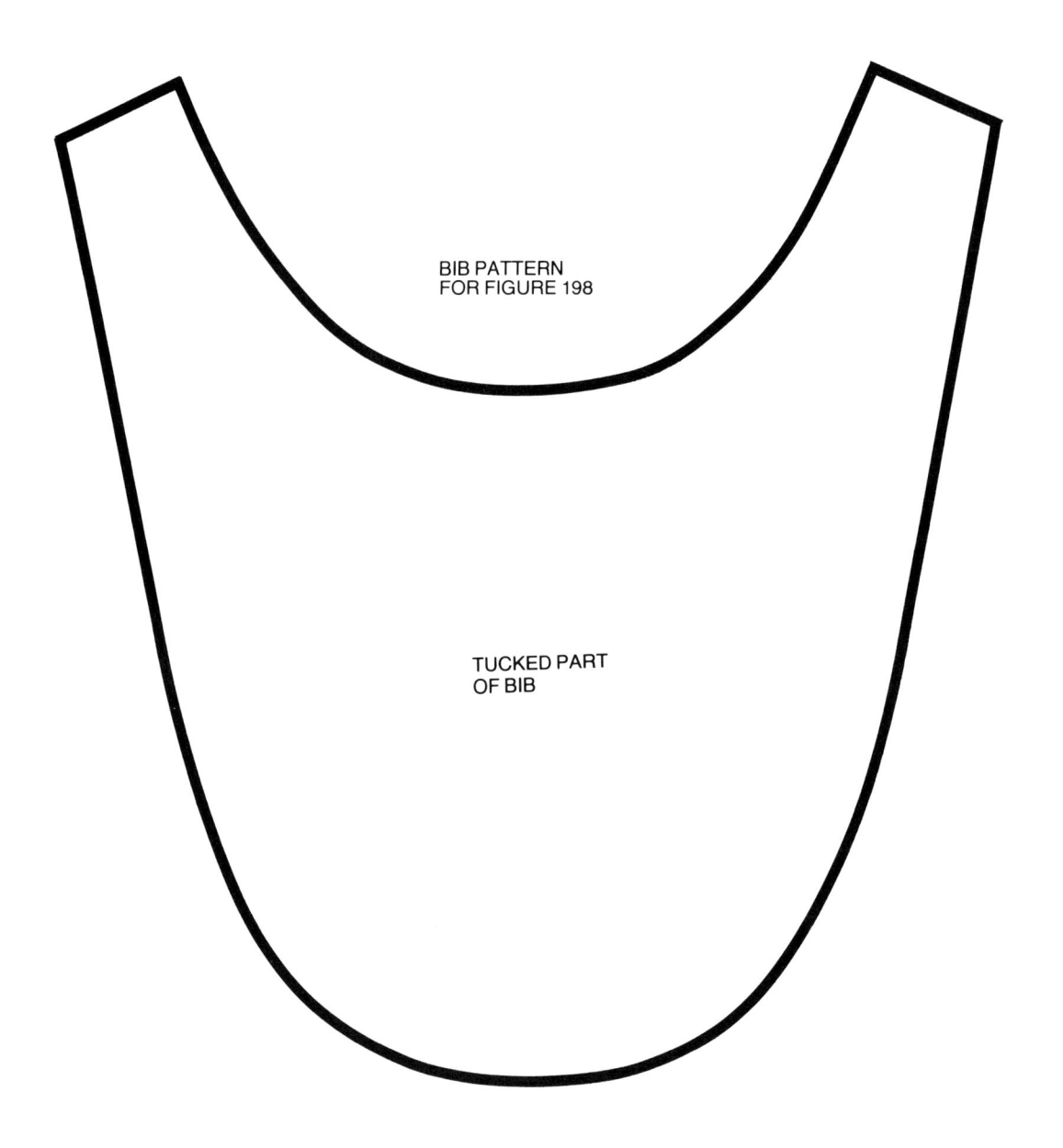

TUCKED PART
OF BIB

Pleated Dresses

This is one of my favorite styles. You can dress it up with a fancy collar or make it plain, with binding or rick rack. The front placket and the cuffs are finished with entredeux and lace edging. (Fig. 199) I have included five collars for you to choose from: (A) Puffing and Lace Collar, (B) Spoked Collar with Embroidery, (C) Collar Outlined with Lace Medallions (Instructions for medallions may be found in Chapter I.), (D) Pointed Petal Collar with Embroidery, (E) Collar with Lace and Embroidered Rectangles at Front.

(B) SPOKED COLLAR WITH EMBROIDERY

(C) COLLAR OUTLINED WITH LACE MEDALLIONS

(D) POINTED COLLAR WITH EMBROIDERY

(A) PUFFING AND LACE COLLAR

(E) COLLAR WITH LACE AND EMBROIDERED RECTANGLES AT FRONT

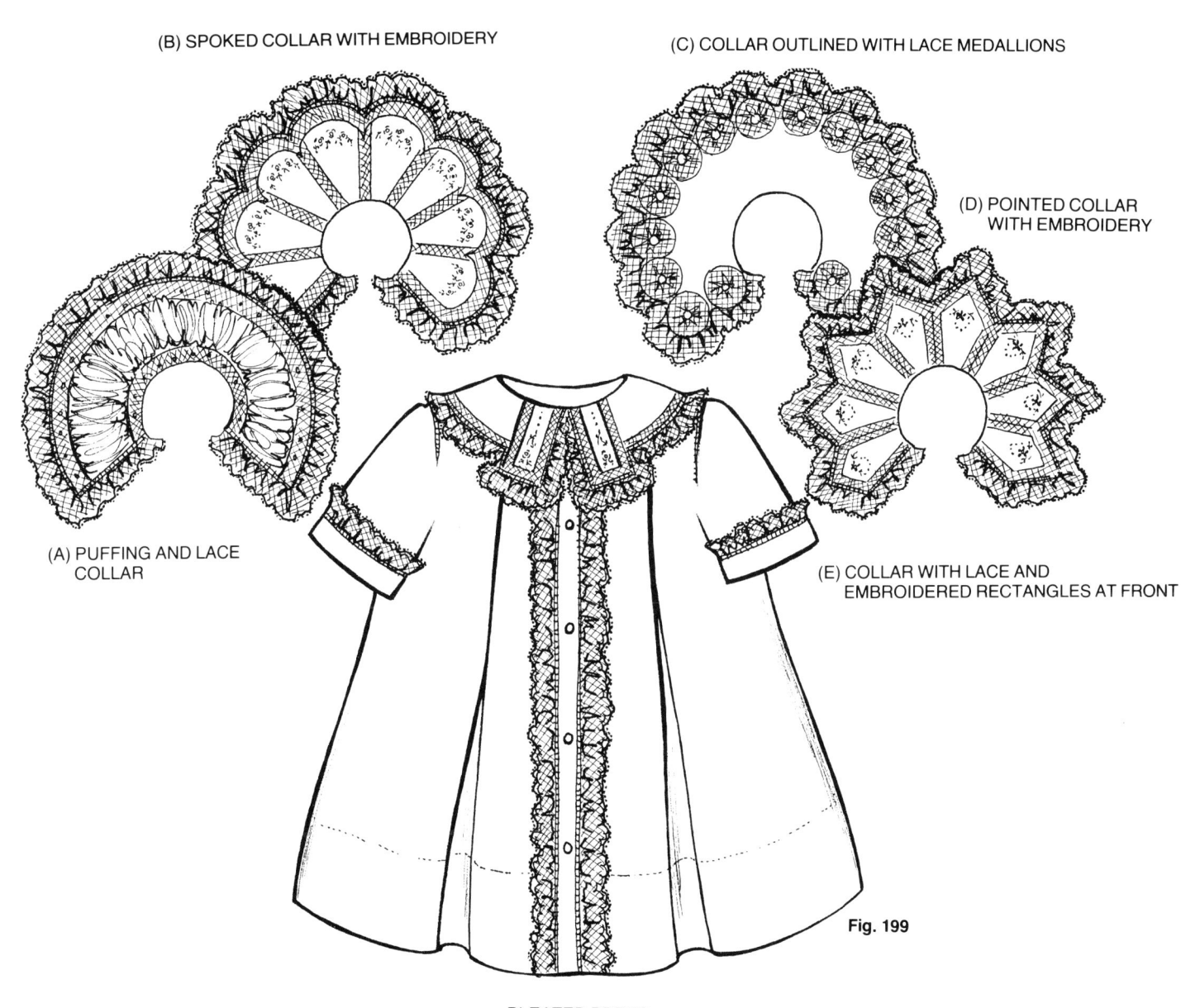

Fig. 199

PLEATED PRESS

163

Collar A: Make a brown paper pattern. Trim away the seam allowance at the neck edge and take the width of the lace edging away from each side of the front. Start at the neck edge with lace insertion; baste to paper (right side down). Baste a row of insertion even with the bottom edge. Measure the distance between the laces and add 1/2 inch to determine the width the puffing should be x two times the bottom measurement.

Roll and whip the top of the puffing strip in equal halves to fit under the top row of insertion. Pin to secure. Roll and whip the bottom of the puffing strip and gather in equal halves to fit above the bottom row of insertion. Pin to secure. Whip the lace to the puffing.

Machine stitch the front sides of the collar as close to the paper as possible. Trim excess away.

Whip entredeux to entire outer edge, excluding neck. NOTE: Use machine stitching as a rolled edge.

Whip gathered lace edging to the entredeux. Attach collar to a finished neck edge.

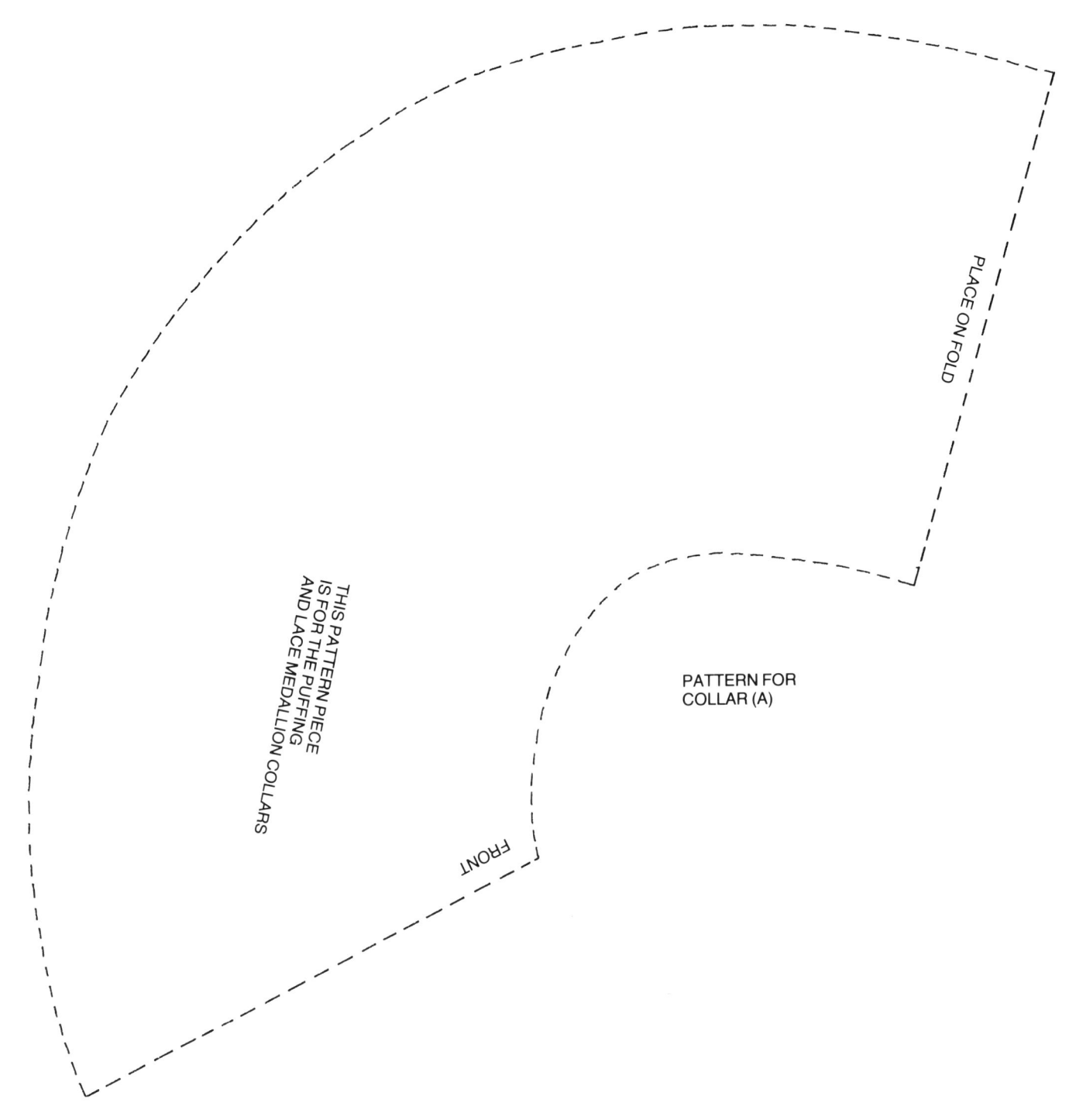

PLACE ON FOLD

THIS PATTERN PIECE IS FOR THE PUFFING AND LACE MEDALLION COLLARS

PATTERN FOR COLLAR (A)

FRONT

Collar B: Draw the outline of the collar on a square of fabric. Do not cut out. Put vertical lace from the neck to the outer edge at an angle. (Do not put lace at front edges.) Tiny baste each side. Secure lace with buttonhole, pin, or zigzag stitch. Trim fabric from behind, 1/8 inch from lace.

Put lace insertion around outer edge of scallops, starting at one neck edge and laying the lace 1/4 inch up on fabric. Miter at points. Secure lace in the same manner as the vertical strip. Trim excess fabric 1/8 inch from lace. Whip entredeux to outer insertion. Whip gathered lace edging to the entredeux. If you desire, embroider before attaching any lace insertion.

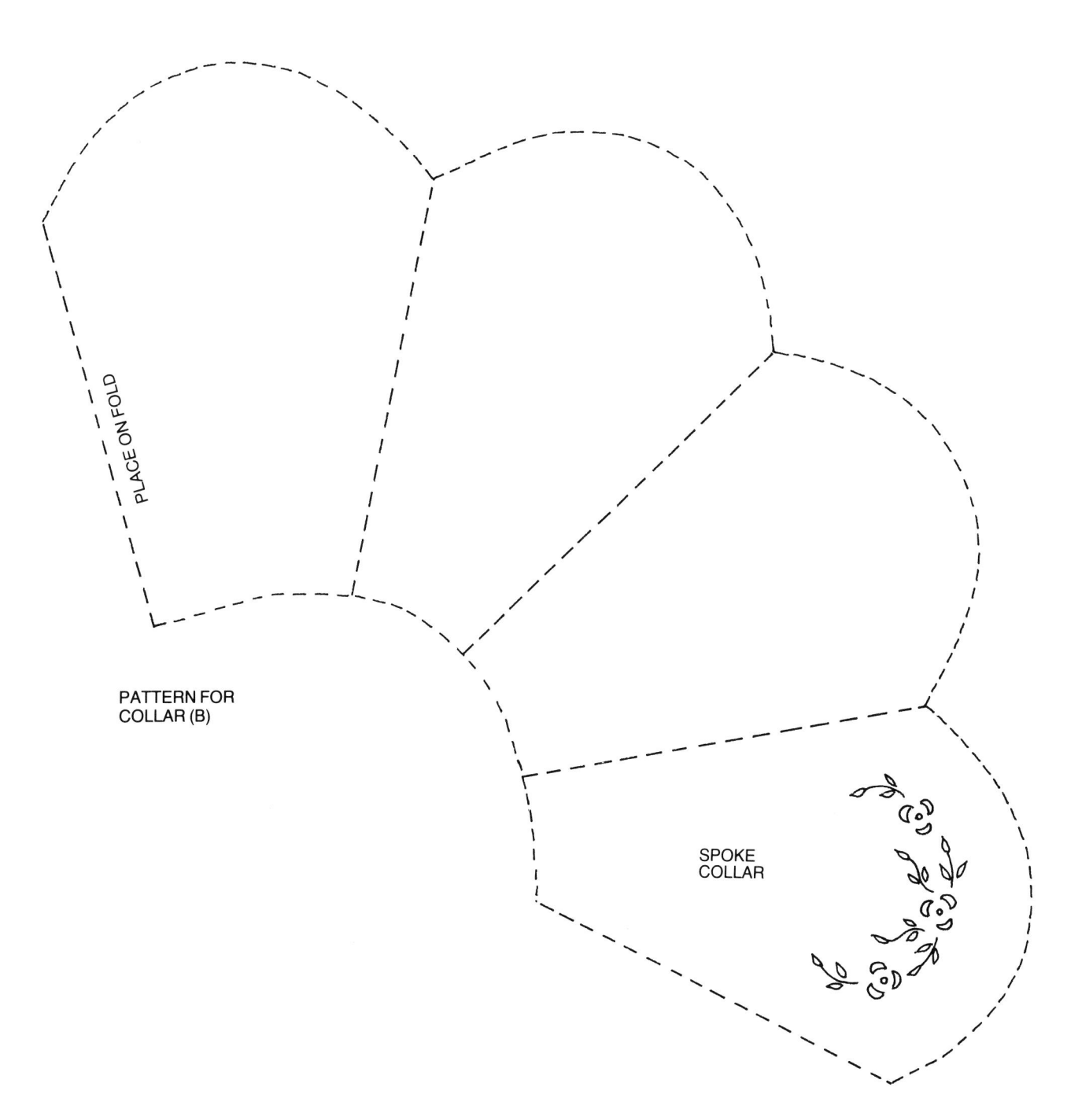

PLACE ON FOLD

PATTERN FOR COLLAR (B)

SPOKE COLLAR

Collar C: Make as many lace medallions as you need to go around the outer edge of the collar. Draw a complete collar on a square of fabric. Place the medallions on the collar. Tiny baste the inside edge. Buttonhole or zigzag over basting. Trim fabric from behind to within 1/8 inch of lace. Whip medallions together at the sides where they meet. Whip gathered lace edging to the outer edge of the lace scallops. Attach collar to dress with bias strip.

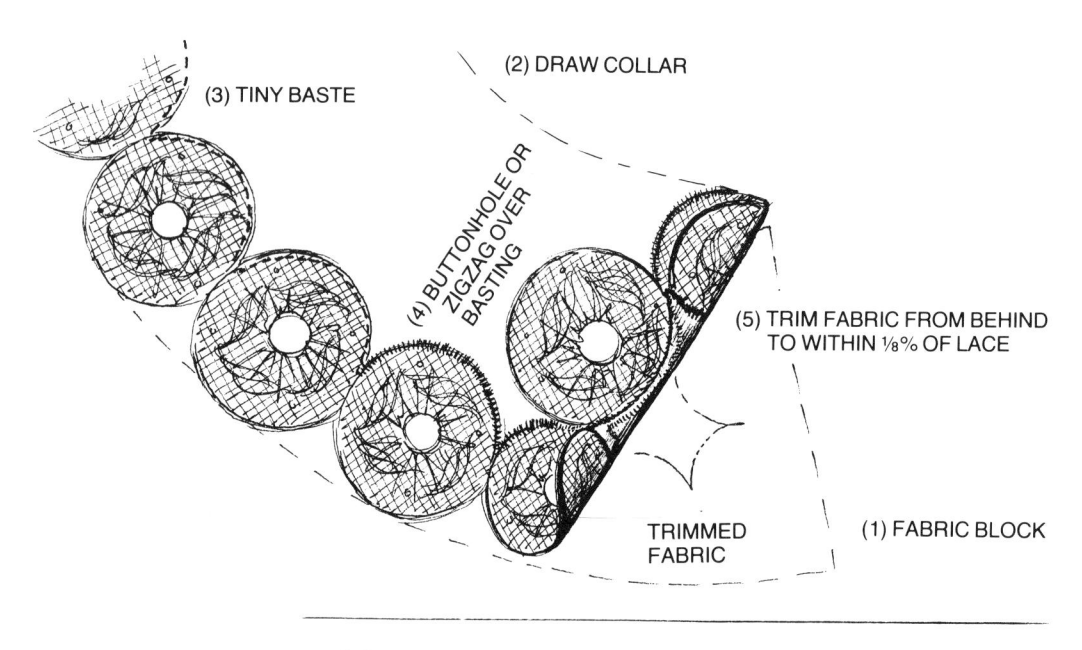

DETAILED DRAWING OF COLLAR (C)

Collar D: Fold a paper collar as you did for B. Cut the bottom edge in points instead of ovals. Mark the lines from the neck to where the points join.

Draw outline of collar on square of fabric. Using a rather narrow insertion, follow the lines on the inside of each petal. Miter the bottom point. Tiny baste the lace insertion on the inside only. Zigzag or buttonhole over basting. Cut the fabric down the center behind the double lace and fold back until you have whipped the two laces together side by side. After this step has been completed, trim all fabric 1/8 inch from stitching line. Whip entredeux to the outer edge. Whip gathered lace edging to the entredeux.

Attach collar to dress with bias strip.

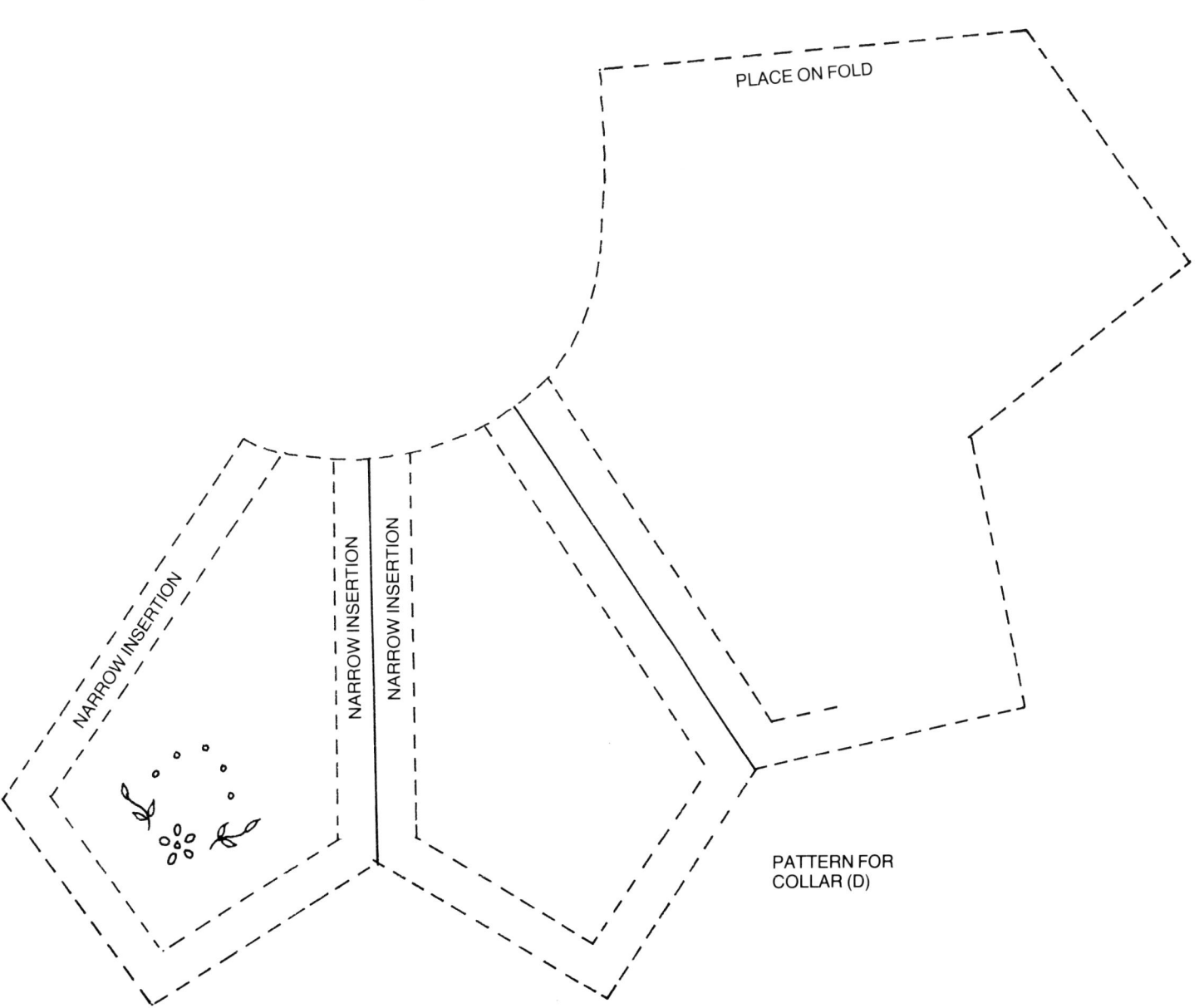

PATTERN FOR COLLAR (D)

Collar E: Make a collar pattern using a wide round collar. Make a rectangle longer than the collar is deep. Lay it on pattern.

Draw the outline of the collar on a strip of fabric. Transfer the embroidery design into the rectangle. Put lace insertion around three sides of the rectangle starting at the neck edge. Tiny baste and secure lace on the inside. Start the bottom insertion. (Let insertion extend under the lace on the rectangle where the two meet.) Tiny baste and secure on the inside line. Trim fabric 1/8 inch from lace. Whip entredeux to the outer edge of the lace. Whip gathered lace edging to the entredeux.

The collar is attached to the dress with a bias strip.

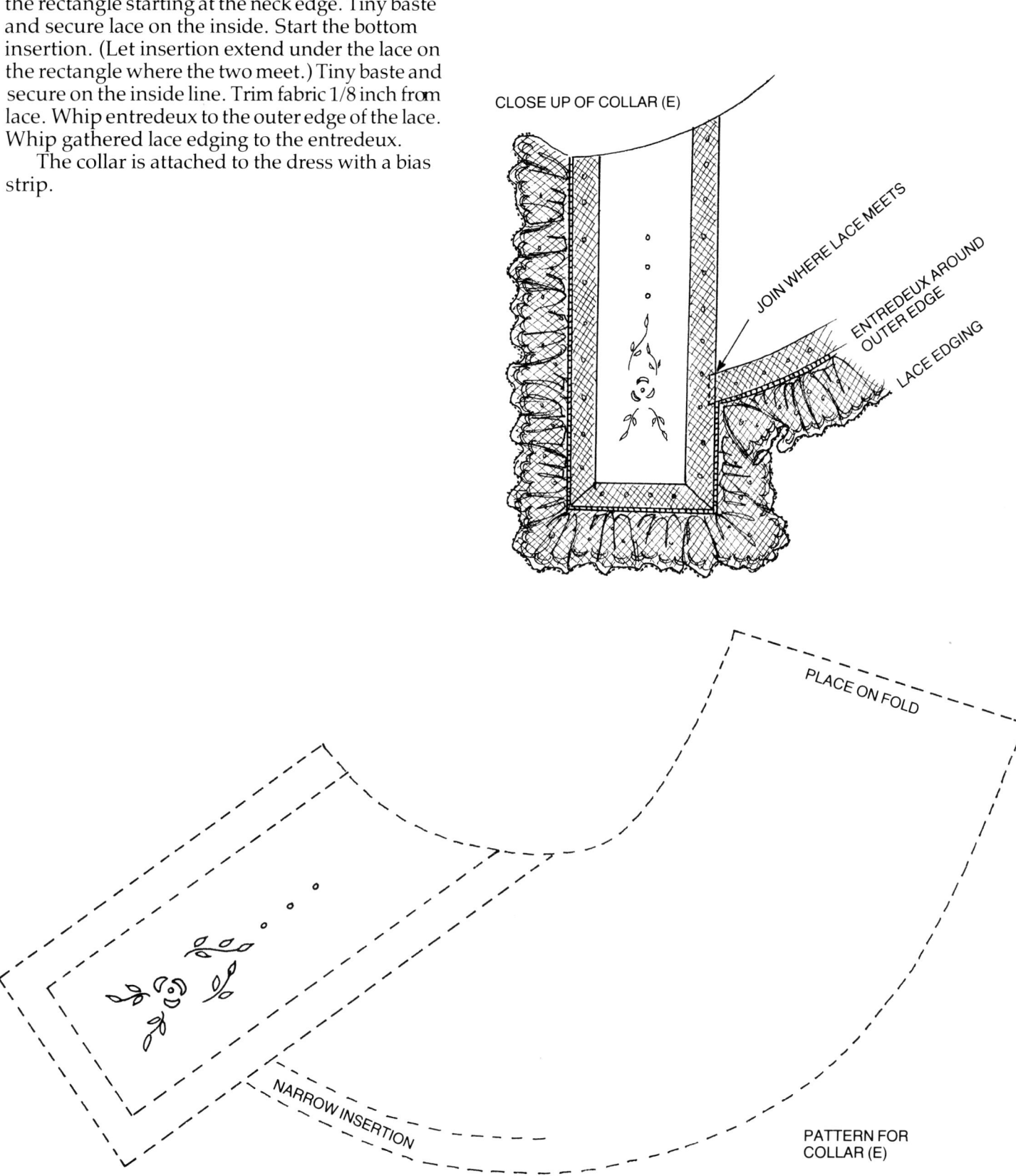

This would make a nice christening boy dress for someone who is older. It would be ideal for his first birthday.

The dress is made on a square yoke. Cut the back on the fold and add a placket to the front.

The skirt has three pleats on each side of the front and six across the back. (Turn pleats toward the armhole.) The placket is trimmed with entredeux and edging.

The square collar is made of batiste with a band of puffing and lace across the front and back edges. It is edged with entredeux and lace edging. The cuffs are trimmed to match the collar.

The front is fastened with small pearl shank buttons. The belt is sewn in at each side and buttons in the back. (Fig. 200)

PLEATED DRESSES

MADE FROM SQUARE YOKE PATTERN

WITHOUT COLLAR

BACK

FRONT

Fig. 200

Make a bib front using wide entredeux, narrow eyelet insertion, or lace spaced between strips of fabric. The sides should be fabric. Whip gathered lace or eyelet edging to the shoulder edge of each entredeux or eyelet strip. (Fig. 201, 202)

Pleat a strip of fabric (length needed to finish dress front) and sew across the bottom of the bib. (All pleats go the same way.) (Fig. 203)

Make a tab to extend across bib. Sew in seam when attaching plain sides. Sew a long strip of fabric, width and length needed, to either side of the bib and pleats. (Fig. 204)

BACK VIEW

Fig. 201

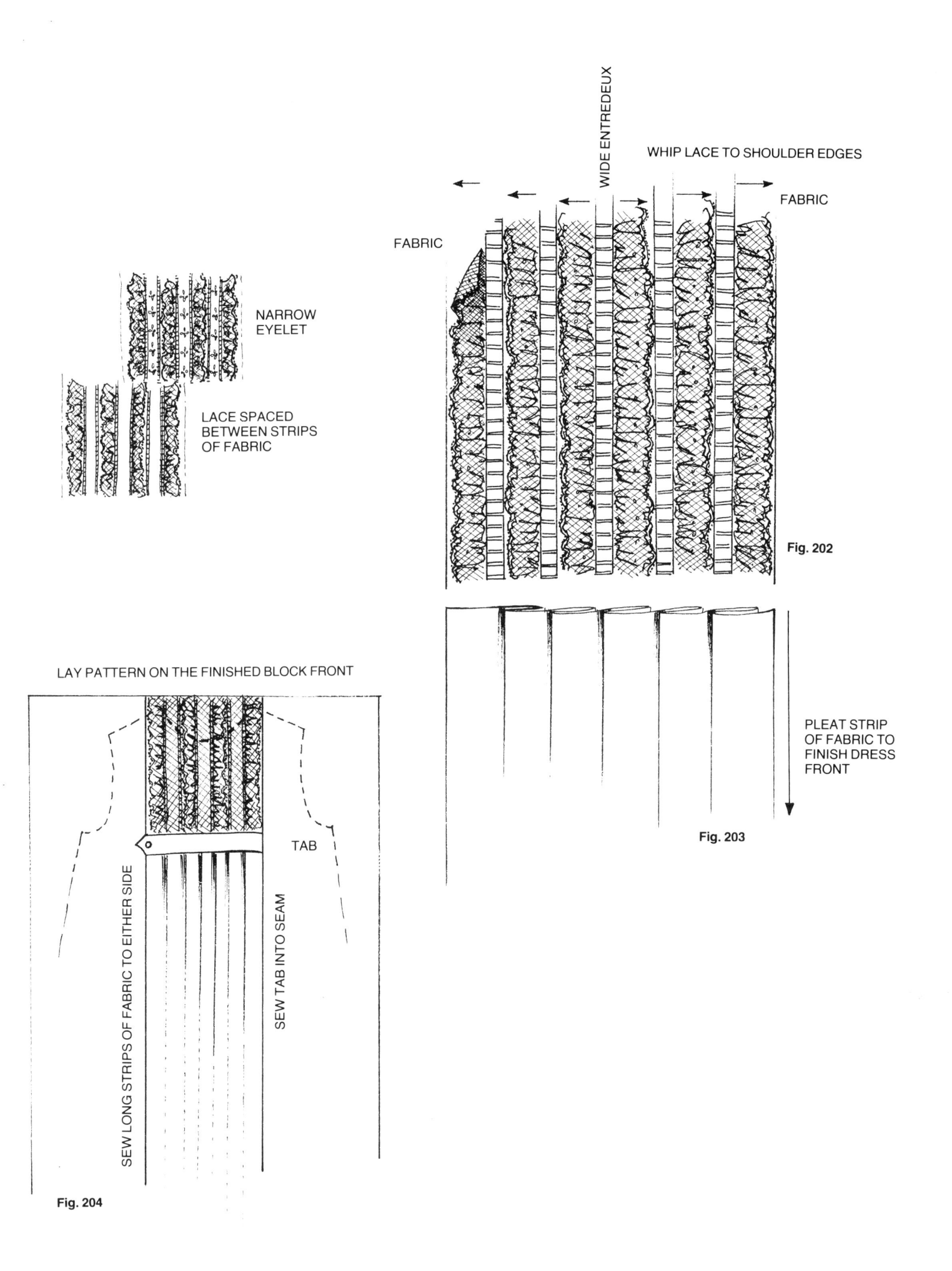

NARROW EYELET

LACE SPACED BETWEEN STRIPS OF FABRIC

WIDE ENTREDEUX

WHIP LACE TO SHOULDER EDGES

FABRIC

FABRIC

Fig. 202

PLEAT STRIP OF FABRIC TO FINISH DRESS FRONT

Fig. 203

LAY PATTERN ON THE FINISHED BLOCK FRONT

TAB

SEW LONG STRIPS OF FABRIC TO EITHER SIDE

SEW TAB INTO SEAM

Fig. 204

171

BLOCK OF FABRIC FOR DRESS FRONT

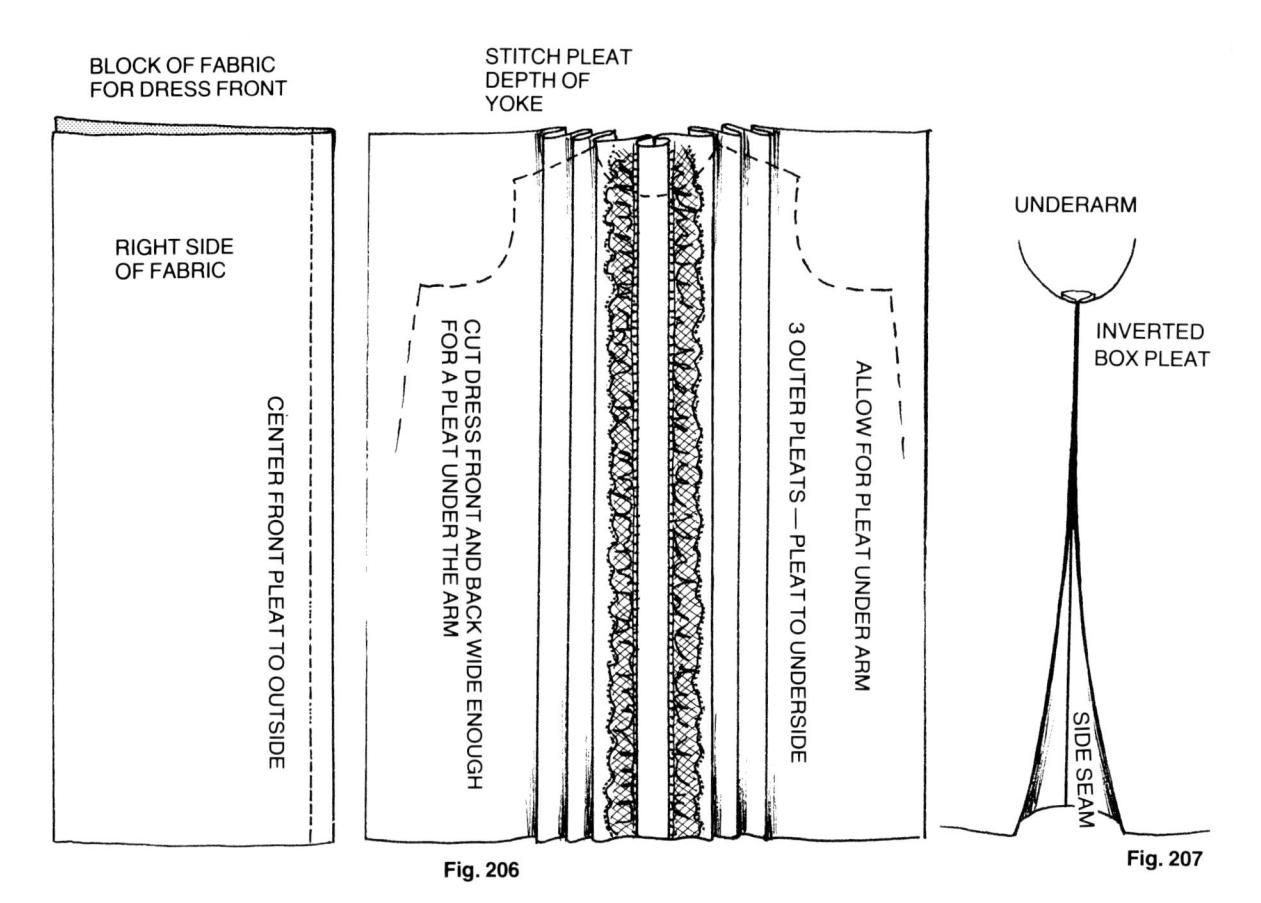

RIGHT SIDE OF FABRIC

CENTER FRONT PLEAT TO OUTSIDE

STITCH PLEAT DEPTH OF YOKE

CUT DRESS FRONT AND BACK WIDE ENOUGH FOR A PLEAT UNDER THE ARM

3 OUTER PLEATS — PLEAT TO UNDERSIDE

ALLOW FOR PLEAT UNDER ARM

Fig. 206

UNDERARM

INVERTED BOX PLEAT

SIDE SEAM

Fig. 207

ALTERNATE VIEW BERTHA COLLAR

FABRIC RUFFLE EDGED WITH LACE

BOX PLEAT

BACK VIEW

BOX PLEAT

BELT ATTACHED UNDER TRIM ON CENTER FRONT PLEAT

Fig. 205

Lay the pattern front on the block and draw the outline on the fabric. Machine stitch across neck and shoulders. Cut out.

The back has a placket that forms a center pleat and a box pleat on each shoulder. The peter pan collar and cuffs are edged with matching trim. (Fig. 201)

Sew a front block to construct the front of the final pleated dress. (Fig. 205) Fold fabric and sew a pleat down the front. Open pleat on the right side and press. Whip entredeux and trim down each of the pleats. (Fig. 206)

Stitch three pleats the depth of a yoke on either side. (These pleat to the underside.) Cut the front wide enough for a pleat under the arm. (Fig. 207)

The back opens all the way down. It has a box pleat on each shoulder.

The belt is attached under the trim on the center pleat and buttons in the back.

The collar and cuffs are trimmed the same as the center pleat.

Tiny pearl shank buttons can be sewn on top of the pleat for added trim. This dress is also nice with a bertha collar.

Side Opening Dress

This dress has a side opening edged and trimmed with lace eyelet or tatted trim. The back has a center box pleat with a tab. (Fig. 208)

The square batiste collar is split in the front and back.

Make a band of lace (eyelet or tatted insertion) the length needed to go across the front and back edges of the collar. NOTE: Subtract the depth of the band from the fabric collar before joining. Roll and whip bottom edge. Apply entredeux. Join to band. (Fig. 209)

Machine stitch or zigzag across shoulder, front and back edges. Use this stitching as a rolled edge. Whip entredeux to the outer edges of each collar piece. Whip gathered trim to the entredeux.

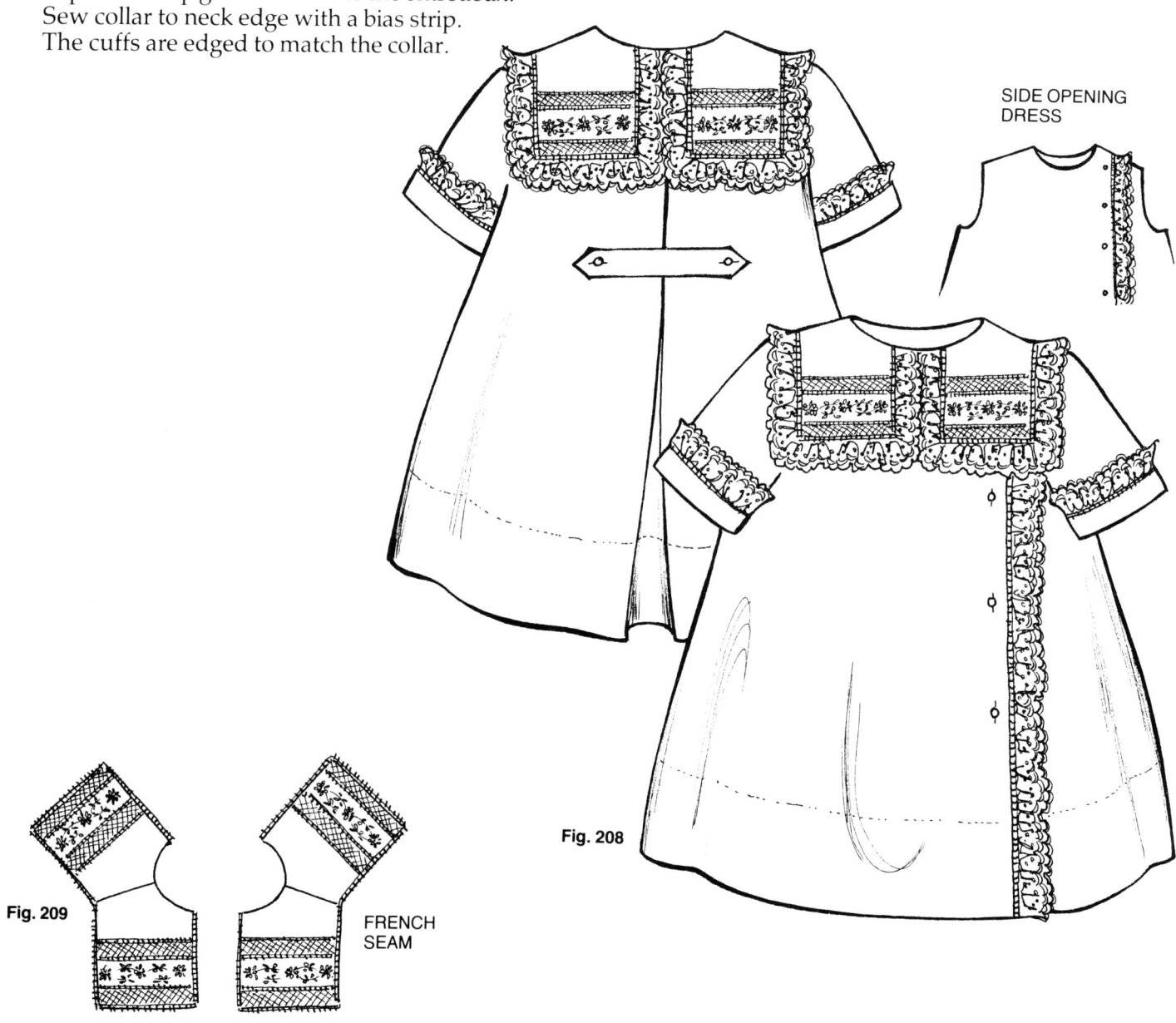

Sew collar to neck edge with a bias strip.

The cuffs are edged to match the collar.

SIDE OPENING DRESS

Fig. 208

Fig. 209

FRENCH SEAM

WHIP ENTREDEUX TO OUTER EDGES EXCLUDING NECK EDGE

Acknowledgements:

Research and Editing
    Carol Cook Hagood

Old Photographs
    Eulalia Reynolds Halston
    Ruth Davis Bonham
    William Oliver Stone

Offset Lithography
    Walker Printing Company, Inc.
    Montgomery, Alabama

A special thanks to Jim Inscoe for allowing us to photograph our subjects at Jasmine Hills Gardens, Montgomery, Alabama.